1598036

Shadows of War

Shadows of War

BRITISH WOMEN'S POETRY
OF THE SECOND WORLD WAR

Edited and Introduced by
ANNE POWELL

SUTTON PUBLISHING

First published in 1999 by
Sutton Publishing Limited · Phoenix Mill
Thrupp · Stroud · Gloucestershire · GL5 2BU

British Library Cataloguing in Publication Data
A catalogue record for this book is available from the British Library

ISBN 0 7509 2257 5

 ™ ALAN SUTTON™ and SUTTON™ are the
trade marks of Sutton Publishing Limited

Typeset in 12/15pt Garamond.
Typesetting and origination by
Sutton Publishing Limited.
Printed in Great Britain by
Biddles, Guildford, Surrey.

For Women

Seeking for light among the shadows of war,
Probing with numb fingers between the ruins,
For warmth in memory, and for lost fires,
And for a path among the litter of ashes,
These women paint their nails and brave the day.

Under the snood of Winter their bright faces
Are frozen and crystal with tears willed to the eye.
Dancing under the holly their laughter hardens
As snow falls and is rigid upon the branches.
These are your girls, these are your flowering daughters,

O brave cold world of sons whose loved arms
Are fossilled with war or clasping the wrists of steel,
Or tenderly wiping the frozen mouths of guns.
Their passionate limbs are stretched under guttering stars
While you rape with steel and fire to assuage your dreams.

SYLVIA READ

In November 1944 Sylvia Read's fiancé, Peter Albery, left England for active service in Europe with the Royal Warwickshire Regiment. 'For Women' was written shortly afterwards. On 28 February 1945 Peter Albery was shot in the spine by a sniper in the last battle of the Reichswald; he was paralysed from the waist down. In May 1945, after three months in hospital, he and Sylvia Read were married.

In memory of my Father and Mother
Basil and Ambrosine Simons (Beaver and Bruno)
who suffered in the shadows of war

and

for my beloved children
Jonathan, Rupert and Lucinda
with my love always

Contents

1941 ──────────

1942 ——————

1943 ——————

1944

1945 ────────

Preface

'Blast this man Hitler!' my father wrote in September 1939. A senior lieutenant in the Royal Navy, he was the commanding officer of HM Submarine *H 34* on patrol off the north-west coast of Scotland. From then on my parents wrote to each other every day they were apart although the details of daily events and cryptic references to the war did not always pass the censor.

My mother's childhood had been deeply affected after her father was killed commanding his battalion during the Battle of the Somme when she was five years old. Tall and beautiful, she lived a precarious life as a model and professional ice-skater until marriage in March 1934 brought her security and a happy-go-lucky naval way of life for the next five years. In September 1939 all this changed. A few weeks after war broke out she and I arrived in Dunfermline to be with my father when he came on leave. By then air raids had started. We sheltered in basements when the sirens sounded but on some occasions there were no early warnings. On one October afternoon as she pushed me on a swing in the park, my mother watched 'a battle in the air . . . planes all over the place . . . the sky like a cobweb with the anti air firing guns all exploding . . .'. A few days later my parents were grieving for a close friend, my father's best man at their wedding, who was one of almost 800 men lost when HMS *Royal Oak* was sunk by a U-boat in Scapa Flow. My mother wrote in a letter:

> It seems so strange when one thinks we're living through a war, we who are so peace-loving. War is a thing we've both heard so much of and never realised till now its full horror. The awfulness of it makes itself more known every day . . . It looks like a long struggle ahead. How sad everything seems in life now, so utterly different to our once happy, carefree lives. I can't believe I am the same person at times. It all makes me feel so old and serious. But we have had a marvellous life together and I am so happy with you . . .

In the middle of November 1939, on her twenty-eighth birthday, my mother was told that my father was unconscious in Scapa Flow. He had returned from patrol and after reporting to the depot ship he fell down a hatch, which in the blackout he had not realised had no ladder. He received multiple fractures to his skull and was not expected to live. My mother spent weeks in hospital at his bedside and then cared for him over many months of convalescence. During the summer of 1940 we were at my grandmother's house on Gower in South Wales. I can remember being woken as plaster from the ceiling covered my bed when a mine exploded on the beach a few hundred yards across the sand dunes; and I am still haunted by the mystery surrounding a German Heinkel that came down in Oxwich Bay sometime over those months but which was never spoken about and was not recorded. In January 1941 my father received a shore appointment at HMS *Ambrose* in Broughty Ferry, Scotland. It was a bleak time for my parents – my father's active service in submarines was over and they were continually hearing that submarine contemporaries and other naval friends had been lost at sea. In May 1941 my mother's sister heard that her husband had been killed in Crete. One of the few times of celebration was in October 1942 during the visit of the Crown Prince of Norway to members of the Royal Norwegian Navy stationed at HMS *Ambrose*. During lunch it was announced that my mother had given birth to a son and as the new baby was toasted the Prince asked to be a godfather. A year later my father was appointed to the submarine base HMS *Dolphin* at Gosport and we rented a cottage in Selsey on the Sussex coast.

We lived just above the beach which was a forbidden area and protected by barbed wire. On several occasions our thatched cottage was badly shaken and windows blown in by explosions from falling bombs and Doodlebugs. My mother brought treats and an air of fun to the nights spent in the Morrison shelter; with a few biscuits and squares of chocolate in a tin and 'special' books these noisy nights became happy adventures for a ten-year-old child oblivious of her mother's responsibilities and fear.

Everyday life for women at home was difficult and exhausting with travel restrictions, no private cars, food and clothes rationing, hours spent queueing. Loneliness, uncertainty and anxiety were ever present. The BBC offered solace through wireless programmes: Tommy Handley's ITMA ('It's That Man Again'), Vera Lynn (the 'Forces Sweetheart'), Gracie Fields and 'Children's Hour' became legends.

Wives on their own with their children formed a close-knit band of friendship in Selsey. The local cinema provided occasional entertainment: *Gone With the Wind, In Which We Serve* and any romantic film with Stewart Granger or Veronica Lake and their contemporaries were popular and *Target for Tonight*, produced in 1941, had an important impact on morale. Squadron Leader 'Pick' Pickard featured as the pilot in the film and the phrase 'Target for Tonight' soon became a national catchword. His wife, Dorothy, lived in Selsey and in February 1944 she heard that her husband was missing after the raid on the prison at Amiens. In May my mother picked lilac and lilies of the valley for a friend, 'ravaged with grief' after she was told that her husband had been shot after escaping from Stalag Luft III in Sagan, Silesia. On 24 March 1944 seventy-nine prisoners went through a tunnel; three were caught near the exit, three succeeded in returning to England but the remainder were recaptured. Fifty were shot without trial. Tom Kirby-Green's widow did not hear the news until almost eight weeks later.

From January 1944 Selsey was subject to very strict security regulations. Residents were issued with special passes. No visitors were allowed into the village unless they were service men home for leave or officials on business of 'national importance'. My grandmother was refused permission to visit us and sent instead 'a box of primroses and violets so sweet and fresh smelling of Wales'. There were good reasons for these exceptional restrictions. A United States Naval Headquarters had been established in Selsey and in the early spring months of 1944 American troops started to arrive. I remember small groups of friendly, laughing sailors who came for tea on our lawn on warm spring and early summer afternoons. They showed my mother snapshots of their families and brought gifts of sweets, chocolate and cigarettes. Also, in 1943, an Advanced Landing Ground had been constructed at Church Norton a few miles from where we lived. At first squadrons of Spitfires and Typhoons were based there; on D-Day South African, Belgian, New Zealand squadrons and Free French Spitfires provided cover for the landing beaches.

Parts of two highly secret artificial harbours – code-named Mulberry – were assembled in Pagham Harbour on the outskirts of the village. At the time local residents could only speculate as to the purpose of the giant structures of concrete and steel that appeared out of the water.

Immediately after the D-Day landings these Mulberries, equivalent in length to 6 miles of pier, were towed across the Channel by over a hundred tugs. A week later over 70,000 troops, 10,000 vehicles and 17,000 tons of weapons, fuel and food had been disembarked from the floating harbours. At that time my mother wrote 'our poor little house shakes and the doors and windows rattle day and night from the bombing on the French coast'.

By the middle of August 1944 the beach at Selsey had been cleared. We bathed almost every day, combed the high-tide line for driftwood and searched for treasure. The most exciting discoveries were the emergency ration boxes washed ashore from aeroplanes and ships. Their tragic implications did not touch the imagination of a young girl.

On 8 May 1945 my mother poured half a glass of sherry for me and a whole glass for herself and a friend and together we celebrated the first day of peace in Europe. Three months later Japan surrendered. But like millions of couples who survived the war years my parents were left emotionally scarred for the rest of their lives.

*   *   *

Acts of sacrifice and heroism were made by women under many circumstances during the Second World War. When we lived in Mons, Belgium, between 1975 and 1978, we were priviledged to know a Belgian woman whose bravery during the war continued in a unique way until her death in 1990.

Madame Ninette Hélène Jeanty, her husband Paul, a distinguished Brussels lawyer, and their sixteen-year-old son, Claude, were arrested by the Gestapo in the summer of 1943 for sheltering an English airman in their attic. Claude was released but four months later his parents faced the Luftwaffe military court, notorious for its severity and for imposing the death sentence on the head of the house.

An article in the German criminal code stipulated that a man might escape the maximum penalty if his wife was insane. In prison Ninette Jeanty feigned madness and eventually convinced the military court of her insanity. Her husband's death sentence was commuted and he was deported to Germany. In May 1944 Madame Jeanty was taken to Duren asylum and committed to the section for 'almost incurables'. In hideously overcrowded wards the inmates were treated as subhuman. Later the patients were transferred to an asylum in Bonn where the conditions were even more appalling. In January 1945 Madame Jeanty confided the story of her sham madness to the director of the asylum. At great risk to himself he put her in isolation and lent her his piano to play.

In the spring of 1945 Ninette Jeanty was repatriated. After months of uncertainty she discovered that her husband had been one of 800 prisoners murdered by the guards at Sonnenburg as the Russian Army advanced in March. Gradually she realised that her time in confinement had given her a personal understanding of human misery and that neither revenge nor bitterness would heal the wounds inflicted by Nazi domination in Europe. 'Now was the time to re-build if there was to be any future for the world', she wrote.

One of Ninette Jeanty's first steps was to appear as a witness for the defence in the trial of the man who had betrayed her to the Gestapo. Between 1946 and 1949 she returned many times to Germany. At first she was attached to the Judge Advocate General's Department of the War Office and was able to intercede on behalf of some of her former enemies. She visited and brought practical help to imprisoned Belgian collaborators and to Germans convicted of war crimes. These included former SS troops who had taken part in a terrible massacre on 10 June 1944. On that day a battalion of the SS Das Reich Regiment reached the little village of Oradour-sur-Glane, some 12 miles from Limoges. In a reprisal for a Resistance attack on German reinforcements for the Normandy battlefield they murdered 642 villagers, including 200 children. The men were shot in barns; the women and children locked in the church and burnt to death when the village was set on fire. In 1953 Ninette Jeanty attended the trial of the SS men in Bordeaux. They had been waiting in gaol for eight years. Ten of the prisoners were Germans and twelve were Alsatians, who had been forcibly conscripted in the SS regiment by the Nazi authorities when they were teenage boys. At the end of the trial the sentences were severe. The village of Oradour-sur-Glane has never been rebuilt and its ruins are a memorial to that horrific day of retribution.

In 1951 Ninette Jeanty gave the first of her famous 'colloquies' — meetings attended by distinguished figures held in the spirit of international reconciliation. She also devoted her time to helping intellectual refugees, destitute students and displaced persons from all over the world. They came to her flat in Brussels and later to her home in Cambridge where she lived with her second husband, Canon Charles Raven, former Master of Christ's College, Cambridge, an eminent theologian, botanist and pacifist. Her radiant spirit of forgiveness and reconciliation touched us each time we met her and in the letters she wrote after we left Belgium. Her message never wavered. 'What I am trying to do is to pass love on.'

*   *   *

I read Ninette Jeanty Raven's remarkable book *Without Frontiers* after we met her twenty-three years ago. I then became fascinated by women's experiences in the Second World War and read many memoirs, letters, diaries and slim volumes of poetry that had been written either during or after the war. In 1989 I started to research for this anthology.

The poems in *Shadows of War* are placed in chronological order of the war years and reflect many different attitudes, reactions and emotions experienced by 131 women who came from all walks of life. They wrote as civilians — actresses, teachers, professional writers, artists, nurses, factory workers, employees of the BBC, mothers at home with their children — and as 'poets in uniform' — members of the Armed Forces and nursing services, the Women's Land Army, various branches of the civil defence and the Women's Voluntary Service. For many women the act of writing a poem was part of the healing process. They wrote from home and overseas with humour, compassion, nostalgia, loneliness, boredom, grief, a deep sense of their faith, and hope for the future. There are poems that refer to the loss of HM ships; specific air and land battles; the agony of parting from loved ones; husbands, lovers, sons, brothers and friends killed in action; the birth of babies; friendships and love affairs; the seasons of the year; life on the Channel Islands during the German occupation; anxiety and death in air raids; the Nazi persecution of the Jews; and the horrors of Belsen and Hiroshima.

Over the war years there was a huge demand for books and magazines but limited paper supplies greatly reduced the number of titles published. Even so, a great many of the poets included in *Shadows of War* had at least one book of poetry published between 1940 and 1950.

Some became part of the literary scene during and after these years; many were already established writers before 1939.

Barbara Cartland, a prolific writer of popular novels, continued her output throughout the war. Edith Sitwell's earliest poems were published in the *Daily Mail* in 1913 and by 1939 she had written some thirty works – poetry, plays, biographies and a novel. Her poems 'Still Falls the Rain' and the three 'Poems for an Atomic Age', written during the war years, reflect the depth of her anguish at world events. Marie Carmichael Stopes, the pioneer of birth control, published her controversial *Ideal Marriage* in 1918. It sold over a million copies. In November 1924 a Marie Stopes birth-control clinic opened in North Kensington with Dick and Naomi Mitchison on the committee. By 1939 Naomi Mitchison had become a well-known author. At Carradale, her Scottish estate on the Kintyre peninsula, she looked after her family and evacuees, managed the farm and wrote her diary for Mass-Observation. This social research organisation recruited men and women from all over the British Isles to keep a continuous record of their everyday lives. She also started her historical novel *Bull Calves*. This was prefaced by her long and powerful poem, 'Clemency Ealasaid' in which she compared her grief after the death of her day-old baby daughter in July 1940 to the tragic events in war-torn Europe. Phyllis Shand Allfrey was Naomi Mitchison's secretary in 1938. She was politically active as a member of the Labour Party and with the Fabian Colonial Bureau and wrote most of her poetry and short stories in London during the war. After weeks of indecision she and her husband sent their two children to the USA for the duration of the war. In June 1940 Vera Brittain, and her husband George Catlin, also sent their two children, John and Shirley, to the United States for safety. Vera Brittain, celebrated for her pacifism after the First World War, was as committed to the pacifist cause during the Second World War. In 1942 her book, *Humiliation with Honour*, was published. It was written in the form of letters to her son John based on her Christianity and Pacifism. The book sold 10,000 copies within three months.

The predominantly female residents of a war-time Dorset village gave Sylvia Townsend Warner the background for *The Corner that Held Them*, her novel about the cloistered life within a fourteenth-century convent that she wrote during the war years. The impact of events on civilian life, before and during the war, when she lived in Romania and Egypt, were later vividly portrayed by Olivia Manning in *The Balkan Trilogy* and *The Levant Trilogy*. From their stone cottage in the hills of North Wales, the poet and artist Brenda Chamberlain and her artist husband John Petts ran the small Caseg Press. The poet Alun Lewis, while serving in the Royal Engineers, wrote asking them to bring out a series of cheap broadsheets with poems and engravings. He hoped these, like the ballads in the seventeenth- and eighteenth-century chapbooks that pedlars circulated around villages, would 'reach the people with beauty and love'.

The two leading literary magazines during the war years were considered to be *Horizon*, edited by Cyril Connolly, and *Penguin New Writing*, edited by John Lehmann. In June 1940 Connolly observed that 'Poetry is still the natural national form of self-expression', but for the November 1941 issue he received poems that were 'so bad' they 'should never have been written' and published no poetry at all. However, Mr Connolly pledged to publish women writers such as Anne Ridler and E.J. Scovell, 'who have by-passed both academic asceticism and rhyming journalism'. There were other popular and important literary magazines at this time. Reginald Moore edited the widely circulated *Modern Reading* from the cottage in North Wales where he lived with his wife Elizabeth Berridge and their two small children. In July 1940 Keidrych Rhys, the editor of the literary magazine *Wales*, was a gunner in the London Welsh Regiment. He spent his first leave with his wife, the poet Lynette Roberts, in the little white-washed cottage they rented for 3*s* 6*d* a week in Llanybri. They read through 'piles of other people's manuscripts' and he gathered together the first of his two anthologies *Poems from the Forces*.

Over forty poetry anthologies were published during the Second World War but women were not well represented in any of these except in two slim volumes; *Poems by Contemporary Women*, which included the works of twenty-nine poets, and *Poems of the Land Army* in which twenty land girls were included. Six of the poets in *Shadows of War* edited wartime anthologies. Patricia Ledward was co-editor of *Poems of this War by Younger Poets*, published in 1942; Honor Arundel was one of the editors of *New Lyrical Ballads*, published by Tambimuttu in his Editions Poetry London in 1945; Nancy Cunard edited *Poems for France: written by British*

Poets on France Since the War, published in 1944; Theodora Roscoe and Mary Winter Were edited *Poems by Contemporary Women*, published in 1944; and Vita Sackville-West was editor of *Poems of the Land Army: an Anthology of Verse by Members of the Women's Land Army*, published in 1945.

There is a wide range in the style and literary merit of the poems in *Shadows of War*. Some stand on their poetic value alone; others, written in the urgency of the moment, offer an historic testimony on events of the time; many combine both these attributes. During the war years the Irish scholar Helen Waddell worked on her translations of the Latin poems of medieval Europe whose significance lay in their 'courage and their poignancy: indeed in their bare existence'. Her assessment is as true for the lyrics written over 500 years ago as for the poetry and verse written by women during the Second World War:

. . . They are like the inscriptions scratched on dungeon walls or prison windows, the defiance of the spirit of man against material circumstance . . .

Anne Powell
Aberporth
April 1999

1939*

INTRODUCTION

During the 1930s Nazi Germany's re-armament and expansionist programme went from strength to strength. Hitler, who had become Chancellor of Germany in 1933 and lawfully Head of State the following year, believed that France and Britain were unprepared for another war and was resolved to reunite all Germans in a Greater Reich. From 1933 until the outbreak of the war the official policy of the German government permitted and encouraged emigration of Jews from Germany, Austria and Czechoslovakia. In March 1936 Hitler's troops occupied the demilitarised Rhineland and two years later Germany had annexed Austria. Hitler also claimed the Sudeten, an area of Czechoslovakia inhabited by Germans, and by September 1938 he was prepared for an invasion of Czechoslovakia and delivered a violent verbal attack on that peaceable country in a speech at a Nuremberg Party Rally. Unlike France, Great Britain was not bound by treaty to defend Czechoslovakia if she was attacked by Germany but on 15 September the British Prime Minister, Neville Chamberlain, flew to Munich and then travelled by train to Berchtesgaden to meet Hitler. After intense negotiations Chamberlain and the French Premier Edouard Daladier signed an agreement with Hitler in Munich in which he agreed not to attack Czechoslovakia if the Sudeten was ceded to Germany. Chamberlain returned to London believing he had secured 'peace for our time', but Czechoslovakia had been weakened, abandoned and betrayed.

By the beginning of 1939 Hitler had brought over 10 million people under his absolute rule and he continued on his offensive path. On 15 March his troops entered Prague. In the House of Commons Neville

---

* Main events in the various war zones, civilian life in the United Kingdom and episodes that have particular relevance to poems in *Shadows of War* are covered in the seven short introductions to the individual war years. These are thumbnail sketches but in the Select Bibliography I have listed some excellent reference books for more specific background reading on the war.

Chamberlain condemned this act of aggression and gave a guarantee that an attack on Poland would not be tolerated by the British government. In April Italy invaded Albania and the following month Benito Mussolini, the Italian dictator, signed the Pact of Steel with Germany which guaranteed military support for each other. They became known as the Axis Powers. Britain, who was by this time making active preparations for war, introduced conscription. On 23 August 1939 Josef Stalin and Hitler signed a Non-Aggression Pact between Russia and Germany and two days later the Anglo-Polish alliance was signed. Hitler was undaunted and at dawn on 1 September Germany delivered her *blitzkrieg*, 'lightning war', which combined air and ground attacks, against Poland. Mobilisation of British forces was ordered a few hours later. At 9 a.m. on 3 September 1939 Sir Neville Henderson, Britain's ambassador in Berlin, delivered an ultimatum to the German Führer. Unless his assurance to abandon the advance on Poland was received by 11 a.m., a state of war would exist between Britain and Germany. Hitler did not reply to the ultimatum.

In homes throughout the land families gathered round the wireless and listened in shocked silence to the Prime Minister's sombre words. As his broadcast ended air-raid warnings were sounded. Although war had seemed inevitable, the reality was appalling after only twenty years of peace. That evening France also declared war on Germany, and the Commonwealth countries India, Canada, Australia, New Zealand and South Africa soon followed. In mid-September Russia invaded Poland from the east and by the beginning of October the country was defeated, occupied and partitioned. During September and October the British Expeditionary Force was safely conveyed across the Channel to support the French, but little fighting took place and the next few months became known as the phoney war. At the end of November the Russian Army invaded Finland but was temporarily halted by the bitter winter weather.

At sea the Royal Navy bore the brunt of casualties during the first months of the war. On the day war was declared the British liner *Athenia*, was torpedoed and sunk in the Western Approaches despite Hitler's orders for U-boats to obey the Hague Convention – 128 people, including 28 Americans, lost their lives. On 17 September the aircraft carrier, HMS *Courageous*, was sunk by a U-boat in the Bristol Channel.

Scapa Flow, a large natural harbour in the Orkneys, was considered a safe base for the Fleet and the strategic point from which the Royal Navy could control the exits from the North Sea. The blockade line north of the Orkneys was composed of armed merchant cruisers and supporting warships. On 14 October 1939 a U-boat penetrated the defences and sank the battleship HMS *Royal Oak* as she lay at anchor with the loss of almost 800 lives. Two days later the Luftwaffe attacked the British Fleet for the first time and warships lying in the Firth of Forth were bombed. As a result twenty-five men were killed and four enemy bombers brought down. British shipping losses continued. During the autumn the German pocket battleship *Admiral Graf Spee* attacked merchant ships on trade routes in the South Atlantic and Indian Ocean. She was eventually brought to action by the cruisers HMS *Exeter*, HMS *Ajax* and HMS *Achilles* off the mouth of the River Plate. Badly damaged, the *Graf Spee* took refuge in Montevideo, a neutral harbour. As the time limit for her respite came to an end the British warships lay in wait outside territorial waters for the German ship to emerge. On the evening of 17 December she left harbour, steamed slowly seawards and then blew herself up. Although her captain had received full authority to scuttle his ship he felt responsible and heartbroken. That evening he shot himself.

On the home front air-raid precautions (ARP) were taken and shelters were dug; gas masks were issued; petrol was rationed; black-out regulations were strictly enforced; and as the men left home to join ships, regiments and air bases, over 1½ million mothers and children were evacuated from towns to the country. In October the pianist Myra Hess gave her first lunchtime concert at the National Gallery. People flocked here for comfort as the reality of another war increased. A large proportion of the British population had suffered personal loss in the First World War. Vera Brittain, whose fiancé and brother had been killed, was a dedicated pacifist and a founder sponsor of the Peace Pledge Union. The first of her letters to 'Peace Lovers', many of which were written from shelters during air raids, was sent on 4 October 1939.

. . . I hope to play a small part in keeping the peace movement together during the dark hours before us. By constantly calling on reason to mitigate passion, and truth to put falsehood to shame, I shall try, so far as one person can, to stem the tide of hatred which in war-time rises so swiftly that many of us are engulfed before we realise it. I want repeatedly to examine those popular slogans and hate-images by means of which we work up one another's emotions. I shall try to keep unimpaired the rational view we had of those whom we now call our enemies, and their needs and hopes, before our blood became heated, or we had suffered at their hands as they have suffered at ours . . .

TERESA HOOLEY

Christ at Berchtesgaden

If Christ went to Berchtesgaden,
(Christ, Who tore devils out of Magdalen, Who drove them headlong from the
    mind of the man dwelling amid the tombs),
If He saw Hitler,
Abandoned of good,
Screaming, blaspheming, raving,
Would He not stand
Strong and lovely as the face of the mountains outside,
Quiet as when He stooped and wrote with His finger in the dust,
Compassionate, all-knowing,
Gathering power of God as a chalice is brimmed with living wine by a priest;
Would He not say:
Come out of the man, thou unclean spirit,
As He said of old time?
So the devil would depart, howling, from his servant,
And better days would dawn for holier men.

THEODORA ROSCOE

Written After Visiting Germany in March, 1939

I loved Germany,
Loved the big, sweeping fields,
And the old farmhouses with their striped walls.
But it is different now;
Behind the welcome of friends
Stalks a shadowy figure,
Cruel, suspicious, menacing,
Tempting them to sell their souls,
To worship material force,
Bringing darkness where there was light,
Dragging them to destruction,
For brother is divided against brother,
Son against father.
It urges them to close their hearts.
To the cruelty of persecution,
To the call of humanity,
It moves secretly, sometimes in gentle disguise.

* * * * *

O, music loving people,
Strolling down the alleys in your Grosser Garten,
Bring back those happier days,
Thrust the menacing figure into the background,
Strangle it,
Before it is too late.
Be free again!
Be beloved!

HELEN WADDELL

From her home in London the poet and scholar Helen Waddell wrote to her sister: '. . . I could not go into the garden without a kind of trance of deep strong delight. The pear was out, and the cherries, and the light was a still gold, as if June were in the heart of April, and I began writing a thing in my head, not finished yet, and very poor, but it will show you what was in my mind —'.

April 20th, 1939
(HITLER IS TO ADDRESS THE REICHSTAG ON APRIL 28TH)

Earth said to Death,
Give these a little breath.
Give them eight days to feel the sun,
To see the limes in leaf . . .
Give me eight days,
And I will pour the silence of June
Into this April noon,
Wine of October in the vine still curled.
Then let you come.
Darkness shall find them sleeping undismayed,
Who shall make them afraid
Who saw eternity
In the brief compass of an April day?

SAGITTARIUS

Nerves
(SEPT. 2ND, 1939)

I think I'll get a paper,
I think I'd better wait.
I'll hear the news at six o'clock,
That's much more up to date.

It's just like last September,
Absurd how time stands still;
They're bound to make a statement.
I don't suppose they will.

I think I'd better stroll around.
Perhaps it's best to stay.
I think I'll have a whisky neat,
I can't this time of day.

I think I'll have another smoke.
I don't know what to do.
I promised to ring someone up,
I can't remember who.

They say it's been averted.
They say we're on the brink.
I'll wait for the 'New Statesman',
I wonder what they think.

They're shouting. It's a Special.
It's not. It's just street cries.
I think the heat is frightful.
God damn these bloody flies.

I see the nation's keeping cool,
The public calm is fine.
This crisis can't shake England's nerves.
It's playing hell with mine.

VERA BRITTAIN

Vera Brittain was at her cottage in Allum Green in the New Forest, when Neville Chamberlain's announcement that Britain was at war with Germany was broadcast on the wireless.

Sunday September 3rd
His voice sounded old & trembled – and suddenly, as I sat on the camp bed in the study listening between the two children, I found that the tears were running down my cheeks – I suppose from some subconscious realisation of the failure of my efforts for peace over 20 years for I had expected the announcement . . . went out in the forest; in the sunny quiet of the gorse and heather it was impossible to take in the size of the catastrophe . . .

September, 1939

The purple asters lift their heads
Beneath the azure autumn skies;
Above the sunflower's golden cup
Hover the scarlet butterflies.

Not in the sandbagged city street
Where London's silver guardians soar,
But through the cottage garden throbs
The aching grief of England's war.

JOAN BARTON

First News Reel: September 1939

It was my war, though it ended
When I was ten: could I know or guess
What the talking really said?
– 'Over the top. At the front.
Sealed-with-a-loving-kiss.
Train-loads of wounded men
At the old seaside station.
Two million dead' –
Child of the nightmare-crying 'Never again'.

The same 'I' sits here now
In this silent throng
Watching with dull surprise
Guns limbering to the line
Through umber sheaves,
Guns topped with dappled boys
And crowned with beckoning leaves,
Like floats for some harvest home
Of corn or wine;

A self removed and null
Doubting the eye that sees
The gun in its green bower,
Yet meticulously records
At each load, discharge, recoil,
How the leaves spin from the trees
In an untimely shower
Over the sunlit fields, and are whirled away
To the edge of the sky.

No mud. No wounds. No tears.
No nightmare cries. Is it possible
It could be different this time?
Far-off that passing bell
Tolls 'Different.
Yes always different. Always the same':
As the guns roar and recoil
And the leaves that spin from the trees
Deck boys for a festival.

VITA SACKVILLE-WEST

From her home Sissinghurst, in Kent, Vita Sackville-West recorded her impressions of the first weeks of the war: 'With the prospect of devastation hanging over us, the impression of fecundity produced by the country-side during the past fortnight strikes one as painfully ironical. All crops seemed to come to fruition at once: the corn, the apples and the hops. These things happen every year, but this year one noticed them more keenly than usual . . .' (From Vita Sackville-West's Country Notes in Wartime.*)*

September 1939

Sick to our souls we dumbly wait
As though some wild disordered star
Broke from its place, and from afar
Rushed downward like a streak of fate.

Nothing remains but active faith
And courage of a high despair,
In moments when we grow aware
Of noble death that is not death.

'Every evening I go my rounds like some night-watchman to see that the black-out is complete. It is. Not a chink reveals the life going on beneath those roofs, behind those blinded windows; love, lust, death, birth, anxiety, even gaiety. All is dark; concealed . . . I wander round, and towards midnight discover that the only black-out I notice is the black-out of my soul. So deep a grief and sorrow that they are not expressible in words.' (From Vita Sackville-West's Country Notes in Wartime.*)*

Black-out

Quiet. The tick of clock
Shall bring you peace,
To your uncertain soul
Give slow increase.

The blackened windows shut
This inward room
Where you may be alone
As in the tomb.

A tomb of life not death,
Life inward, true,
Where the world vanishes
And you are you.

War brings this seal of peace,
This queer exclusion,
This novel solitude,
This rare illusion,

As to the private heart
All separate pain
Brings loss of friendly light
But deeper, darker gain.

ANNE RIDLER

'This was written very soon after the declaration of war, so long anticipated and dreaded. My generation, who were children in the First World War, had debated so much about the justice of going to war under any circumstances, that we could not but compare our own state of mind with that of our forebears – e.g in the wars with France. "Deo gratias Anglia Redde pro victoria", as the anonymous Agincourt poem has it. Laurence Minot celebrated the battle of Crècy.' (Letter from the poet.)

Now as Then
SEPTEMBER 1939

When under Edward or Henry the English armies
Whose battles are brocade to us and stiff in tapestries
On a green and curling sea set out for France,
The Holy Ghost moved the sails, the lance
Was hung with glory, and in all sincerity
    Poets cried 'God will grant to us the victory'.
For us, who by proxy inflicted gross oppression,
Among whom the humblest have some sins of omission,
War is not simple; in more or less degree
All are guilty, though some will suffer unjustly.
Can we say Mass to dedicate our bombs?
Yet those earlier English, for all their psalms,
Were marauders, had less provocation than we,
And the causes of war were as mixed and hard to see.
Yet since of two evils our victory would be the less,
And coming soon, leave some strength for peace,
Like Minot and the rest, groping we pray
    'Lord, turn us again, confer on us victory.'

DALLAS KENMARE

September, 1939

(1) War
I have seen Arras and Reims and Ypres –
Arras the sad, the shrapnel-pock-marked,
Reims, the city of ghosts,
Ypres, the stricken, the silent.
I have seen phantom broken trees,
pointing gaunt fingers in accusation;
also I have seen the ugly mud-labyrinths,
where those they still called men supported life like animals –
and I have seen mile upon mile of little crosses, white and
    black –
graves of the English and the German dead.

And it has come again,
the agony that I cried must never be,
the spectre that haunted my days relentlessly –
for I could never forget
Arras and Reims and Ypres,
wan cities of the dead,
nor the pitiful broken trees,
and the twisted lives of the sons of God –
English and German and French –
nor the illimitable fields of small crosses,
white and black.

LILIAN BOWES LYON

A Son

A middle-aged farm-labourer lived here,
And loved his wife; paid rent to hard eternity
Six barren years, till thorn-tree-blessed she bore
A son with a bird's glint, and wheat-straw hair.
Sweet life! Yet neither boasted.
The boy was a tassel flown by gaunt serenity,
Hedge banner in the September of the War.

A jettisoned bomb fell; at noonday there,
Where take my dusty oath a cottage stood.
Great with unspendable centuries of maternity,
'At least he had struck seven', she said, 'this year—'
Of different grace; of blood.
The man looks bent; yet neither girds at God,
Remembering it was beautiful while it lasted.

PHYLLIS SHAND ALLFREY

In mid-September 1939 Phyllis Shand Allfrey and her two children were staying with Naomi Mitchison (q.v.) and her family at Carradale House on the Kintyre peninsula in Scotland. One evening after dinner they played the record of Beethoven's Fifth Symphony *on the gramophone.*

Beethoven in the Highlands

Like conscript soldiers, her fingers march on the keys
While an unrhythmic grief assaults her throat.
Out in the bay listless, irresolute seas
Whip the andante to a single note.

War of the heart, and battle out of reach!
Landscape of Argyll seen through pensive glass,
Will the machine-gun bullets litter this beach
And shrapnel scar the children on the grass?

The scherzo now; for it is yet too soon
To press the Marche Funêbre or to bombard
The greyness of a Highland afternoon
With that crescendo pitiful and hard.

The great deaf German sings to deafened ears,
And darkened minds anticipate the shriek
Of anti-aircraft guns and loyal cheers
Stop the offensive! Let adagio speak . . .

Those first grave chords, fluted and clarion, pierce
The bogus hatreds and the native pride.
Brothers in music, halting, deny their fierce
Sick passion for the Rhineland or the Clyde.

The great deaf German groped for this, and more.
Giving his brain and heart as food for sound,
He gave himself for the Argyllshire shore
And gave himself for men the world around.

VIRGINIA GRAHAM

Sound the Trumpet

If, said the Speaker, raising her voice in a rage,
(she was round about fifty years of age)
if you young girls in this country are going to shirk,
then all I can say is, by heaven, you must be made to work!
If you will not go voluntarily into the factories or join the Forces
then you must be driven there like horses!
    We will not tolerate slackness, it is our duty to see
that every young woman under the age of thirty-three
is usefully employed making guns or aeroplane parts
and so on. There must be no excuses, no faint hearts.
    The youth of England must show the world
why the Union Jack has never yet been furled!
If Russia can do it, surely we can do it too?
I want you – she pointed at the auditorium – and you and you!
    After a sip of water, the Speaker reluctantly resumed her seat,
and the women clapped vigorously and stamped their feet.
They were enthusiastic, they screamed each to each,
Wasn't that inspiring? Wasn't that a really *fine* speech?
    and they looked about them with ardent, burning eyes,
and the hall was filled with the sound of their battle cries,
and they beat their pointed umbrellas like tom-toms on the floor.
    (Their ages averaged, roughly, sixty-four.)

SAGITTARIUS

The Descent of Man

'An emergency trench . . . can be rapidly made in a garden. The depth suggested is 4ft. 6in. The roof should slope slightly so that rain-water may drain off and should be covered with two or three inches of earth to hold it down.' – The Times, Sept. 26

For this, man's handiwork was wrought,
For this he heavenward aspired,
For this his philosophic thought
Of universal truth inquired,
And all his science comes to this
Derogatory Nemesis.

The long achievement of the mind,
The Law's majestic edifice,
Arts for man's benefit designed,
All time's inventions come to this,
That people with immortal souls
Must crawl like beetles into holes.

Emancipated from the ape
So long to wear creation's crown,
A little surface soil we scrape
And living in the earth lie down,
Abandoning the godlike view
To squirm below as vermin do.

With drains and ditches for our tomb
We scurry underground to hide,
And there await the insect's doom,
In torrents of insecticide.
As man's exterminating bomb
Rounds off his epic martyrdom.

SARAH BRYAN

I Admired Him Digging

I admired him digging
They were making an air-raid shelter
and a young workman was digging
the sullen, yellow clay.
With a curved rhythm that did not falter
came the thrust of the spade, the tugging,
the lift and the cast away.

In admiration
I saw his strength with the earth.
In his task was a close relation
(he sang as he worked away)
with our newly invented death,
but he was entirely immortal –
Man and the wrestling clay.

With sinews hardened,
his frame's rude grace appearing,
he worked as Adam gardened;
his strong hands caked with grime,
in the dirty slacks he was wearing,
(flax hair was curved at his brow)
he was beautiful, carved in time.

Alexandra Etheldreda Grantham

War

Beyond all speech the agony and grief
Which in an ever widening torrent reach
Right round the world, beyond hope of relief,
  Beyond all speech,

Beyond the power of God to heal. Men preach
Christ's gospel, but descend to deeds, the chief
Satanic lord of hell would fear to teach.

It should be filled with love the passage brief
From birth's mysterious source to death's dim
    beach
Beyond the fog that hides the fatal reef,
  Beyond all speech.

SHEILA WINGFIELD

From 'Men in War'

Shouts rang up the street
War War it has come
Like leaves they were blown
A spear from its corner
A summons on paper
Or buckle to thumb

In the dark of a room
Old fears were known
By wrinkled up cheeks
And by young wives
Who bending at waist
Must kiss them alone

But light were their feet
As thoughts were broken
And barriers thrown –
Out of copse out of brake
Out of field they were flown
To the tap of the drum.

Goodbye the milkcart pony
Standing in the sun;
The creaking basket
Of a baker's round;
And summer's garden besom
Sweeping on the ground
Then pausing; work unfinished
And work done.

Goodbye to the inn's warmth
Of views on beer and crop,
Where each man's talk's
As well known as his gait;
Goodbye to what the village
Knows and hears; to that late
Word at a lit door
Of a small shop.

Goodbye such emptiness
As loiters up and down
To show its friends
The new pup on a string,
Or with some tight-held flowers
Goes mutely visiting –
On Sundays, in the cleanness
Of a town . . .

FREDA LAUGHTON

The Evacuees

There is no sound of guns here, nor echo of guns.
The spasm of bombs has dissolved
Into the determination of the tractor.

Our music now is the rasp of the corncrake
And the wedge-shaped call of the cuckoo
Above leaves tranced in the lap of summer.

We have discovered the grass, curled in the ditches.
We have combed it with rakes in the hayfields,
And coiffed it in lion-coloured stacks.

We have stroked milk, warm and gentle from the cow,
The placid primitive milk, before bottles
Sterilise its mild wonder.

We have met the bland smile of eggs in the willow-basket;
Returned the stolid stare of cheeses ripening on the shelf;
Warmed ourselves at the smell of baking bread.

We have seen food, the sacrament of life,
Not emasculate and defunct upon dishes, but alive,
Springing from the earth after the discipline of the plough.

EDITH PICKTHALL

At the beginning of the war, Edith Pickthall joined the village branch of the Red Cross Detachment in Mylor, near Falmouth, Cornwall. Mylor was a reception area for evacuees.

Evacuee

The slum had been his home since he was born;
And then war came, and he was rudely torn
From all he'd ever known; and with his case
Of mean necessities, brought to a place
Of silences and space; just boom of sea
And sough of wind; small wonder then that he
Crept out one night to seek his sordid slum,
And thought to find his way. By dawn he'd come
A few short miles; and cattle in their herds
Gazed limpidly as he trudged by, and birds
Just stirring in first light, awoke to hear
His lonely sobbing, born of abject fear
Of sea and hills and sky; of silent night
Unbroken by the sound of shout and fight.

CHLORIS HEATON ROSS

Sunday Tea – 1939

Blinds drawn on rain; the fire's capricious flames
Kiss here an ambered cheek, deep-slippered toes,
Swift knitting pins, dark oils in gilded frames,
While muffins' cheering vapours tempt the nose.

Cups chatter busily; the shadows kiss;
Smiles barter: 'Sugar, please!' for 'Pass the toast!'
Our talk grows murmurous with tea-drugged bliss;
The old, sweet gift of laughter lifts our host.

Mad fairy tales the crumpled news-sheet screams –
We chat of wars and leagues and exiled kings,
Then turn our minds to weightier, present themes,
To horses, golf . . . the copper kettle sings.

The black, voluptuous cat yawns distantly
And England nods in peace at Sunday tea.

SYBIL POWIS

Peace Ironical
(ARMISTICE DAY, 1939)

The sea swings idly, full and bluish white
Like skimmed milk. Over the reeking boats
That lie like whales immobile on the beach,
The avid gulls poise, plunge, retreat, return.
Nets, newly-oiled, are stretched on shore to dry,
A creamy film, fine, delicate as lace.

The sun, May-warm, shines on the frothy lip
Of the long bay, lights up the squat mill's sails:
The air speaks peace to-day; this purring sea,
This clear-swept blue dabbled with puffs of cloud
Seem freshly made, unvoyaged, without speck.

Yet peace is but illusion. We have seen
The tilted hulls of ships go slowly down;
Men rescued, injured, dazed with nothing left
But life grown now precarious and full
Of dangers hiding subtly in the deep.

Here we have seen, like giant chestnuts, round
Spiked mines thrown up by the protesting sea
Lie ominous along the empty beach.
The sky too has its menace: the dull sound
Of thrumming engines, high, invisible,
Strikes fear, and the dark monotony of night
Torn by the siren's undulating scream
Breathes out suspicion. The bland moon
We eye distrustfully, we who like moles
Grope in the tunnels of our blackened streets.

Moth-like, the pale gulls flutter round the masts.
Behind them, facing seaward in a square
Of green a slender cross is raised,
Its base inscribed: round it the massed
Poppies lift their silent scarlet cry
And mock this peace. Our sunlit quietude
Is shattered by their poignant irony.

MINNIE HASKINS

King George VI quoted this extract from a longer poem in his Christmas broadcast to the Empire in 1939.

God Knows

And I said to the man who stood at
the gate of the year: 'Give me a light
that I may tread safely into the unknown.'
And he replied:
'Go out into the darkness and put
your hand into the Hand of God. That
shall be to you better than light and
safer than a known way . . .'

1940

INTRODUCTION

On 8 January 1940 every man, woman and child in the United Kingdom was issued with a food ration book. With the exception of tea, people were required to register with one particular retailer for basic food – sugar, meat, fats, bacon and cheese. The adult allocation for the first week was 4 oz bacon or ham; 4 oz butter; and 12 oz sugar. Meat was not rationed until March. Children, invalids and expectant mothers were allowed one pint of milk per day. Bread, potatoes, vegetables, fruit and fish were not rationed. By July the weekly ration of tea was 2 oz per adult. Shortages became more acute when food supply ships were sunk and the weekly allowance per person varied accordingly. The housewife had to adapt to these difficult times; she spent many hours queuing for food and then had to eke out small quantities with the help of hints and recipes given on the wireless, in newspapers, leaflets and books. Puddings and cakes were made without eggs and fruit preserved without sugar. On 3 June 1940 Naomi Mitchison recorded in the Diary she kept for Mass Observation:

> Unfortunately all the rhubarb we'd been bottling is beginning to go. Everything seems to unless there is masses of sugar in it, which is so maddening. We have a certain amount of sugar saved, but of course it won't be easy after the present ration. The cut in butter will be no hardship, as nobody really knows the difference except me. I am trying to have cheese dishes etc., as much as possible . . . We have bought about half a big jar full of eggs laid down in water-glass; I am getting smoked haddock once a week from Campbeltown which helps with that. The hens are not laying very well . . . Have laid in some more soap, and coffee, which we can't get locally . . .

The 'Dig for Victory' campaign was launched in December 1940. People were encouraged to grow their own vegetables in gardens and allotments – the number of the latter increased from 815,000 in 1939 to 1½ million in 1943. Pig and poultry keeping became popular and every available acre was farmed for food. The Women's Land Army, prisoners of war, conscientious objectors and civilian volunteers replaced the pre-war farm labourers who were now in uniform. During 1940 the Women's Institutes produced 3 million pounds of jam; 150 tons of canned fruit and 150 tons of pulped fruit and chutney.

At the outbreak of war over 70,000 'enemy aliens' in the United Kingdom had been placed in specific categories. In May 1940 rumours of fifth columnists became widespread and aliens, many of whom were refugees from Nazi oppression, were interned in camps, sent to the Isle of Man or deported. However, by the summer of the following year, a more reasonable attitude prevailed and only some 5,000 were still interned; many served in the forces after their release.

During April and early May 5,000 Polish officers, prisoners of war of the Russians since September 1939, were massacred in a small wood near the village of Katyn. This act of appalling barbarity became the subject of major political controversy between Germany and Russia, each denying responsibility. It was not until 1992 that President Yeltsin finally admitted that the Russian secret police (NKVD) had committed the crime on the direct orders of Stalin.

Swedish iron ore was recognised as being vital to the German war effort. This commodity was imported via Norway and the North Sea, particularly in winter when the Baltic Sea was frozen. Under the pretext of helping Finland, Britain and France planned to support Norway but Germany moved first and on 9 April 1940 occupied Denmark and invaded Norway. Caught by surprise, the British government, in a poorly organised campaign, landed forces in Norway on 14 April. Individual units of the three services did very well, particularly the Navy which, in the First and Second Battle of Narvik, sank or disabled a large part of the German surface fleet at heavy loss to themselves. At the beginning of June the Norwegian campaign was abandoned, troops were evacuated and King Haakon and his government sailed for exile in the United Kingdom aboard the cruiser HMS *Devonshire*. On 8 June the aircraft carrier HMS *Glorious* together with her two escorting destroyers *Ardent* and *Acasta* were sunk by the German battleship *Scharnhorst*.

On 10 May Neville Chamberlain received a vote of no confidence in the House of Commons and Winston Churchill became Prime Minister. On the same day Hitler launched his invasion of Holland, Belgium and

France; the Luftwaffe bombed towns and airfields and Panzer Corps marched on the offensive. Five days later the Dutch Army surrendered and on 28 May King Leopold announced the surrender of the Belgian Army. The Allied rearguard, outmanoeuvred by the speed of the German thrusts, tried to prevent them from reaching the retreating allies on the beaches at Dunkirk. The RAF, heavily outnumbered, lost 177 aircraft. The Luftwaffe flattened the town of Dunkirk, ferociously attacked the stranded men and sank or damaged many of the rescue craft. Against these formidable odds almost a thousand ships and privately owned small boats evacuated the men across a calm channel to safety. Between 26 May and 3 June 338,226 Allied troops were rescued.

The battle for France that followed lasted seventeen days. On 14 June the Germans entered Paris. Eight days later, unable to continue effective defence, France signed a humiliating armistice with Germany in the same railway carriage used for the 1918 Armistice. German casualties on land and in the air were estimated at 127,000; those for France at 290,000 with 1.9 million men prisoners of war. Winston Churchill told the House of Commons 'The Battle of France is over. I expect the Battle of Britain is about to begin.' Britain was concerned that the still considerable French Navy might fall into German hands. Negotiations with the French at the Algerian ports of Mers-el Kebir and Oran failed and on 3 July the Royal Navy were forced to attack. Most of the ships were crippled, 1,297 French sailors were killed and the French were naturally bitterly resentful.

On 19 June Churchill ordered troops to be withdrawn from the Channel Islands as they were not considered defensible. About 30,000 islanders were evacuated and some 60,000 remained. On 28 June 1940 Guernsey and Jersey were bombed by the Luftwaffe and two days later a German detachment landed at Guernsey airport. The occupation of Alderney and Sark followed. Newspapers were censored; property, transport and supplies requisitioned; teaching of German became compulsory in schools. Alderney was heavily fortified and parts of the island turned into labour camps. Life for the Channel Islanders was to be harsh for the remainder of the war.

The Luftwaffe had been attacking British shipping in the Channel during June and July. Hitler's plans for the invasion of Great Britain, code-named Operation Sealion, depended on the RAF's defeat by the Luftwaffe.

On 10 July the German airforce switched their operations to eliminate the small British fighter force. They attacked control radars and airfields but Fighter Command, with an excellent control system, held them off. There were heavy losses on both sides. The Battle of Britain that followed was to prove one of the turning points of the war. The RAF pilots, 'The Few', were strengthened by young men from Canada, Australia, New Zealand, South Africa, Ireland and the United States; and Free Polish, Free French and Free Czech pilots made up fighter squadrons. The battle in the sky was at its most intense during August and September 1940. On 24 August London was bombed and Churchill ordered an attack on Berlin the following day. Hitler's angry retaliation, as the daylight air battle was at its peak, came with preliminary bombing raids on Birmingham and Liverpool followed by a raid on London on the night of 7 September. This change of tactics proved to be a serious German blunder. The blitz on London initially lasted for fifty-seven consecutive nights. Underground stations and a variety of public shelters provided some protection for Londoners; class barriers were forgotten in the shared suffering and appalling conditions among the debris and devastation; civilian women worked as air-raid wardens, firefighters, drivers of ambulances and mobile canteens, as members of the Women's Voluntary Services. Soon these amenities were applied in the provincial cities ravished from sustained bomb attacks. On the night of 14/15 November over 400 German bombers destroyed Coventry cathedral, much of the city centre and numerous armament factories; 380 people were killed and 865 injured. The terrible air raids on London and other cities continued but the threat of invasion receded after Hitler, frustrated at not gaining air supremacy among other factors, postponed Operation Sealion indefinitely.

Italy declared war on the United Kingdom and France on 10 June 1940 and on 27 September joined Germany and Japan in signing the Tripartite Pact. The following month an ill-prepared Italian Army invaded Greece. On 11 November 1940 British sea power in the Mediterranean was firmly established after twenty-one torpedo-carrying Swordfish aircraft from HMS *Illustrious* successfully attacked and crippled the Italian Fleet in the port of Taranto. By skilful offensive use of limited resources General Wavell defended Egypt from a superior Italian force and defeated them at various points along the North African coast, notably Sidi Barrani on 9 December.

RUTH PITTER

Seagulls in London, January, 1940

They stormed upon me like catastrophe.
All fear of man was gone: scenting the food,
The harpy-crowd gathered and broke on me.
These, bred in solitude
Among the sea-pink in the salt sea-marsh,
Moated about by creeks of quaking slime
Lonelier than mountain deserts, now with harsh
Throats besought alms at this most bitter time.

My hands, cold-palsied, felt their crooked bills,
Their pirate sails struck on my stiffened cheek;
Their cold wet feet touched me with fleeting chills
Frail and inadvertent, that seemed to speak
For all the fury, of existence weak;
And one was lame,
Lagged on the turn, got nothing when he came.

Heart-withering hunger! how the terror whips
The shrinking mind! knowing ourselves curtailed,
More steel, less grain loading the threatened ships,
We, for whom plenty never yet has failed,
Feel the frore shadow of what famine now
Clutches the bowels of both foe and friend,
And while all Europe shudders in the snow
Dare not foresee, nor think upon the end.

And I am moved to ask you to forgive
If I have hope: if like a stubborn seed
The heart turns tough, determined still to live,
Made a mere dormant centre of the need
For bare existence, of the will to be:
If this is hardness, O forgive it me!

Pardon the faith, that will not be denied,
One with my life, and needing not a name,
That like these wings over the rushing tide
Beats upward, and not knowing whence it came
Battles with *hunger, anguish, and the sea*!
If this is folly, O forgive it me!

DALLAS KENMARE

Chestnut-buds and Hazel-catkins

'This world is word, expression, news of God.
Therefore its end, its purpose, its purport, its
meaning is God and its life or work to name
and praise Him.'
                    Gerard Manley Hopkins

Now it is February, the war five months old,
and I turn to my chestnut-buds, proudly swell-
    ing, bravely showing green;
to hazel-catkins, already golden, already shedding
    pollen –
chestnut-buds and hazel-catkins, victorious to-
    gether in a rough green vase.

'Escape,' is it, in a world of war, of stark
    actualities, to turn to green growing things?
To find a consummate answer in the relentless
    growth of the chestnut-buds,
the passionate assertion of life in the pollen-
    dusted catkins?
This is no escape, this is reality –
the ugly world of war, of hate and of death is
    illusion, because denial of life.

Therefore I turn with passion to my chestnut-
    buds and my hazel-catkins,
I turn with worship to the undeniable evidence
    of creation,
I reject utterly the negating principles of des-
    truction and death.

I will not listen to talk of war and of infamous
    wastage;
I turn triumphantly from the evil manifestations
    of science, from the death-inventions –
in turning to my chestnut-buds and my delicate
    life-pregnant catkins
I turn to God, Whose concern is ever with
    creativeness.

ROSAMOND PRAEGER

War
(MARCH 24 1940)

I hear the soldiers marching on the road,
    And overhead their grim machinery roars.
Wild lights go flickering across the world,
    And Death is knocking on a million doors.

And this is Easter. Lovely, delicate things
    Are pushing upwards through the warming earth,
The resurrection of the hidden Power,
    That fosters in us life, and love and mirth.

What is the darker Power that dogs us here,
    And piles on Man intolerable loads?
I see the war-planes crashing from the clouds,
    And mangled men upon a thousand roads.

AUDREY BEECHAM

Norway

Once the sound of its drum has burst the eardrums
And the loud shriek anguished at last to silence
Love of itself is vanquished;
But the relinquished
Hold of the lover sleeping binds the mind
To levels lower and to those more stale
Than pools of stagnant rain beneath the earth.

Spain, our ace, was tricked by molten gold:
And our sly trail unrolled on Europe's map
Slugged action, flounders now through snow
To race the waiting bomb-burst of our hearts.
The rhythmical stop-go
Of fate's two eyes suffice to hold us back
From any courage which would jeopardize
The bonds that hold our honour to a rack.

O England, may your blight of boredom melt
Like sweat of love, and may your wind ride up
Above the doldrums of a boring war
To blast the flags that flap in national shame
Out of the sky
And cheer the hands that fail
And fall from masts.

MAY DOLPHIN

May Dolphin's son Humphrey was a prisoner of war between 1940 and 1945.

Norway, 1940

The lilies and the foxgloves wave their heads
Under the limes where they grow tall and straight.
Twice have they bloomed, once fallen, since you went,
You and your comrades, to that northern land
Where bombs were dropped on undefended heads
And men lay dying on the crimsoned snow.
Yet some survived, came home, and told their tale;
Others, like you, wait in an alien land
And send brave messages of hope and cheer.
But always to my heart the flowers say,
'Will they be back next spring, or next, or when,
That we may bloom to give them welcome home?

Uncensored

What can I tell you as I censored write
That you may read the thought between the lines –
The rose's colours are a warm delight,
The winds, as ever, whisper in the pines?

Maybe, in prison camps they say to you
Your rose-bed is a dream which spectres haunt,
And the deep hollow where the lilies grew
Is the abode of shadows, tall and gaunt.

Yet, in the script which alien eyes have scanned
You'll find a bouquet that will tell you much,
So much that none but you will understand,
Remembering a rose, a scent, a touch.

SYLVIA LYND

RAF, May, 1940

Heard the squadron flying home
At midnight high among the stars;
Never did tale of Greece or Rome
Tell of such heroes or such wars.

Legend nor boast nor history
Proclaims such deeds as these achieve,
Who daily fight Thermopylae,
Who snatch the glove from Death, and live.

Perseus and Bellerophon,
They, too, were fighters and had wings,
They fought with monsters and they won,
And in the stars their glory rings.

Castor and Pollux keep their station,
Neither do we dispute their claim
If a more glorious constellation
Should mark a still more glorious fame.

Instead of Bear, or Wain, or Plough,
Splendid to see in night's great dome,
Give to those stars a new name now,
Call them the Squadron Flying Home.

PHYLLIS SHAND ALLFREY

In the spring of 1940 Phyllis Shand Allfrey took her two children to live with friends in the United States for the duration of the war. She was reunited with Bernd von Arnim, whom she first knew in Buffalo, New York, early in the 1930s. Although she was torn between her love for him and her loyalty to her husband Robert, she decided to return to England and Robert. She sailed from New York at a time when the U-boat threat in the Atlantic made every voyage a dangerous undertaking.

Cunard Liner 1940

Now, for the last time, total solitude.
The ship hangs between explosion and quiet forward driving,
The faces of the passengers are grave.
Oh what is this sobriety which so denudes us
Of the sarcastic cough, the cackling laughter,
The thin flirtation and the importance of black coffee after?
Of course, we are all being British, all being ourselves,
All knowing we carry Empire on our shoulders:
But even so, we are exceptionally grave.
Voices: 'My husband's heavily insured.'
'I said to stewardess, get baby into the boat!'
'I carry pneumonia tablets in my old army bag.'

Yes, friends, but if we had no time to scramble
For babies, tablets and insurance papers,
What would the U-boat's dart, the spurting mine
Mean to each one of us? The end of *what*?

The end of helpless dignity for the army officer!
The end of dancing for the golden girl:
The end of suckling babies for the mother:
The end of study for the gangling youth:
The end of profit for the business men:
The end of brave sea-faring for the crew:
But for so many it would be the end of nothing,
Of nothing nicely done and dearly cherished.

And for myself? O darling, for myself
It would be life's most true and fatal end;
It would be the conclusion in my brain
And my most spirited heart and my fair body
Of you – the last rich consciousness of you.

BARBARA CARTLAND

In the 1935 General Election, at the age of twenty-nine, Barbara Cartland's brother Ronald won the parliamentary seat for the Conservative Party in the Birmingham constituency of King's Norton. Ronald Cartland, MP, joined the 53rd Worcestershire Yeomanry, Anti-Tank Regiment, Royal Artillery and arrived in France with the British Expeditionary Force in April 1940. On 15 May he wrote to his mother: '. . . the fog of war is pretty impenetrable. We shall win in the end, but there's horror and tribulation ahead of all of us. We can't avoid it . . .' The Worcestershire Yeomanry had all their anti-tank guns put out of action at Cassel. They were making for the coast when Ronald Cartland was killed by a bullet from a German tank. He was the first Member of Parliament to be killed in the war.

To Ronald
KILLED NEAR CASSEL, 30 MAY 1940

On the 'Dunkirk beaches' of England's story
She finds her soul and her greatest glory,
For the men who love her are always the same,
Ready to die in freedom's name.

The vision that once our fathers knew
Has been born again. Can we make it true?
So that out of the muddle and sins of the past
England may find her peace at last?

MARY DÉSIRÉE ANDERSON

Mary Désirée Anderson, Lady Cox, lived in London during the war.

Dunkirk

For many days it seemed as if the sky
Held back its breath in anguish, and the sea
Seemed frozen by our fear, for storms meant death
To countless thousands whom this calm set free.

Our whole world dwindled to that narrow beach;
We watched a miracle with hearts of stone,
Then, awestruck with relief, we turned once more
To seek for friends — and found ourselves alone.

PAMELA HUNKA

The Time of Dunkirk

We rode through the rain
And it blew in our faces
The scent of the may blossom
Came from the hedges
The wheels of our bicycles
Whirred on the roadway,
And we heard in the distance
Sound of the gunfire.

We laughed at the rain
(Sheltered in an old factory)
We watched and we saw it teem
Over the marshes,
And we saw some old ships
Far away on the river;
And the rain on the iron roof
Sounded like gunfire.

I know we were happy
For we were all young there,
A bright moment of youth
Like a raindrop it shone there
Soon will it fall
Like a tear in the mud there;
And our dreams shall be silenced
By sound of the gunfire.

TERESA HOOLEY

Regatta

The little ships of England,
　　In fifteen-eighty-eight,
(The Armada in the Channel,
　　King Philip at the gate,)
From Sussex and from Hampshire
　　Sailed out with pennons high,
Like terriers at the heels of Drake,
The furious fighting ships of Drake
　　To victual and supply.

Three hundred years and over
　　Drew onward to a Day –
(The foe across the Channel
　　Our fighting men at bay.)
Ghostly, through listening shires
　　Drake's drum began to roll:
Like terriers on the Navy's heels
The little ships on dauntless keels
　　Set out with steadfast soul.

The little ships of Dunkirk
　　Drove forward into hell:
Death on the beaches, death from the air –
　　Machine-gun, bomb, and shell.
Yacht, trawler, barge and coaster,
　　Battered and scored and black,
Snatched life like Lazarus from the tomb,
Snatched victory from the jaws of doom,
　　And brought the Army back!

PEGGY WHITEHOUSE

From A Democrat's Chapbook

. . . To my house (I being born under Cancer)
Came a lieutenant, stationed here, for rooms.
Came a lieutenant, stationed here, from Dover
When tension was in the white sky
And beautiful as silver fish were wheeling the formations,
Veily with their fins, disturbing the white sky:

Beautiful in their formation, in the days of thousands
Distant and imperative (for we did not know war)
Bright flashed the eyes of the smiling man
With a spectre behind them: (we did not know war)
Gay smiled the lips of this attractive person
With a twist, as he unbuckled his holster. (We did not know war.)

We knew little of the eternal peaceable graves
Only another sort of death.
Hence in the grey eyes the spectre.

'I was not there, I took them off the boats,'
The Lieutenant said. 'And in their pockets were photographs.'
He did not weep, but in his eyes was pity for the dead
Lying lustless now, who went all gay in Paris.
He lusting in his fine smiling, smart and dapper.
That part of him alive.
He seeing this tragedy in death
For it would most be his . . .

DENISE LEVERTOV

Denise Levertov was evacuated to Buckinghamshire where she heard the guns in France during the Dunkirk evacuation.

Listening to Distant Guns

The roses tremble; oh, the sunflower's eye
Is opened wide in sad expectancy.
Westward and back the circling swallows fly,
The rooks' battalions dwindle near the hill.

That low pulsation in the east is war:
No bell now breaks the evening's silent dream.
The bloodless clarity of evening's sky
Betrays no whisper of the battle-scream.

SYLVIA TOWNSEND WARNER

During the war Sylvia Townsend Warner lived at Frome Vauchurch, Maiden Newton, Dorset, with Valentine Ackland (q.v.). She became secretary to the local branch of the WVS. On 13 June 1940 she wrote in her diary:

> *. . . Paris has fallen – has been abandoned . . . For some days the city has been under a pall of smoke from the burning oil-drums in the suburbs. One could not see across the Place de la Concorde. During the last night they blew up the factories.*
>
> *But all day the impression in my mind has been the serenity, the urbanity of Paris. Those wide streets, the air of tranquility and civilisation, must have a queerly austere and reproving look to an invading army, confused with triumph and exhaustion.*
>
> *It seems to me that the Louvre and the Place de la Concorde, and Notre Dame and the bridges . . . must have a look of saying – Yes, here we are. Et puis? And the people who remain: I suppose their blank faces would have much the same impression.*

Road 1940

Why do I carry, she said,
This child that is no child of mine?
Through the heat of the day it did nothing but fidget and whine,
Now it snuffles under the dew and the cold star-shine,
And lies across my heart heavy as lead,
Heavy as the dead.

Why did I lift it, she said,
Out of its cradle in the wheel-tracks?
On the dusty road burdens have melted like wax,
Soldiers have thrown down their rifles, misers slipped their packs:
Yes, and the woman who left it there has sped
With a lighter tread.

Though I should save it, she said,
What have I saved for the world's use?
If it grow to hero it will die or let loose
Death, or to hireling, nature already is too profuse
Of such, who hope and are disinherited,
Plough, and are not fed.
But since I've carried it, she said,

So far I might as well carry it still.
If we ever should come to kindness someone will
Pity me perhaps as the mother of a child so ill,
Grant me even to lie down on a bed;
Give me at least bread.

RUTH PITTER

The Sparrow's Skull

MEMENTO MORI
WRITTEN AT THE FALL OF FRANCE

The kingdoms fall in sequence, like the waves on the
    shore.
All save divine and desperate hopes go down, they are
    no more.
Solitary is our place, the castle in the sea,
And I muse on those I have loved, and on those who
    have loved me.

I gather up my loves, and keep them all warm,
While above our heads blows the bitter storm:
The blessed natural loves, of life-supporting flame,
And those whose name is Wonder, which have no other
    name.

The skull is in my hand, the minute cup of bone,
And I remember her, the tame, the loving one,
Who came in at the window, and seemed to have a mind
More towards sorrowful man than to those of her own
    kind.

She came for a long time, but at length she grew old;
And on her death-day she came, so feeble and so bold;
And all day, as if knowing what the day would bring,
She waited by the window, with her head beneath her
    wing.

And I will keep the skull, for in the hollow here
Lodged the minute brain that had outgrown a fear;
Transcended an old terror, and found a new love,
And entered a strange life, a world it was not of.

Even so, dread God! even so, my Lord!
The fire is at my feet, and at my breast the sword,
And I must gather up my soul, and clap my wings, and
    flee
Into the heart of terror, to find myself in Thee.

IRENE RATHBONE

If You Sank . . .

I

Because you had a radiance beyond others',
Were white, blue, gold,
(The wheat in your fields,
Fleurs de lys on your shields,
Cocks on spires old,
Your skies, rivers' sand, blond bread)
Because you said,
Men are free, they shall know it, men are brothers!

II

Because when fighting gods of murk you smiled,
Blades in the sun,
Feet on the homely soil,
Lived as though pleasure, toil,
Wisdom were one,
Took truth for your worship, not death,
Drew dulcet breath,
We mourned when your lilies were defiled.

III

When they told us your lilies were defiled,
Smelt worse than weeds
We wept; but, ah, waited
For pride recreated,
For grief-forged deeds . . .
And they gleamed, as we waited, they came,
Shamed the world's shame.
You resisted, you rejoiced us and – you smiled.

IV

But thinly now; this night all nights transcends,
Tears blot your blue,
Outrage historic yields
Place in your gracious fields
To horrors new,
Your small ones fall famished, cells deep
The tortured keep,
White innocents are shot, and far your friends.

V

How can we cry, Hold out, be strong and stronger!
We, whom sea saved?
Your hell is unshared by us,
Rescue declared by us
Halts; while enslaved,
Racked, spectral, you strike at the Beast,
See felons feast.
We redden in our island, how much longer?

VI

Yet forced to cry, Hold out! For if you perished,
Though all we stayed,
Earth's heart would beat weakly,
Life's banners droop bleakly,
Feet be afraid.
We tell you, ten roods of your cornland,
Your art-rich torn land,
Your peace-loving blood-sodden bold land
Your vine-sweet old land
Above ten null new continents are cherished.

Ah if you sank
What worth America? We drank,
Drink still, *your* springs, undying France.

CECILY MACKWORTH

Cecily Mackworth helped refugees from Belgium and the north of France at a rest centre at Austerlitz station before she left her home in Paris on 10 June 1940. Her journey south to Marseille took her two months. The long distances she covered on foot in the hot sun were relieved by train journeys, lifts in cars, farm carts and lorries. Towards the end of her eventful and exciting journey, she was offered a lift up by a young French officer in his dilapidated army car. She had just passed a signpost indicating 'Toulouse, 270 kilometres':

> *This was my first contact with the south, for this young man came from Toulon . . . He had passed the war far from the front as supplies officer to a regiment which had remained as rearguard in Central France, and had never seen his own home menaced. The difference of mentality between Southerners and Northerners, which became more and more marked as I moved southward, was so great that after a certain line of demarcation, beginning roughly where the department of Limousin ended, it was almost like going into a separate country. It was not so much a matter of indifference as of inexperience. The Southerners had never felt the direct threat to themselves and, except in a few towns like Marseille, had never known the horrors of bombing raids . . .*

En Route

A man in the café laughed and said: the war is done.
The instant froze and joined the starry way
Of clear, unchangeable things men do and say
That spin in whirling history around a tired sun.

Along the roads the tired people lay,
Death's feet were quiet in a sky of indigo,
It seemed an old song of Touraine from long ago
Still lingered in that centuries-old evening, fragile and gay.

The chequered map of France beneath our feet
Unrolled itself day after clover-scented, azure day,
Incarnate Summer's ultimate and proud display
Before she laid her corn and birds and flowers down in defeat.

SAGITTARIUS

All Quiet
(JUNE 23RD, 1940)

We can take down the map of the war
With the sweep of the Maginot Line
Broad and strong from the sea to the Rhine,
And the cities, the rivers, the forts.
There is no Western Front any more,
The Line was a sham after all.
We shall hear no more 'latest reports'
We can take down the map from the wall.

These cities have gone up in flames,
These cornlands and vineyards are lost,
The Marne and the Seine have been crossed,
There is nothing left now but the names,
The rivers are full of the dead.
It was here the tanks broke through the Gap,
Here they stood, here they fell, here they fled.
It is done. We can take down the map.

The battle is suddenly still,
The life is gone out of the land,
Consigned to the enemy's hand,
Betrayed and surrendered and sold
To be tamed to the conqueror's will.
Now silence and terror descend,
Our friend and our comrade of old
Will not be at our side to the end.

We can take down the map of the war,
From the Rhone and the Rhine to the sea
All's quiet as the grave; there will be
No counter-attack or advance.
The flag is defiled that she bore
And the sword of her forging is blunt.
So peace has been given to France
All's quiet on the Western Front.

WILMA CAWDOR

The Countess Cawdor was the wife of Lieutenant Colonel The Earl Cawdor who commanded a battalion of the Queen's Own Cameron Highlanders of the 51st (Highland) Division in France between January and June 1940. She was an ardent friend of the Free French forces. The poem was written at Cawdor Castle in Scotland.

A Curse

Here in this house the Fighting French are held
As loved and honoured brothers. He who expects
Our welcome, speaks of France within these walls
With faith in her fair name – or else corrects
His ignorance . . . For otherwise he falls
Under a Cawdor curse, by which, expelled
From here, he must Be Mindful of mischance
Until again the cock crows, *Vive la France*!

MARY DÉSIRÉE ANDERSON

National Gallery Concert
DAME MYRA HESS

Who has not walked in gardens some wild June,
When midnight skies were mountainous with cloud,
And seen how dauntlessly the silver moon
Sailed through some vaporous breach and, proud,
Across the space of immemorial years,
Smiled on our infinitely trivial fears?

Who has not walked through darkened woods in June
And felt their silence did bespeak a threat,
Until the fount of Philomel's faint tune
Pulsated through the shadows and so set
The leaden stillness of the sultry air
Alight with rhythms, amorous and rare?

Who can forget how, that disastrous June
When every day led hope in headlong flight,
We craved for beauty as the final boon
Before our day was overwhelmed in night,
Drank music with parched souls and, for a while,
Forgot the tempest in an artist's smile?

THEODORA ROSCOE

At the National Gallery Concerts

They come as to a shrine,
Eager, expectant,
Wave upon wave of pilgrims seeking rest –
Rest from the cares of war;
Exiles there are, and those once persecuted.
And as the music floats from lofty dome
The listening crowd is one –
One soul set free.
Pity and love flow through them with sweet force;
Wisdom, forbearance, hope surge in their hearts,
And courage triumphs over all dismay!

JOAN BARTON

Newgale Sands 1940

Every year
There is a short season
When the summer 'buses from the market town
Routed to the farthest rock of western Wales
Stop where the road swoops down upon the shore
At Newgale Sands:
The wind-rutted bungalows
Taking their crazy shutters down
Hoist the gay semaphores
That signal summer,
The sun blares in through doors
Blistering on sandy hinges,
Down in the bay
The rocks stare motionless
Into the August mirror of the sea.

But in June
When the honey honeysuckle is thickest on the bush
The wind blows off the sea
And no-one comes,
In any year
No season has begun then.
Only this year we know it never will begin,
None will come but those
Like us, to say goodbye, sisters to brothers,
Lovers to lovers.

This quite deserted year
We saw Newgale sands as men
Shipwrecked see the waiting island,
Two miles of bay still wet
At mid-day from the morning tide
Under the thick English summer sky
Which only lets the warmth through not the sun;
There was a noon tide bearing on the land
The unremitting roar
Of endless breakers racing
With furious hair after the fretted surf

Scattered like whitened bones on the flat sand;
And here, entangling the noon light,
A fresh stream glancing
Ice-cold out of the generous rock
For those thirsty and ragged landing

From the sun-baked boats,
And then the caves
Shelter for fires of driftwood
Within the echo, like a thousand underground falls,
Of never-quietened waves;
Limpets on the rocks, and the warm pools streaming
With drowning weed, hiding crabs and crayfish,
Razor shells for knives,
And at last the green land, the turf
Growing to the cliff edge
Promising cornfields, promising sheep with black faces, honeysuckle,
And the wild strawberries scarlet in the hedge
The size for birds' eyes.

We were content to be like castaways,
Idle while the vast sea rushed in
Grinding over the scrupulous sands
Whose every grain swam magnified and clear
Before our downward dazzled gaze,
Gallons of green waves
Spouted over our hot skins their delicious pain
Forcing sharp cries
Out of our heedless mouths,
With endless, endless, soporific roar
Falling on the ear,
On heart, on brain,
Sorrow and thought . . .

We were content to be like castaways,
Recognizing we had found an island
Midway between dangers,
Content, we rested there.

DORIS BURTON

Children of War

We are children of war!
We lie on the top of the cliffs;
Far below, the blue-green waves of the sea
Sparkle and dance in the light of the sun.
We gaze at the yellow sands.
They tell us
Once children made castles and forts,
And dug deep holes with their spades,
Fetched water in bright coloured pails,
Whilst they laughed and shouted and ran.
They bathed in that shimmering sea,
Sailed boats, and caught tiny crabs on the rocks.
What joy!

But for us
There are coils of rusty barbed wire,
And spiked iron guards.
There are mines – they blew up a dog!
Oh, yes, it was killed quite dead.
So we may not go to the shore.
We are children of war!
Who lie on the top of the cliffs
And gaze at the sea below.

RUTH PITTER

The Compost-Heap

Miss Twigg is out to win the war
    By all the means she may;
She rakes the parish, near and far,
    For all that can decay;
With a thankful smack on the juicy stack
    She adds to it each day.

Her finer feelings she will sink
    In maiden sacrifice;
She does not blench, she does not blink,
    But patriotic tries
Bravely to think the complex stink
    Is really rather nice.

With all the clippings of the grass,
    And leaves from every tree,
She swells the richly-festering mass
    Almost in revelry,
And adds a spot of you-know-what
    And a little oh-dear-me.

She finds the oddest things to add,
    (Especially at night),
A cabbage that is really bad
    Is glorious in her sight,
An ancient boot, a mouldy fruit
    Is just exactly right.

And with the heap her passion grows,
    And every sense invades;
She goes to pluck each fullblown rose
    Almost before it fades;
When her own stuff is not enough
    She makes nocturnal raids.

But at her big tom-cat's demise
    She felt her bosom racked:

His germs, his nitrogen, his grease
    Were what her treasure lacked,
But a friend's peace after decease
    She felt should be intact.

But still she could not bear the waste:
    So in a dress-box fair
The remnant of her pet she placed,
    And then interred him there,
Satisfied then his nitrogen
    A good result would bear.

Her heap is now memorial
    To Tibby and her love;
A wreath adorns each several wall,
    A big one lies above;
In the rich bed above his head
    Is stuck a plaster dove.

Ah friends who plough and friends who dig
    Tough clay or blowing sand,
Don't laugh at good old Ethel Twigg,
    But give a helping hand;
I wish that all would feel the call
    To help neglected land!

LILIAN BOWES LYON

Headland, 1940

The Atlantic clangs, a hammer against the headland.
Lungs of my generation, wait for the stroke,
The wave's long tension tattering into smoke;
Breathe turmoil, with this headland that is England.

Surf in the cove has woven a scantier garland,
Scalding the ribs of a trawler mined in May.
Roll on, my soul; reveal the spindrift boy,
The men like matchwood, broken against the foreland.

THEODORA ROSCOE

Old Dorset Women and Tanks

In the waiting bus at Wareham
Sit a row of old village women,
Ready to drive into Corfe.
They are laden with baskets and bags.
Thundering by roar tanks,
Great inhuman, brutal weapons of war,
With gargoylish figures peering out of the turrets.
But the old women never turn their heads to look;
They nod and prattle together.
What matters these noisy tanks to them?
They who have been marketing?
Their interest is the business of living
An old, old business.

* * *

Soon the bus moves on,
Moves to beneath the line of hills
Clear cut against the sinking sun.
They too are indifferent to warfare,
For many wars have passed beneath their heights.
They and the old women, belong to the
eternal order of things.

Naomi Mitchison

On 4 July 1940 Naomi Mitchison gave birth to her seventh child at Carradale House. The following day her baby daughter died.

> *4th to 7th . . . The septum of the heart had not closed properly. It would not have made any difference if she had been ten days later at full term. If she had lived it could not have been for more than a few months or years of a very wretched kind of existence. It was just one of those things which do happen . . . I said I would like one of the boats to take her out to sea . . . The silly thing is that I realise perfectly that much worse things are happening at this moment to thousands of people (and indeed have done so for a long time), but one cannot generalise as simply as that. I at least cannot change pain into love. And all the little things hurt, hurt, hurt, and there is nothing to be done . . . She was part of me, and wanted, all these months, and warm, and one said what a nuisance, but lovingly, and now the whole thing is ended . . .*

Clemency Ealasaid

JULY 1940

Mi Ritrovai in una selva oscura
    Blindly, gingerly, beginning to grope through the prickly future,
    With only thorns left on my white rose
    To jag and tear at the heart suddenly,
    Hands out, I move.
    Knowing that inside those shut drawers, the woolly coats and the vests,
    The cuddly shawls and the flannels, all, all, wait cold and folded.
    When I go down to the room I left last, in pain and happy,
    They will come and put them away, sorry for me, hoping I may have forgotten,
    As though forgetting were possible.
    Having imagined beforehand, very precisely and very gently,
    The white cot by my bed, the old cot with the new green blankets,
    The new dark soft head, the faint breathing, the warmth and love,
    The ghost of the cot is still there when I turn to my right.
    And when I turn to my left, there is the sea, there is Carradale Bay, and sea-
        deep,
    Dark and alone where the Cluaran dropped her, my dear, my daughter,
    Not in my arms, not in my womb: in the box Angus made, a small weight.

Round about, says the Boyg
    Thinking of these things, wrongly, archaically, personally,
    I must retract, I must say to myself

She was not yet human, not individual, cannot be lonely,
It is only my projection of love onto her,
Only the months of bearing, the pains of labour interpreted,
And interpreted wrongly.
Because I had touched her, kissed her, been happy for a few hours,
I had built up a structure of love and vanity, my pride, my youngest.
That was irrational, and, because irrational, wrong.
Peer Gynt, for ever projecting and protruding his self onto the world,
Symbol of the individual, of capitalism, of commercial progress,
He is finished. But the Boyg in the Dovrefelt
Still remains above half-starved, half-beaten Norway,
And will remain.

You said to me: Come back, come back, mother – knowing
That I was not wholly here, but half pulled down, half drowned in the sea
    tangle,
Beside my baby, where the waves covered, in the wake of the Cluaran.
I must, I will, come back.

These twenty centuries of bourgeois bargaining,
Since Jesus, himself a Jew, saw through it, saw there must be
No scales of corn-growing justice, but only love,
Have left their mark on me.
Now I am trying to bargain, to say take her death, my grief,
But save me the others, from bombs, shells, from pandemic
Disease, save me children and husband, save Ruth, Dick, Taggy and all of
    them,
Clutching out for lives on the spread bargain counter, clutching them to my
    heart,
But looking up I see
No bargainer on the far side of the counter, nothing: only another
    projection:
Round about, says the Boyg.

Roll up the map of Europe
    Should we try to make sense of a senseless situation?
    Over-simplifying, after the habit of the orthodox,
    Catholic or Marxist. Shall we try to make sense of Oran?
    Try to make sense of inevitable hatred
    From mothers of French sailors, babies who had lived
    Through the years of hope and pride and delight, boyhood and manhood,
    Now murdered by the Ally, perfide Albion?
    How make a bargain on that? Roll up the map of Europe.

The lights have gone out: the concentration camps are full: the men and
    women
Who thought themselves safe have been betrayed to the vultures,
To Himmler, Goering, Franco, to those whose faces
Express Satanic possession. Paris is dead.
Only the bones remain. Paris of the Commune
Dead as the sailors at Oran. This winter we hope to starve
France, Belgium, Holland, Denmark, Norway, Poland:
Harvest of dead babies, disease, hatred: no sense.
My breasts tingle and stab with milk that no one wants,
Surplus as American wheat, surplus and senseless.
Not her soft kind mouth groping for me. Useless, senseless.
If my baby had been starved by England, would I ever forgive?
Roll up the map of Europe.

Carradale
This was to have been a binding between me and Carradale.
Weeper of Carradale Glen, fairy hare, cleft rock, did none of you speak?
How shall I stay here, how go on with the little things,
How not hate Carradale, the flowery betrayer,
Dagger in fist?
How be crushed into such humility as can continue
The daily work, alleviation of meals and sleep and slight laughter?
How, having known happiness, not see it anywhere?
I should have been happy before, in Highland May
Of blossom and bird-song. Ah, how not be happy
When one could not foresee?

Time and the hour runs through the roughest day
The roughest day is not yet. This was a rough day
For me and perhaps for Carradale. But the roughest day,
The day lived through by Macbeth who had been king,
Some say a good king, and by Gruach, my ancestors,
Hangs now in the future, the unturned page, the history book
So far unwritten, and we, single-sighted,
Not having seen the ghost funeral nor identified the bearers,
Imagine it next week or next month, Ragnarok, the doomday.
Who knows what each shall lose? Who knows the issue?
Will there be another birth, a fair one, or is West Europe
Too old, too old for that, as I shall be too old
For another bearing
Before the roughest day is past: as I am now
Unable to imagine the new times, because of the blackness

Steadily ahead of me, the still curtain
Over my dancing daughter, my innocent, my small one.
Ah darkness of the spirit, lift, lift, let the hour run through you!
The roughest day is to come. We shall perhaps
Live through it, or others will. In a hundred years
Things may be seen in order, making sense, drawing a new map:
Human endeavour going roundabout, unselfishly,
May, arriving suddenly on the Dovrefeld, see ahead, make fresh ski-tracks.
In a hundred years
The French sailors at Oran, the Scottish dead at Abbeville,
The tortured in the concentration camps and all the leaders,
The ones who thought themselves godlike, forgetting the Boyg,
And I, and my children, and all the people of Carradale,
We shall be dead, at last out of the running of events and hours. The page
    will have been turned,
The history written, and we, anonymous,
Shall be condemned or not condemned, gently upbraided
For folly of not foreseeing, for dithered watching of hours
While the roughest day runs by.
But the trees I planted in the heavy months, carrying you,
Thinking you would see them grown, they will be tall and lovely:
Red oak and beech and tsuga, grey alder and douglas:
But not for you or your children. What will it matter then, forgotten
    daughter,
Forgotten as I shall be forgotten in the running of time,
Maybe a name in an index, but not me, not remembered
As I alone remember, with what tears yet, the first kiss, the faint warmth
    and stirring?
The waves will cover us all diving into darkness out of the bodies of death,
Vanishing as the wake of a boat in a strong current.
The hot tears will be cooled and the despair of the middle-aged, rolling up
    their map,
Will be forgotten, with other evil things, will be interpreted,
Will be forgiven at last.

Dame Scholastica Sybil Hebgin

Dame Scholastica Sybil Hebgin was a nun at the Benedictine Stanbrook Abbey in Worcestershire.

From the Home Front (July 1940)

Our bread-trays, spoons & mustard pots have gone to serve the King,
The saucepans joined the RAF, the wash-bowls on the wing.
The kettles, funnels, ladles, jugs, will shortly learn to fly.
The pastepots, mugs & tumblers too are heading for the sky.
T'will need more metal yet perhaps to make a Spitfire spit,
But here's a dozen bottle caps arrived to do their bit.
Our peaceful pots & pans unite to change their state & thus,
While <u>we</u> took care of <u>them</u> before, now they'll take care of us.

CAMILLA DOYLE

Camilla Doyle lived in the Cathedral Close in Norwich during the war years.

War Time Garden

By day we live amidst the calm
Contented hum of bees
Wheeling around the buddleia stems
And through the privet trees.

By night we strain our ears to hear
The shrilly gasping planes
Wheeling around the shattered roofs
And splintered window panes.

RUTH TOMALIN

Needlework made a welcome diversion during air-raids. Ruth Tomalin wrote that 'in one incident a German crew died when their aeroplane, carrying a landmine, crashed at Stansted Park in Sussex wrecking the nearby Chapel and its pictorial window . . .'.

Embroidery, 1940

The day the shattered Germans lay in shreds
among the placid nettles at the gate,
I took a skein of sunset-coloured threads
to make my brave Red Admiral a mate.

When snarling dog-fights trailed across the blue,
and men went home at night to count their dead,
over the gold-eyed purple iris flew
a Tiger Moth in goblin green and red.

I cannot see the Painted Lady's wings,
embroidered apricot and veined in buff,
without remembering quite other things
that happened while the land-mines did their stuff.

'England can take it!' runs the gallant line:
and later, as we gossip of the blitz,
we shall imagine everyone felt fine,
just waiting to be blown to little bits.

We may forget; but here they testify
the passive agony of long suspense –
the rose, the orchid and the butterfly:
good Lord deliver us from that pretence!

The sickening dive of planes, the dripping glass,
the bloody fire-bomb singing to the kill,
are sewn in delicate bright wings and grass,
and writ, in satin-stitch, upon the squill.

PRISCILLA NAPIER

Priscilla Napier's husband was in command of the destroyer HMS Jackal at the outbreak of war. He took part in the Norwegian campaign and in Arctic convoys and spent many days continuously on the bridge without rest. He became increasingly exhausted but refused to go on sick leave until he was carried ashore dying of septic endocarditis. He died in August 1940 a week before their third child was born.

From 'To Michael, Dying'

. . . Soft night, soft coolness of the evening quiet,
Sweet healing hand of summer and of sleep,
Stirred, murmuring trees, that past the instant riot
And tumult, their caressed perfection keep;
Aloof unravaged country for whose peace
A total happiness is well forsworn,
And splintered cities for whose far release
The torment and the loss is fairly borne –
For these the sternest pain
We do in full accept, and would accept again.

You that were strength itself are weakness now,
Stretched in long fever of the wearied heart,
You that with resolute and smoking prow
Endured through winter's rage the heaviest part;
You whom no clamorous seas could overleap,
The mounting waves of poison overwhelm,
And fiercer tides to vaster oceans sweep
The rudder of your proud and steadfast helm,
Against whose vicious spate
With calm and mocking courage you yet navigate.

Not in the thunder and exhilarance
Of surface action wounded; but in these –
Perennial days of stony vigilance,
Interminable nights in the scorpion seas,
In the long roar of storm's besieging rumpus,
In the black minefields and the fog's eclipse,
Straining past mortal stature to encompass
The enormous ocean with the too scant ships,
On without sleep or rest
Till the worn flesh defaults before the will's behest.

You that are life itself draw near to death,
Life's very being fails, while the warm land
Murmurs and shines with summer's lavish breath;
The quivering oats are reaped, the corncocks stand,
And blue with afternoon, the slope hills run
Their feathered promontories in Tamar's gleam,
The valleys mist and clear, the glowing sun
Lights the curved haunches of the reaper's team,
And evening rings the cry
Of garrulous homing rooks, night-blown across the sky . . .

HILDA KATHERINE WILLIAMS

The following two poems were written in Jersey during the years of German occupation.

The Sun and the – Luftwaffe

Sun-bathing in suit of grasshopper green,
Alone in a war-time garden;
In sunshine so warm
Reclining one's form,
Oh! it's bliss, and I don't care who knows it!
Above roars a plane,
Dips low down again –
Some young pilot who's bored and who shows it!
So he swoops low to see
Who's so care-free to be
Reclining like me,
All drenched with the sun,
Unperturbed by the Hun,
Sun-bathing in suit of grasshopper green,
Alone in a war-time garden!

The Cage

A Prisoner of War;
A bird in a cage –
Wings clipped – no more free to blissfully soar
In sunshine so brilliant,
In radiant blue skies,
O'er wide waters winging,
For sheer joyousness singing!
– A bird of passage,
– A migratory bird,
Ecstatically flying in the bright beams of the sun!
Now, a bird with wings clipped,
Unable to soar;
A bird in a cage –
A Prisoner of War.

Margaret Elizabeth Rhodes

Guernsey

And has September come
As warmly, as brownly
To the small sandy coves,
The water's cool shadows,
To the cliffs of home?
I could sleep now, if only
I knew still September
Had come as in other days
To the sweet, clean cows in the meadows,
And the green fields of the sea
That my heart loves.

Silence folds close the bays;
What eyes now peer in the pools,
What voices and laughter
Now startle the gulls?
The lanes take their secret ways,
None follow after;
The peace of September falls
From its blue sky,
But no, not as it used to be,
Not as we remember,
You and I.

ANNE RIDLER

Anne Ridler wrote this poem after saying farewell to her husband in London. He was working at the Bunhill Press and part-time in the auxiliary fire brigade as he waited to be called up; she went into the country for the birth of their first child.

At Parting

Since we through war awhile must part
Sweetheart, and learn to lose
Daily use
Of all that satisfied our heart:
Lay up those secrets and those powers
Wherewith you pleased and cherished me these two years:

Now we must draw, as plants would,
On tubers stored in a better season,
Our honey and heaven;
Only our love can store such food.
Is this to make a god of absence?
A new-born monster to steal our sustenance?

We cannot quite cast out lack and pain.
Let him remain – what he may devour
We can well spare:
He never can tap this, the true vein.
I have no words to tell you what you were,
But when you are sad, think, Heaven could give no more.

JILL FURSE

The actress Jill Furse married the writer and glass-engraver Laurence Whistler in September 1939. He was called up a year later and spent the war years in various training camps. When he was on leave they spent much of their time together at Halsdon Mill, a cottage on the Furse estate in Devon.

The Days that Forced our Lives Apart

The days that forced our lives apart
Are shut up like a fan.
We shall not even speak of them,
Because at last we can.

There's nothing in between us now,
Neither silk nor sheet.
Our lives have come so close tonight,
Even our graves meet.

The Rain Falls Silent in the Garden

The rain falls silent in the garden,
Of other tears compassionate.
Ashes of the declining fire
Whiten a little in the cooling grate.

And you have shut the door and left me
Walled up in silence, like a ghost
Nor book nor candle exorcises,
To haunt one room and think of what is lost.

I cannot read the page you wrote
In the brief hour that was mine.
In present tears the meaning dies,
The words run dark into the candleshine.

VALENTINE ACKLAND*

Valentine Ackland lived with Sylvia Townsend Warner (q.v.) at Frome Vauchurch, Maiden Newton, Dorset, during the war. In the early years she was a member of the WVS, and drove a mobile canteen and was involved in firewatching.

From 'War in Progress'

A running commentary started in Spring, 1940, and continued till Spring, 1943

7 October 1940

One does not have to worry if we die:
Whoever dies, One does not have to bother
Because inside Her there is still another
And, that one wasted too, She yet replies
'Nothing can tire out Nature – here's another!'
   Fecundity par excellence is here,
   Lying in labour even on the bier.

Babes born in air-raid shelters now are called
'Messerschmidt', 'Junker' or, in case they're dated
By names, of obsolete terror and so not mated,
'Barrage' or 'Sireen'. Who but will stand enthralled
   When parish registers yield to the search
   Such treasures sanctified by Holy Church?

Maternity's the holiest thing on earth
(No man who's prudent now as well as wise
Concerns himself with what is in the skies);
Drain-deep below the slums another birth
   Sets angels singing – the other noise you hear
   May be the Warning, may be the All Clear.

* This version of the extract from 'War in Progress: 7 October 1940' comes from the typescript in the Sylvia Townsend Warner/Valentine Ackland Collection in the Dorset County Museum. It differs from the published version in *The Nature of the Moment* which excluded verses 2 and 4.

In any case, the child is born and joy
Enchants the father and uplifts the brother,
Pleasures the sister, and we know the mother
Best pleased of all because another boy
    Is born into the world — Who bothers where
    He'll find himself next minute, how get there?

Comfort ye My people! These reflections
Should help them die politely who must die,
And reconcile those left behind, who sigh
For loss of children or some near connections —
    Reflect! There is no need for grief nor gloom,
    Nature has ever another in Her womb.

Teeming and steaming hordes who helter-skelter
Stampede the city streets, to herd together
Angry and scared, in dark, in wintry weather —
Above ground still? Fear not, there's one deep shelter
    Open alike in Free and Fascist State,
    Vast, private, silent and inviolate.

RUTH PITTER

Wherefore Lament

WRITTEN DURING AN ATTACK ON LONDON, 7 OCTOBER 1940

Wherefore lament, thou fond ephemeral?
    Thy salve is very sure;
Thy wound shall cease, thy wrongs be cancelled all,
    Thine hurt hath certain cure.

Whatever woe thou weepest, it must end,
    And over thee the green
And mindless mantle of the grass shall bend
    As though thou hadst not been.

But thou art not contented with the grave!
    Thou hearest the unborn joy
Groan for the sun, the life it cannot have,
    The large, serene employ.

Thou canst not be a traitor to that seed
    Which the whole world could fill
With myriad blossom; wherefore thou dost bleed,
    And these strong tears distil.

Let the great tempests of the spirit blow,
    Fanning that seed of fire,
Until the flaming tree of life shall grow,
    And flourish, and aspire,

And fill the universe, and bear the stars
    Like birds on every bough;
In whose pure eyes these wild and bitter wars
    Profane the heavens now.

MARY DÉSIRÉE ANDERSON

'Blitz'

In London now Death holds high festival.
The clustered candelabra of the flares,
High in the darkly thrumming vault of heaven,
Hang motionless, then slowly, slowly, drop
Towards the shrinking darkness of men's homes.

In parody of dawn the eastern sky
Flames with the ghastly beauty of great fires.
The moonbeam tentacles of searchlights grope
Through baffling cirrus, while the moon herself
Seems to grow smaller, shrinking from the earth,
Her brightness reddened by the reek of war.

Strangely unreal seems the roar of guns,
The long-continued crash of falling walls,
With snake-like sibilance of splintered glass,
And slowly swelling mushrooms of black smoke
Rising from bursting bombs. With all of these
We are familiar through a thousand films,
And scarce believe them to be bitter truth.
Strangely unreal too the ageless faces
Of those who struggle out of shattered homes;
Faces expressionless through fear and dust,
Dust that was once the fabric of their homes.

I've seen old women, trembling from the shock,
Yet angry only that their limbs should thus
Betray the fear their smiling lips denied.
I've seen young children watch the solid walls
Bend inwards with the blast and then recoil;
Seen their eyes wide with terror and their mouths
Closed far too tightly for such tender lips,
Yet never sound came from them in their fear.

I have seen Death hold festival to-night,
With hideous beauty of dark ritual,
And yet, as plainly, read a Covenant
That Man's unconquerable kindliness
Shall master hate as surely as the dawn
Makes dim the terrors of Death's Beltane fires.

EDITH SITWELL

From 'Still Falls the Rain'
(THE RAIDS, 1940. NIGHT AND DAWN)

. . . Dark as the world of man, black as our loss –
Blind as the nineteen hundred and forty nails
Upon the Cross.

Still falls the Rain
With a sound like the pulse of the heart that is changed
                    to the hammer-beat
In the Potter's Field, and the sound of the impious feet

On the Tomb:
            Still falls the Rain
In the Field of Blood where the small hopes breed and
                    the human brain
Nurtures its greed, that worm with the brow of Cain.

Still falls the Rain
At the feet of the Starved Man hung upon the Cross.
Christ that each day, each night, nails there,
                        have mercy on us –
On Dives and on Lazarus:
Under the Rain the sore and the gold are as one . . .

SUSANNE KNOWLES

Susanne Knowles served in the London Auxilliary Ambulance Service during the war.

The Blitz

Hell is ours. Not in the calculated pain
  We give and suffer, hate for hatred's sake,
The criminal mis-channelling of brain
Whose power is turned to break and break
  and break;
Future, ideas, hopes, inspiration unfulfilled,
Cancelled, made vain; not in the shattered
Wretches death drops on, impersonally killed,
Their dead blood, spilt to no end, spattered
On streets; the paralysis of fear
Or the appalling race to recompense
Death with a wider death; insatiable woe,
Want, miscreation, waste. Not here, but here:
In knowing we chose this unintelligence,
In taking for granted that it could be so.

*Susanne Knowles wrote that the 'long, long hours of inactivity and humdrum daily
routine are the greatest test of character and ability. It is during those hours, if one is to
carry on at all, that an ability to laugh at oneself and one's companions and the red
tape that inevitably ties them together becomes an almost vital necessity . . .'*

The ABC of Civil Defence

A is the Ambulance picking up bits,
B is the Black-out, the Bomb and the Blitz,
C is Control that copes with the trouble,
D, Demolition that digs in the rubble,
E is Equipment (mask and tin hat),
F for Fire service, First-aid-and-all-that,
G, poison Gases that worry our noses,
H the fire Hatchets, the Hydrants and Hoses,
I's the Incendiaries (all mess and fuss),
J is the Jerry who drops them on us,

K is our Knitting, patient row upon row,
L is the London and Lights we mayn't show,
M, Mobile Units that dash in and out,
N for the Nurses they carry about,
O is the Ominous Overhead humming,
P, Purple Warnings that tell us they're coming,
Q for the Questions on Gas and First-aid
R, Rescue Party, Respirator and Raid,
S is the Search Lights, raking the stars,
T for the Telephone, calling all cars,
U is the Uniform screening our charms,
V is our Version of last night's alarms,
W the Warning, the Warden and War,
X the explosives that are more than a bore,
Y is the Civil Defence Youth – and – beauty,
Z is the Zeal which they spend on their duty.

AUDREY HEWLETT

Audrey Hewlett served in the Women's Land Army in East Sussex.

October, 1940

October, with the magic of her brush,
Has washed the landscape with a thousand hues;
The grasses in the bog are green and lush,
And rosy berries cheer the sombre yews.
Along the lane is found the beechnut husk,
Thrown there by boys who picked and had their fill,
Long ere the stars came shining through the dusk
And mist crept up to clothe the naked hill.
The sun gilds gently now the fallen leaves:
His passion sated, he is mellow, soft.
The rays that beat all day on rows of sheaves
Now shyly peep at apples in the loft.
How peaceful seems the world when evening comes,
The autumn smells like incense on the air,
And labourers go weary to their homes
With hearty appetites for simple fare.
The horses plodding slowly up the steep
Feel harness growing heavy on their backs,
And while in woods the birds prepare for sleep,
The mice begin to stir behind the sacks.
The dusk falls gently as a flake of snow,
And silently – until a fearful sound
With moanings fills the air that louder grow
And shatter all the peace above, around.
The wailing siren, with its message dread,
Is heralding the enemies of Right,
Whose monsters come to claim their living bread
And make a phantom of the quiet night.
And those who toil by day can find no rest,
For all the world is sick with greed and lust.
Men seek for truth, then leave the irksome quest,
And Christ's great Cross is trampled in the dust.

ALICE COATS

Alice Coats served in the Women's Land Army in Warwickshire between 1940 and 1945.

October, 1940

To-day I gather from the orchard grass
    Apples and shrapnel – windfalls shaken down
    When angry gusts tempestuously pass.

To-night, above the dark surrounding town,
    Shellbursts and stars will decorate the sky
    With dangerous beauty, devastation's crown.

A lunatic balloon, adrift on high,
    Trailing its shadow by a silver thong,
    Above the sailing leaves goes sailing by.

Sirens and robins share their Autumn song,
    As War and Peace alternately take wing,
    Chanting antiphonally all day long.

And I, impartially hearkening,
    Nevertheless continue, hour by hour
    Confident planting for a doubtful Spring

    The cabbages that others may devour,
    The tulips I may never see in flower.

The 'Monstrous Regiment'

What hosts of women everywhere I see!
I'm sick to death of them – and they of me.
(The few remaining men are small and pale –
War lends a spurious value to the male.)
Mechanics are supplanted by their mothers;
Aunts take the place of artisans and others;
Wives sell the sago, daughters drive the van,
Even the mansion is without a man!

Females are farming who were frail before,
Matrons are attending meetings by the score,
Maidens are minding multiple machines,
And virgins vending station-magazines.
Dames, hoydens, wenches, harridans and hussies
Cram to congestion all the trams and buses;
Misses and grandmas, mistresses and nieces,
Infest bombed buildings, picking up the pieces.
Girls from the South and lassies from the North,
Sisters and sweethearts, bustle back and forth,
The newsboy and the boy who drives the plough:
Postman and milkman – all are ladies now.
Doctors and engineers – yes, even these –
Poets and politicians, all are shes.
(The very beast that in the meadows browse
Are ewes and mares, heifers and hens and cows.)
All, doubtless, worthy to a high degree;
But oh, how boring! Yes, including me.

JANET HILLS

After graduating with a degree in English from Somerville College, Oxford, in 1940, Janet Hills joined the WRNS. She served as an officer in Intelligence and then in the Educational Department.

Autumn by the Sea

    The Autumn's ashes here.
No warmth of berries, and the sunlight grieves
    With no woods near.
The unescapable, the desolate sea,
Rigid through all its changes, deadens me,
And, pale as Autumn seas, the scattered leaves
Break round the long-stalked flowers on homeless land.

    We loved to talk of peace,
And looked to see the rising of a truth
    If war should cease.
Now, in the darkness, listlessly we guess
Towards some future blood-drained weariness.
For we, cut off from grace, must spend our youth
For something we abhor, but know must be.

EILUNED LEWIS

Eiluned Lewis and her husband, Graeme Hendrey, who worked in London, lived in the Surrey village of Blechingley during the war years. She worked for the Red Cross libraries and in the local baby clinic. During the troubled months in France her sense of loss was heightened as she suffered a miscarriage at the time.

France, 1940

Under these brooding skies,
   Still, pewter grey,
Why is it, France, of you
   I've dreamed all day?
On the dark fountain's face
   Fall the bright leaves;
Memory's looking-glass
   Where the heart grieves.

Here are tall forest trees,
   Half dreamt, half known,
Brown as old tapestries,
   Their summer flown;
Here one of Corot's ponds
   Hidden, remote,
Where a small red-capped boy
   Tethers his goat.

Silent these autumn woods,
   Then faint, forlorn,
From some deep castled glade
   Sounds the sad horn;
Echoes of cavalcades
   Ridden away,
Magic of poets' words
   Time can't betray:

Words sown so long ago
   In an old lamplit room
Where a dear Mademoiselle
   Taught them to bloom.

France, it's not true today,
    True that you're gone!
You who are part of us,
    Bone of our bone!

BRYHER

Bryher arrived in London from her home in Switzerland at the end of September 1940. She stayed with the American poet Hilda Doolittle at 49 Lowndes Square for the duration of the war.

From 'Tourist'
ENGLAND, NOVEMBER, 1940

I am not come from Vaud to find
bare branches and willow rind,
even the berries,
Arden-red though they may be,
have no near identity.

> You say it is duck-sleepy
> and so quiet . . .
> is this an answer to my coming back?
> I have no mooring ring
> and feel the sea
> furrowing the flat plain till it rises;
> there were medieval stories
> blowing an island to a lonely west
> of smoky waves and shell transparencies.

The cows, the saplings, are alike
tawny cold at twitterlight
the last leaves flaunt above their ears
tassles over Border spears.

> There is no 'why I came'
> to such deep silence
> and familiar strangeness;
> only if I might speak
> I could explain
> it was a sharing of the secret way
> Marlin preferred
> to the audacious voyage of the air,
> yes, to command of all his flying words;
> though it be over, over . . .
> the wish that was so high I saw it blurred,
> was steadily there that month that was a day.

In her memoir The Days of Mars *Bryher wrote: 'The rationing system in England was absurd. "Bread is unrationed," the bureaucrats said proudly but it was not even sawdust; we wondered what it could contain and we knew it was unrationed because it was uneatable. It turned a particularly livid hue of green within a few hours and was so hard that the populace referred to it as "our secret weapon" . . .'*

Untitled

I wonder what would have happened to Drake
when they asked him the Spaniards to slaughter
had he fed on a diet of parsnip and hake
and a glass of pure water?

We look at the skies and think Nelson was fine,
his speeches and manner we parrot,
But would he have battered those ships of the line
on a chew of raw carrot?

We shiver on roofs between blackout and dawn,
while Whitehall (hush hush) studies Plato.
But I wonder politely just why we were born
to be gay and shout hey
and hurray for the Government Food Control
on the half of a frigid potato?

MARY DOUGLAS

Blitz on Coventry

[14/15 November 1940]

The air was strangely charged that night,
A queer combine of grit and fright;
For we had had grim raids before,
With death brought closely to our door.
Yet still there were the foolish ones
Who, seeking fun, defied the bombs,
And after dusk they strolled about,
Seemed not to fear at being out.
But after this most dreadful night,
When there was demonstrated might
In vilest form conceivable,
Their change was scarce believable –
At least till Time had wiped away
The agony of that fearful day.

'Twas when the light began to fade
(We thought perhaps there'd be a raid),
That soon as warning sirens screeched,
We knew the foe our homes had reached,
For bombs poured down in ceaseless strain,
While guns bit back with might and main:
The ground it shook, the buildings rocked,
While laughing moon stood by and mocked.
Chief among the bombs that fell
Were some that burned like fires of hell,
And though it was as light as day,
They dropped their flares to show the way.
While whistling bombs burst and exploded,
The guns blazed back and then reloaded.
Then household lights were all put out
And window frames were blast about.

Streets of houses caught ablaze,
Thoroughfares became a maze;
Brave firemen sought to do their best,
Fought grimly on, nor thought of rest.

Many a hero braved that night,
And many died in grimmest fight
That lasted till the morning broke
To bring relief to bomb-shocked folk.
For every hour was hard to bear,
And made some doubt that God was fair.
Yet every devastating blow
Had been conceived by men below.

Then near to dawn the raid increased,
And terrified both man and beast.
Many uncouth, ungodly men
Said anxious prayers; and then, Amen!
Although they had not prayed for years,
They prayed for loved ones midst their fears.
Husband and wife, though miles apart,
Drew close together, heart to heart;
And friend sought friend he'd loved so dear
With heart that ached and silent tear.
And people swore, if they came through –
With God's great help – they'd start anew
To make this world a cleaner place,
And make amends for years of waste.

And when, at last, the morning came,
'Twas little that remained the same.
Bombs still burst and streets blazed red
As men strove hard to find the dead.
Out to the roads the people rushed,
With tired hearts, though still uncrushed,
The fire pumps roared, hose lined the street,
And firemen fought terrific heat.
Assistance came from near and far,
Food was brought by van and car;
And as the crowds swarmed through the town
I fancy God in heaven looked down
And pitied man in his grim fight
'Gainst what was wrong, and for the right.
I fancy that He stooped to bless,
A thousand times, to ease the stress
That threatened weigh the warrior down,
'Midst all he'd lost in that sad town.

ANNE RIDLER

Anne Ridler lived 30 miles from London but saw the red sky over the city on the night of the great fire raid on 29 December 1940. The allusion is to Bishop Ken's hymn:

> *. . . Teach me to live that I may dread*
> *The grave as little as my bed . . .*

For this Time

Now that the firmament on high,
Noah's peace-promising sky,
Is given over to an enemy,
And that those durable lights the stars
Fuse and explode, and friendly fires
Are travestied in the bomb's brightness,
And homes made hostile as the darkness;
Now country people look towards town,
And awestruck see the crimson stain
Spread on the cloud, and *London's Burning*
Say in grief as once laughing:
From such a conflict, fire and frenzy,
Where should we turn unless Lord to Thee?
That Thou wouldst teach us to bear calmly
The invisible battles overhead,
And to get us through the night without dread.
Teach us therefore so to live
That we may fear our noisy bed
As little as our more peaceful grave.

VERA ARLETT

Because they belonged to You

They were such ordinary things, but once they
    belonged to you –

A pipe, and a little ash tray, and Macaulay's volume
    of 'Essays'.
Take them away, my heart cried; throw them into
    the ruins!
Cities, cathedrals, burn, and tenement houses tumble;
The Heinkels fall in flames, and the world's a
    screaming nightmare.
– Why have I feeling left for details, for petty
    possessions?
Think of the streets in rubble, the shelters, the buried
    Wardens,
Think of the whole crazed world – then how can my
    eyes be sore
For a pipe and a little ash tray? What can they matter
    now?
Nothing, nothing I answer; nothing can matter now.
– You read that book in the sun; you smoked, and
    you lost the matches –
But why remember such nonsense? The world is on
    fire, is falling.
Yet because they belonged to you, these things have
    staggered my heart.

1941

INTRODUCTION

On 19 January 1941 the British launched their campaign against the Italians in Eritrea. It culminated in the total defeat of the Italian Army in East Africa in May. On the North African coast Tobruk was taken and on 6 February Benghazi was captured by British forces. The following month the German General Rommel, who became known as the Desert Fox, arrived in Tripoli, reorganised his forces and started his advance through North Africa. On 24 March General Wavell's troops were forced into retreat when Rommel captured El Agheila; after the failure of two attacks on Rommel's forces in May and June Churchill sent General Auchinleck to replace Wavell as C-in-C Middle East Command.

At the beginning of March British, Australian and New Zealand Divisions landed in Greece; a month later Bulgarian, German and Italian troops invaded Greece and Yugoslavia. The latter surrendered on 17 April. The Allied-Greek force put up a strong resistance but were overwhelmed and on 23 April the Greek Army surrendered. Almost 51,000 men of the British Expeditionary Force were evacuated from the Greek mainland. Many were redeployed to Crete. Through the successful breakthrough in decoding Enigma signals the British knew of Hitler's plans to attack Crete. On the island General Freyberg was in command of 42,000 men, a quarter of whom were Greek. Crete was attacked by German airborne forces on 20 May; despite heavy losses the Germans captured and held a vital airfield. After bitter fighting the unsupported Allied troops were withdrawn by sea; the Royal Navy suffered severely. In the Atlantic the Royal Navy experienced a further disaster when the German battleship *Bismarck* with the *Prinz Eugen* in company sank HMS *Hood*; *Bismarck* herself was hunted down, crippled and sunk on 27 May.

Barbarossa, the code-name for Germany's invasion of the USSR, was launched on 22 June, with complete surprise in spite of continual warnings to a sceptical Stalin. German troops reached the gates of Moscow at the end of November but by then they were exhausted and ill-equipped to fight a winter war; the determined resistance of the Soviet Army brought the German offensive to a temporary halt. By then, the 'Final Solution' to eliminate all the Jews of Europe was established. It was in Russia that Hitler set up an organised attempt to destroy the Jewish race. Special killing squads followed up the invading armies with orders to eliminate Jews from every town and village. Other arrangements were made in Nazi-controlled Europe and by April 1942, 3 million Jews had been murdered, mostly in specially constructed death camps.

On Sunday 7 December Japan launched a ferocious surprise air attack on Pearl Harbor, the Hawaian base of the United States' Pacific Fleet. The next day the United States and the Allied governments declared war on Japan. Over the following few days Japan invaded the Philippines, Siam, Malaya, the British colony of Hong Kong and Burma. On 10 December the battleships *Prince of Wales* and *Repulse* were sunk off Malaya by Japanese air strikes; on 11 December Germany and Italy declared war on the United States. On Christmas Day the Governor of Hong Kong surrendered to the Japanese Army commander: 11,000 British soldiers were taken prisoner and over 3,000 British civilians interned under brutal conditions.

In the United Kingdom there was no respite from hardship, danger and disruptions to everyday life. In the early months of 1941 heavy bombing raids continued on London, provincial cities and ports, including Plymouth, Portsmouth, Bristol, Bath, Swansea and Glasgow. On 10 May a massive raid on London left 1,436 civilians dead; the Houses of Parliament and many other buildings were badly damaged. German bomber squadrons were then redeployed to take part in the invasion of the USSR, but air raids still continued over the United Kingdom. In the nine months of concentrated bombing on Britain more than 43,000 civilians had been killed, 139,000 injured and over a million houses destroyed or damaged all over the country.

It was not only through air attacks that Germany intended to beat the people of the British Isles into submission. They also planned to ensure that no food, fuel or ammunition reached her shores. During the first half of 1941 German U-boats had considerable success in sinking both warships and merchant shipping by wolfpack tactics against Atlantic convoys. Loss of food and raw materials at sea meant stricter rationing at home. On 1 June clothes, shoes and material, which included sheets and towels, were rationed. Initially each person was issued with sixty-six coupons to last for a year. A pair of trousers required 8 coupons for a man and 6 for a boy; a pair of boots or shoes 7 for a man and 3 for a boy. A dress required 7 coupons for a woman and 5 for a girl; a pair of shoes, 5 for a woman and 3 for a girl. One coupon was needed for 2 oz of knitting wool. Utility clothes were made with very little material; dresses were plain and simple with short hemlines; 'Make-Do and Mend' became the needle and thread slogan. On 1 December a points system, allowing each person sixteen points per month, was introduced whereby many varieties of groceries were rationed. It covered tinned fish, vegetables and meat, including the versatile spam. Many of these goods were sent from the United States as a result of their Lend-Lease Bill which provided aid to the allies.

Great Britain was the first country to mobilise women. By December 1941 the manpower shortage was so acute that a Bill making unmarried women between the ages of twenty and thirty liable for conscription was announced in the House of Commons. They could choose between service in one of the armed forces, the Women's Land Army, Civil Defence, transport and factory work. Conscientious objectors often volunteered for firewatching or work on the land.

Through advertisements in the *Lady* and local newspapers Barbara Cartland bought some 120 second-hand wedding dresses on behalf of the War Office and RAF commands. These were lent to brides-to-be who suddenly found themselves in uniform. 'For one day at least a girl who was never meant by nature to be "a fighting unit" could forget the war, her uniform, her camp, her duties, and be a woman . . .'.

VIRGINIA GRAHAM

Bristol was badly bombed on 16 January 1941. Virginia Graham, a member of the WVS, wrote to Joyce Grenfell (q.v.) describing the raid: '. . . Friday night the planes came over steady from 6.15 p.m. to 6 a.m. and tried to set the whole place on fire . . . They pretty well succeeded & this time chose the part of the city where they should have been aiming for with the original raids – the warehouse & docks . . . Our nerves were stretched like banjo strings for 12 weary hours . . . I'm sick of the sound of guns & the smell of burning houses . . .'. Later she wrote of her experience during a daylight raid.

Air Raid over Bristol

The twelve Hurricanes circle round and round,
and we on the ground
stand in a little knot
and wait, even as they are waiting, for we know not what.
   A woman comes out of 'Chatsworth' and says:
'Anyone here seen Les?'
   'He's out in the van', says the grocer; 'went out
about
ten minutes ago', and then he rather surprisingly places
a pair of field-glasses to his eyes. We turn our faces
skywards again. Phew! What a sight!
   'Well, I hope he's all right',
says the woman,' I hope he won't come to any harm.'
I tuck my Salvage leaflets under my arm.
(Madam, do you keep your pig-food in a separate bin?
It is a sin
against the nation not to preserve each bone.)
   Suddenly over the house-tops we hear a drone.
   Dear heavens, look at them! A hundred or more!
Wouldn't you say a hundred? I retire to the door
of a china shop. 'Hi, Mr Bates, are they Jerries
or ours?' screams 'Sans Souci'. 'Jerries?'
taunts the grocer, peering through his glasses again.
'Good Lord, no, they're ours – positive.' With disdain
he smiles, 'I'd know ours anywhere'.
   Immediately the air
is rent by wildest gun-fire. Across the sky
the twelve Hurricanes fly
like angry wasps. There is a lot of noise,

so, with what I hope is poise
I retreat into the china shop rather fast
and am at once cast
into a sort of iron dungeon under the stair-
case by the proprietress. Her mother is already there,
with a Tinies' night-light.

It is very hot and tight,
and instantly I realize we shall not survive,
and that I shall be buried alive.
Therefore I give a tremendously British smirk,
and say 'Oh, well, I suppose it's all in the day's work'.
    Mother clicks her tongue and says 'It does seem a shame!'
and I remember I have not put my husband's name
on my identity card.
    The floor is remarkably hard.
    'Kit
will be having a fit
at school', says the proprietress, and gives a heave.
'They have *superb* shelters in *all* the schools, I believe',
I reply, and very carefully remove some candle-grease
from the crease
of my coat-lining.
    There is a shrill tormented whining
coming nearer and nearer,
clearer and clearer.
All that is British in me falters and flies,
I put my fingers in my ears and close my eyes.
It is aiming straight for the shop's portal.
We shall not die, we are immortal
(and, please, besides your dustbins
put, *separately*, all your tins).
    No, I am not dead, I feel well, and wonderfully clever.
The proprietress remarks appropriately, 'Well, I never!'
and crawls out on all-fours.
    We rush to the doors
to greet
'Chatsworth' and the others who are scouring the street
for shrapnel. They are oh, so merry.
Yes, it was a Jerry,
fell Fishponds way,
they say,

'Well', I murmur, 'thank you so much, I mustn't stop.'
I bow to the proprietress of the china shop,
and now that I mysteriously feel such a credit to the nation
I hand her a leaflet on Salvage from the Corporation.

LYNETTE ROBERTS

Lynette Roberts lived in Tygwyn, a little white-washed cottage in the centre of Llanybri, a small Welsh village some 7 miles from the market town of Carmarthen. Her husband, Keidrych Rhys, was called up in July 1940 and she spent most of the war years on her own with their two small children. Over the three nights of the February blitz on Swansea 230 people were killed.

From Gods with Stainless Ears

. . . Night falling catches the flares and bangs
On gorselit rock. Yellow birds shot from
Iridium creeks. – Let the whaleback of the sea
Fall back into a wrist of ripples, slit,

Snip up the moon sniggering on its back,
For on them sail the hulls of ninety wild birds
Defledged by this evening's raid: jigging up
Like a tapemachine the cold figures February
19th, 20th, 21st. A memorial of Swansea's tragic loss . . .

Author's Note: Swansea Raid. February 19th, 20th, 21st, 1941, when several members of the NFS of Birmingham said the intensity of the raid was worse than their own Midland tragedy. The severest hardship was: no room for Welsh evacuees. In our village we had accommodated forty-five from east London, so that we were compelled to refuse children whose parents we knew.

The New Perception of Colour

AND I SHALL TAKE AS MY EXAMPLE THE RAID ON SWANSEA

I, that is XEB07011 pass out into the chill-blue air
and join XEBN559162 her sack apron greening by the
light of the moon. I read around her hips: 'BEST CWT:
CLARK'S-COW-CAKES H.T.5' I do not laugh because
I love my peasant friend. The night is clear, spacious,
a himmel blue, and the stars minute pinpricks. The
elbow-drone of jerries burden the sky and our sailing
planes tack in and out with their fine metallic hum.
'Oh, look how lovely she is caught in those lights!'
'Oh!' From our high village overlooking the Towy

we can see straight down the South Wales
Coast. Every searchlight goes up, a glade
of magnesium waning to a distant hill which
we know to be Swansea. 'Swansea's sure to
be bad; look at those flares like a swarm
of orange bees.' They fade and others
return. A collyrium sky, chemically washed
$Cu (DH_2)$. A blasting flash impels Swansea
to riot! Higher, absurdly higher, the
sulphuric clouds roll with their stench of
ore, we breathe napthalene air, the pillars
of smoke writhe, and the astringent sky lies
pale at her sides. A jerry overhead drops
two flares, the cows returning to their
sheds wear hides of cyanite blue, their
eyes GLINTING OPALS! we, alarmed, stand
puce beneath another flare, our blood
distilled, cylindricals of glass. The
raiders scatter, then return and form a
piratic ring within our shores. High
explosives splash up blue, white, and green.
We know all copper compounds are poisonous,
we know also where they are.
Bleached, Rosie turns to fetch in
the cows. I, lonely, return to my hearth,
there is a quiet clayfire with blue flames
rising that would bring solace to any heart.

NAOMI MITCHISON

The first severe raid on Glasgow and the surrounding areas came on the night of 13/14 March 1941 when more than 500 Clydebankers were killed and over 600 injured. Naomi Mitchison went to Glasgow to help search for Jim McKinven, a young man from Carradale on the Mull of Kintyre, who she had encouraged in his first attempts at writing poetry. He was in a house that received a direct hit during the raid and when his body was dug from the rubble she stayed to comfort his parents.

Jim McKinven: March 1941

You came on summer evenings
With your head away in a cloud
Your eyes mazy with staring
At sheep or tree or mountain:
And your mind longing and caring
For what lies behind the lock,
Not to be said aloud,
Nor fully brought to words.
With your blue exercise book
And filled pages of writing
In a boy's pencilled hand,
You would be looking to me
To read and understand
Catching the thing below it,
The thought you had almost said.
I told you to write as you could,
With the Scots words in your head,
And you would grow to a poet.
Still those calm evenings remain
Forever untouched by pain;
Nothing can kill the past.
What was, is still good.

There have been boys like you,
Brave and handsome and gay,
Or sad with the old sadness
Of high hills at break of day
When the heather is drenched with dew
And the birds scarcely wakened:
Sadness that is sweet too,

That lies in the wild mouth of singing,
That is part of being a Scot.
These boys have died or been killed,
By the English, by poverty, by drowning at sea,
And some were good and some not,
But all had lain once on a mother's knee
And for all a mother's long mourning
And a place not to be filled,
And a sore pain to the last.
Yet they had lived and been happy,
They had become part of the river
Of folk's lives which is Scotland.
Nothing could change the past.

So for you too, part of that river,
Ah, part of Scotland forever,
For you too, no forgetting,
But remembrance, surely with joy,

Neither resenting or regretting
The careless step of a young boy
Whose eyes are fixed and far,
Beyond parents,
Beyond friends,
On the moon glens where his dreams are
And the known world ends.
And remembrance with delight,
That will someday not be pain,
Of the child's body stretched gently at night
Under the father's roof and the fierce rain,
When the storm went where it would;
And the child's smile at the hearthside.
What was, is still good.
And remembrance with right pride,
Of growth and strength and the mind forming
And shapes beginning to show
As the words drifted fast
Through the head of the young poet.
Ah good and sure to know,
However cruel the present,
Nothing can hurt the past.

MABEL ESTHER ALLAN

This poem was written in March after the bombing of Wallasey in Cheshire.

I saw a Broken Town

I saw a broken town beside the grey March sea,
Spray flung in the air and no larks singing,
And houses lurching, twisted, where the chestnut trees
Stand ripped and stark; the fierce wind bringing
The choking dust in clouds along deserted streets,
Shaking the gaping rooms, the jagged, raw-white stone.
Seeking for what in this quiet, stricken town? It beats
About each fallen wall, each beam, leaving no livid, aching place
    alone.

JOYCE GRENFELL

March Day, 1941

Taut as a tent the heavenly dome is blue,
Uncrossed by cloud or tossing twig or 'plane,
A measureless span infinitely new
To fill the eye and soar the heart again.
Deep in the wintered earth the shock is felt:
Glossy sweet aconite has shown her gold
And string straight crocus spears, where late we knelt
To lodge their bulbs, are waiting to unfold.
The ragged rooks like tea-leaves in the sky
Straggle towards the earth with awkward grace;
A robin in a silver birch nearby
Thrusts up his carol through the naked lace.
   I've known this day for thirty years and more;
   It will go on as it has done before.

FRANCES BELLERBY

*Frances Bellerby lived in Plash Mill, Upton Cross, a thatched, white-washed cottage
on the south-east edge of Bodmin Moor in Cornwall.*

The Airman Asleep on the Rocks

Gently the sky leans over, and the sun
Lays lightest blessing on forgotten face
Of the surrendered sleeper. Here he lies,
The black rock folding this defencelessness,
The pale air sculptured to this limber death.

Above a line of weed at the sea's edge
Broken light leaps, shaking a dazzling glitter,
A March-mad glitter, wild as crazy fishes
At mindless, spendthrift, wastrel, silver play!

The children, sand-intent, stay unaware
Of this fantastic glittering dance of light
Bordering the sea, where weed is thrust and pulled.
The children build with urgency. They run
Hither and thither, as for very lives.
And years may go before they've time to pause
And see – in March, some harebell afternoon –
The glittering shattered light above the weed,
And think: Has all this happened once before?

In the forsaken face the sad eyelids
Fashion small mounds, like graves. The parted lips,
The loosened hands, have given up the ghost.
Oh Holy Ghost, oh lovely Ghost, return!
Flood back, sweet Senses, and annihilate
The grave enchantment of this pictured death!
Still he'll have time to watch the dancing glitter,
To puzzle, clouded, half-remembering . . .
Kingfisher-flash, renew the child, intent,
Building with sand to outlast Eternity.

EILUNED LEWIS

London Spring, 1941

If I could paint I'd show you
Something I saw today;
A house bombed, blasted sideways,
The roof blown clean away;
A bath perched near a chasm,
A waste of broken floors,
The staircase turned to matchwood
And twisted, tortured doors.
While in the neighbour's garden,
With slender fence and tree
Dividing all its modest length
From dark catastrophe,
A little Moses cradle
Was placed upon the ground
And in it slept a baby
So pink and sweet and round,
With no-one there to mind it,
To fuss or fear, not one!
But all the jolly crocuses
Wide open to the sun.

MARIE CARMICHAEL STOPES

The Doll

ENGLAND 1941

In a flowering hawthorn tree,
Swaying with the topmost may,
In the glowing light of day,
Hanging lightly, swinging free
Up against an azure sky
There's a child's doll caught on high.

Swinging from its golden hair
Threaded in the may flower sweet,
With its little slippered feet
Flickering and dancing there;
Only bees can reach it now
In the scented hawthorn bough.

Did its laughing owner throw
Her doll so high among the bees
Loading pollen in the trees?
Or did she wish her doll to go
Above the very topmost sky
To tell her how bright angels fly?

In the silence by the gate
The brook still ripples through the green
Of Stellaria's fragile sheen,
Burbling softly as of late;
And the white ducks paddle slowly
Hunting creatures still more lowly.

Swaying by your golden hair
Doll, you're tangled very high,
Looking down from childhood's sky,
With your blue eyes in a stare,
Glassy eyes, set gazing fast
On the future and the past.

Now I've turned the cornered lane,
See the thing at which you're staring
With your hard glass eyes not caring:
All your view I'll see again
And again. Reflecting years
Mirror it in crystal tears.

Looking from your flowering bough
Over lawn and cobbled path
You're dumb where elemental wrath
Shattered, as a clod by plough,
Wall and lintel, hearth and bed,
Mounding splinters splashed with red.

Yet the hawthorn's scented foam
Breathes unscathed so very near,
As though great beauty knows no fear
Of the spurting scattered loam
Or of screaming sudden flash
With the spluttering earthward crash.

Did it happen in the night,
Hidden by the purple dark
That this home was laid so stark
By one blinding flash of light?
Yesterday the cottage stood
Garden-girdled in a wood.

Crumpled now to mouldering heap
The house is like an ant-piled mound
Of refuse mandibles have found,
But this was gathered in one leap:
Wrenched from their appointed place
Parts obliterate home's grace.

Hanging by your golden hair
In the hawthorn, your fixed eyes
Gaze on this, your world's new guise
Quite unmoved, you dance up there
Only swaying when the breeze
Flirts with springing hawthorn trees.

The wind has turned you in your tree:
A mark shows on your blue silk skirt:
Is it stain of loam-spread dirt
Flecked with grey and red I see?
No, no, no, no, no, I stand
Gazing at a baby's hand.

Severed from its little wrist,
Clutching your blue skirt so fast
The small hand hurtled through and past
All the shattered debris-twist
Of the cot and nursery,
To the hawthorn's greenery.

Little hand thus raised alone
Held mid flowers by golden hair
Above a home beyond repair,
Must I make my heart a stone?
I weep, and turn, to watch the sky
Flock-full of metal made to fly.

SHEILA SHANNON

The Artist's Vision
ON A SHELTER PICTURE BY HENRY MOORE

The artist sees the world in composition:
in colour, pattern, rhythm, line and light,
and we in Moore's tube shelter sketch are seen
as solid half-recumbent female figures,
still, statuesque, devoid of all emotion,
shining in splendour of soft magenta and green.

Majestic, superhuman; as if some God
were in the act – creating us from stone;
leaning towards life, yet only half alive,
half patient, malleable, enduring rock.
No heart will drive its pulse along our veins;
no tears will gather in our vacant eyes;

No weariness has ever weighed us down
Nor hunger ached in us, nor cold has curled
its paralysing fingers round our limbs,
nor pain, nor joy, nor love have ever known,
but soulless megaliths we lie entranced
in limbo's circle, lost between the worlds.

GRETA BRIGGS

General Wavell wrote: 'I read these verses in an Egyptian newspaper while flying from Cairo to Barce in Cyrenaica at the beginning of April 1941, to try to deal with Rommel's counter-attack. I was uncomfortable in body – for the bomber was cramped and draughty – and in mind for I knew I had been caught with insufficient strength to meet a heavy counter-attack; reading this poem and committing it to memory did something to relieve my discomforts of body and mind.'

London Under Bombardment

I, who am known as London, have faced stern times before,
Having fought and ruled and traded for a thousand years and
                                                    more;
I knew the Roman legions and the harsh-voiced Danish hordes;
I heard the Saxon revels, saw blood on the Norman swords.
But, though I am scarred by battle, my grim defenders vow
Never was I so stately nor so well-beloved as now.
The lights that burn and glitter in the exile's lonely dream,
The lights of Piccadilly, and those that used to gleam
Down Regent-street and Kingsway may now no longer shine,
But other lights keep burning, and their splendour, too, is mine,
Seen in the work-worn faces and glimpsed in the steadfast eyes
When little homes lie broken and death descends from the skies.
The bombs have shattered my churches, have torn my streets
                                                    apart,
But they have not bent my spirit and they shall not break my
                                                    heart.
For my people's faith and courage are lights of London town
Which still would shine in legends though my last broad bridge
                                                    were down.

PAULINE RICE

April Blitz

Looking back over my shoulder
into the mirror of yesterday,
I find myself still a ghost
smiling inwardly at the thoughts
of strawberries on midsummer's eve.
Yes, even in the small brick sepulchre
of a draughty street shelter.
Five companions, hushed with identical dread,
littered the concrete floor
like praying monks in mundane English garb,
while I stood, believing myself unafraid,
by the sack-cloth opening,
listening to the steady thud of bombs,
the wails of sickly children;
feeling the earth revolt at the intrusion
of an unwanted stranger,
treading with heavy feet into the rendezvous
of moon-eyed roses.
A snow-queen sentinel,
with flames for thoughts
and a void where the heart should be.
Only the head, only the head remained,
dynamic will opposing falling steel,
trusting inexplicably the human atom;
I, the inexorable,
felt Christ laugh within me,
and laughing in unison
found desire to sob out the aching void
beside cool running waters.
When will there come an end
to the breaking of air, of starry air?
To the tiger's roar torn from the dusty souls
of falling houses,
leaving unwholesome gaps
among the streets' brick molars?
An appeal to God?
A burnt offering of silent prayers
for the weakness in man?

I have no gods, only a blind faith in my own ego,
a sure faith in the fingers round the brush.

At Number Nine, twelve feet away,
where cooled the wrinkled sheets
not long since warm,
Picasso hung upon a wall
and played his visual symphony.
Looking out within myself,
yet standing from the shell apart,
I watched five bodies on the floor
who wished to die, and kneeling tried to pray.
At twenty-two I did not want to die,
Although a hundred years seemed added to the score,
and when the knowledge came
that Number Nine had fallen like a child's house of cards,
hearts downward faced . . . the smirking knave on top . . .
when the final knowledge came
that all I loved lay patchworked in the dust,
I did not pray.
Let me repeat myself;
only the head, only the head remained
of one who stood and watched with dusty eyes,
the head supplanted by a spinning-wheel
weaving abundant stuff
torn by a swift thought-shuttle,
subject for surrealism.
The proud masterpiece
crushed like a complicated jigsaw puzzle
under a carved bronze bust
minus a nose.
Dust into dust
where crashed and tumbled
concertos on to symphonies,
weeks of boring grind paid out in music discs,
and treasured every one.
I did not pray
as Jack fell down the hill,
I did not follow after.
A thought strand, swift as light,
illumined the spinning-wheel,
that counted all the unborn weeks,

the working hours that press
the silver lucre in my palm,
the slow waiting time before my treasure
is restored again.

So small a happening
in this world volcanic with such wild emotion,
a little thing
assuming giant proportions in the minds
of five who prayed
and one who stood,
a snow-queen sentinel.
It happened yesterday,
And yet to-day is yesterday,
to-morrow is to-day.
Time is changeless,
only the human moon waxes and wanes,
sand in the hour-glass trickling away,
adding the sliding months
to two and twenty.
The house is different now,
two ancients sharing half of it.
There is no studio.
Pictures are out of fashion
I am told . . . therefore
the walls have vacant stares.
They call me highbrow and put
my music-box upstairs;
father just sits . . .
Pierrot without a grin;
the knitting needles click,
the wool unravels from its ball.
I paint in corners when the fire is bright,
I write this while the house is hushed,
poised, ear-cocked for every sound.
The fire is out,
but I am free to think of strawberries
on midsummer's eve,
torn books, Picasso hanging on the wall . . .
Only the head, only the head remains.

CLEMENCE DANE

During March and April Plymouth suffered heavy bombing raids.

Plymouth

I've just been down to Plymouth. Did you know
that lovely place before the trouble started?
Well, you'd be broken-hearted
if you could see it now, I tell you that,
The mess the 'planes have made!
Acres laid flat!
It's cruel – day and night, raid after raid!
And how the people stick it out, God knows!
I wouldn't know.

But there they are, and, stubborn, there they stay.
They work all day
between the bombs. At night – this moved me most –
an hour before the sun goes down
they flock, the ruined people of the town,
to listen to the band,
(light music, nothing grand)
and dance, or watch the dancing, on the Hoe.

Who dance? Oh – sailors – girls from a canteen –
men at a warden's post –
a smiling couple from a salvaged home –
or others who've lost everything. They come
for company, to change their thoughts, to rest:
and shabby clothes don't matter on the Hoe.

The waters darken, purple dyes the west,
the hilltops lose their green,
the stars begin to glow.
Black-out! As home they go
the 'planes are heard afar.

This was the second summer of the war;
yet every night, sedately,
most innocent and stately,

the boys and girls were dancing,
were dancing on the Hoe.
The boys and girls of Plymouth
were dancing on the Hoe.

OLIVIA MANNING

Olivia Manning and her husband, a British Council lecturer, escaped from Romania and arrived in Athens in October 1940. They were evacuated on an old steamship after the Germans occupied Greece in April 1941 and spent the rest of the war in Cairo.

From 'Written in the Third Year of the War'

The men that went out of Athens on the bright day in spring
When everyone had a flower or a flag, and the Greeks were
    carrying the bearded sailors,
Like classic heroes, aloft on their shoulders.
The men that went out that day waved from the lorries,
And when we cried 'Good Luck!' called back to us 'We're
    off to Berlin.'
Those that began returning a week later had nothing to say.
The clouds hung low, bagged with wet, and the wind stripped
    petals from the trees.
They stared with blank eyes over the lorry sides, the bandages
    muddy on their heads.
We watched with compassion and bewilderment.
It seemed a long way to bring the wounded. We were not
    told how close the Germans followed.
When the lorries stopped and the men slid down like old
    men, blind, without response for us,
We felt then a thing unknown to our generation, the sorrow
    and terror of defeat . . .

PEGGY WHITEHOUSE

From A Democrat's Chapbook

The wave, at Greece, caught up a little country
And heroes died on hills, and were not sung:
The obstinate heroes fought a three-times army
And kept it back, for twice the allotted days:
And heroes died among the groves of Ilex,
Or by the olive terrace: and the vine
Uprooted tossed. And as of old ran blood
The seas.

Across those seas
By boats, at night, men rowed,
The little army,
Beached: in some low bay, at Crete;
The shingled pebbles lapped by long, low waves
As gentle as the little waves at home;
And voices gentle in the gentle night
So low and humid with the salty splurge
Of the crushed sea-plants: and mimosas ache
Of yellow scent. And bay.
And tamarisk. And other foreign trees
That crossed the moon.
                    The voices gentle
And quiet the rocked boats on even keels
Drawn up the shingle: as a whisper cuts
Long silence. But their own particular sound
More urgent than a whisper; cut of cloth, or cord
Through hawser.
This was the flight of the men the wave had thrown
To hang like flies, on rocks, or gulch-like valleys . . .

. . . And while on Crete a friend of mine, a tall woman
Yes, strange, not some unknown, a girl, a friend,
Met in the London summers, in the green-leafed squares
Her house there, and her people: Greek
And eminent. And she a 'society girl'
Finding in drawing-rooms the setting for her snaky hair
Black as Medusa's: and hearthed fires

For the long limbs the background —
Deceived and tricked the enemy. A nurse
Who put the first things first: and showed that power
For good can turn ill things to good,
And turn even evil to the use of good:
Showed white endurance as the old Greek women showed it,
Strong, tall, and vehement, and powerful: and such courage as
    lives;
There, hidden in a gully, by a rock
With countless wounded men, in rows, in caves
And waterless, and foodless, without help,
And she, the single woman: one her race
had bred for this. — A story bright, and fine,
And clear as all the old Greek stories . . .

JULIETTE DE BAIRACLI-LEVY

Killed in Action

His chair at the table, empty,
His home clothes hanging in rows forlorn,
His cricket bat and cap, his riding cane,
The new flannel suit he had not worn.
His dogs, restless, restless, with tortured ears
Listening for his swift, light tread upon the path.
And there – his violin! Oh his violin! Hush! hold
your tears.

For N.J. de B.L.
Crete, May 1941

ELEANOR WELLS

During the war six high explosive bombs fell on the British Museum. However, the greatest amount of damage occurred on 10 May 1941 when dozens of incendiaries pierced the roofs of the south and west wings. The following areas were badly affected: the Roman Britain Room, the Central Saloon and adjoining Prehistoric Room, the main staircase, the Room of Greek and Roman Life and its annexes, the Medal Room, the Greek Bronze Room and the First Vase Room. The intensity of the fire destroyed the roofs, buckling the massive cast iron girders. Although the Museum's collections were evacuated during late August and September 1939, in August 1940 an exhibition of duplicate antiquities, casts, models and reproductions was arranged 'not only for the instruction and entertainment of visitors, but also as a possible sacrifice to the perils of war'. This suicide exhibition was mounted in the Prehistoric Room and the Central Saloon on the first floor. It fulfilled its destiny on 10 May 1941 . . . (A letter from an archivist at the British Museum.)

For the Undefeated

I

Imperilled stands the day. Up the bright street
The shadows slowly creep and darken slowly
The sunlit pavement and the yellow leaf.
Windless, the trees are heavy in the air,
The flags hang silent, and the clouds come on
As imperceptibly as time. Dangerous
Are these approaching thunderheads and these
Attendant lightnings, and the night that falls
Unnoticed, terrible, in the heart.

In the city men walk with canes tapping
Like blind beggars, and the open windows
Bring in no light, nor do they throw the lamplight
Into the garden. Talk is in whispers.
We have locked our valuables away,
And forgotten how to spell in our own language.
Dust gathers on the piano and the violin case,
And when we kiss one another it is furtively in
        corners.

A bomb fell on the Museum among the Impressionists
And the plaster casts of Greek gods.

The librarian burned his books. The post office
Stopped sending letters except for the government,
And the radio stopped playing Brahms.
Night fell, and the doctor broke the test tubes in his
       laboratory,
The lawyer couldn't keep up with the legislature,
The Broadway stars went back on the road,
And the rain fell all night upon the city,
And the darkness over it was like mist.

II

Do you remember, Maximilius, the rain
Falling in Gaul, and the legions marching,
Footsore, south to the Alps and Rome?
Three weeks from home, Maximilius,
And the Huns behind us. Have you forgotten
The skins across their shoulders and the horns of deer
Stuck in their helmets, the great knives,
The war cries shrilling in the blood?
Rain was falling in Appia and the night
Drew down behind us as we fled.

Do you remember, Maximilius, the darkness
Gathering in Rome?
               Have you forgotten, Crito,
The killing of brothers and the Thracian hordes
Walking within our temples? Do you remember
Dusk here in Athens among the olive trees,
Dusk in the markets, in the streets, between
The radiant pillars of the Parthenon? Crito,
Remember how the evening came and stole within,
Chilling as hemlock.
             Do not forget, Atahualpa,
The Spanish horses prancing in the golden sun,
Nor the slaves bearing ingots for the conqueror.
Remember always in your heart, O King, the vines
Creeping among the caryatids of temples, the crumbling
Of the walls of Cuzco, and the black midnight
That seized you, strangling, here upon your altar.

III

Under our portals now the shadows lengthen,
And our fires turn swift to ashes. Into our keyhole

Seeps the ancient dust. What we have saved of silver
Tarnishes, and the towers we built to stand forever
Mock us. In our factories men put away their tools,
And we close our books, shut off the radio, eat
A last meal, for night has come.

      But if night falls, believe me,
Dawn will return. If we must sleep
Let it be as children, dreaming of tomorrow,
Or as lovers sleep, waking in the night to rise
And go out into the gardens and walk
In darkness among the flowers, not seeing colour
But knowing the rose also is awake.
            And many of us, sleepless,
Will sit together through the long night, talking
Of friends remembered and dead poets and the earth
Warm in the spring between our fingers. Some
Will die in the slow hours of returning day,
Some have already fallen asleep never to wake, some
Will always sit patiently in the shadows waiting
For yesterday to return.
            The darkness claims us.
Let us climb the hill and look for tomorrow.
We will sleep in the meadows where the sun,
Rising, may find us early. We will know,
Even in darkness, that the earth turns beneath us,
And we will dream of our seeds in the earth
And of the harvesting of them, and of the dawn
That will dazzle the treetops when we wake.

LYNETTE ROBERTS

During the heavy bombing raid on London on 10/11 May 1941, the twelfth-century
Temple church received a direct hit. The roof over the chancel was destroyed, the interior
of the Round and the choir were burnt out, and the tombs of the Knights Templar badly
damaged. On a visit to London, Lynette Roberts saw the destruction; the widowed
mother of one of her friends helped to save some treasures from the ruined church.

Crossed and Uncrossed

Heard the steam rising from the chill blue bricks,
Heard the books sob and the buildings huge groan
As the hard crackle of flames leapt on firemen
    and paled the red walls.

Bled their hands in anguish to check the fury
Knowing fire had raged for week and a day:
Clung to buildings like swallows flat and exhausted
    under the storm.

Fled the sky: fragments of the Law, kettles and glass:
Lamb's ghost screamed: Pegasus melted and fell
Meteor of shining light on to a stone court
    and only wing grave.

Round Church built in a Round Age, cold with grief,
Coloured Saints of glass lie buried at your feet:
Crusaders uncross limbs by the green light of flares,
    burn into Tang shapes.

Over firedrake floors the 'Smith' organ pealed
Roared into flames when you proud widow
Ran undaunted: the lead roof dripping red tears
    curving to crash.

Treasure was saved. Your loyalty broke all sight,
Revived the creed of the Templars of old;
Long lost. Others of the Inn escaped duty
    in black hats.

Furniture out, slates ripped off, yet persistently
Hoovering the remaining carpet, living as we all do
Blanketed each night, with torch, keys, emergency basket
  close by your side.

From paper window we gaze at the catacomb of books,
You, unflinching, stern of spirit, ready to
Gather charred sticks to fight no gas where gas was
  everywhere escaping.

Through thin library walls where 'Valley' still grows,
From Pump Court to dry bank of rubble, titanic monsters
Roll up from the Thames, to drown the 'storm' should it
  dare come again.

Still water silences death: fills night with curious light,
Brings green peace and birds to top of Plane tree,
Fills Magnolia with grail thoughts: while you of King's Bench
  Walk, cherish those you most love.

*Towards the end of May, Lynette Roberts visited the poet Alun Lewis, who was serving
in the Royal Engineers at Longmoor Camp in Hampshire. She later sent him a poetic
invitation.*

Poem from Llanybri

If you come my way that is . . .
Between now and then, I will offer you
A fist full of rock cress fresh from the bank
The valley tips of garlic red with dew
Cooler than shallots, a breath you can swank

In the village when you come. At noon-day
I will offer you a choice bowl of cawl
Served with a 'lover's' spoon and a chopped spray
Of leeks or savori fach, not used now,

In the old way you'll understand. The din
Of children singing through the eyelet sheds
Ringing 'smith hoops, chasing the butt of hens;
Or I can offer you Cwmcelyn spread

With quartz stones from the wild scratching of men:
You will have to go carefully with clogs
Or thick shoes for it's treacherous the fen,
The East and West Marshes also have bogs.

Then I'll do the lights, fill the lamp with oil,
Get coal from the shed, water from the well;
Pluck and draw pigeon with crop of green foil
This your good supper from the lime-tree fell.

A sit by the hearth with blue flames rising,
No talk. Just a stare at 'Time' gathering
Healed thoughts, pool insight, like swan sailing
Peace and sound around the home, offering

You a night's rest and my day's energy.
You must come – start this pilgrimage,
Can you come? – send an ode or elegy
In the old way and raise our heritage.

CONSTANCE SCOTT

On 24 May 1941 the German battleship Bismarck *sank the battle-cruiser* HMS Hood *in the Denmark Straits. There were only 3 survivors from a crew of over 1,400 men. Three days later the* Bismarck *herself was sunk by a combined force of British warships and naval aircraft.*

HMS *Hood*
TO THE DEATHLESS MEMORY OF ALL WHO SERVED ABOARD HER

I used with pride to think my window frames
    The sweetest scene a little window could,
Flowers everywhere, the children at their games:
    Sometimes so naughty, then so 'darling-good,'
But now I only see a list of names,
    Through blinding tears, his dear name . . . and
       the Hood . . .
Never again will he stride up that path,
    Nor help me plant the flowers with boyish glee,
I shall not hear him whistle, no, nor laugh:
    Except in dreams and aching memory.
But I am sworn to duty all my life,
    I hear him ask this last love-gift of me:
'Yes, yes, I swear it, as a sailor's wife,
    God helping me, *our son shall serve the Sea.*'
    I am *so* cold, will you make up the fire?
    Yet these are roses, what a sad, mazed June!
Where are the children? Do not let them tire
    You kind folk out: I shall be better soon . . .
I shall, in time, learn not to blame the sea
    (When God created it He found it good);
I must be brave to join that company,
    The silent, tragic widows of the Hood.

OLIVE HALLETT

A Good Laugh
(WHIT SUNDAY, 1941)

[25 May 1941]

My mirth is of quite recent date,
For on Whit Sunday (rather late)
I sat in bed with morning tea
And listened to the B.B.C.
Broadcasting news at nine o'clock.
I must confess I had a shock
On hearing the announcement made
So calmly by the Board of Trade.
It seemed to me a sorry way
To start a Whitsun holiday.
But as the voice went bravely on
To tell us just what should be done,
My thoughts flowed in a happier vein,
And when it started to explain
The kind of tokens to be used,
Well then I really was amused.
Just fancy buying crepe-de-chine
With coupons labelled 'Margarine!'
(If there had been a rationed hat
Would it be 'Lard or Cooking Fat?')
Oh, how I laughed as I began
To work out this new clothing plan.
One gown or frock or woollen dress
And I'm eleven coupons less.
For five, it seems, I'd have to choose
Between a blouse and pair of shoes.
I know I must go very slow,
For it would be a cruel blow
And place me in a fearful fix
If I had spent the sixty-six
And then discovered I was short
Of something which I should have bought.
But still I'm having lots of fun
In finding things that can be done

With garments given up for dead.
So that when all is done and said,
This scheme which took us by surprise
May be a blessing in disguise.
To me, it cannot be denied,
It has a very funny side.

RUTH TOMALIN

In May 1941 there were unusual swarms of ladybirds in Sussex and heavy air raids over London.

Ladybird, Ladybird

'Ladybird, ladybird,
fly away home . . .'
leopard-winged ladybirds,
why do they roam?
the children were singing
the summer refrain,
'Ladybird, ladybird,
fly home again!'

Outside, a tired woman
lingered to say,
'You wouldn't know of
a place I could stay . . . ?'
weary, with bundles –
life had gone West.
'Bombed out last night, dear.
I – just need a rest . . .'

(Children and ladybirds
singing of flight . . .)
'I had two kiddies, dear –
until last night . . .'
Oh, ladybird, ladybird –
so it goes on –
Your house is afire
and your children are gone.

V.H. FRIEDLAENDER

Trivial Detail

Floating on the water in the A.R.P. bucket
Was a round reddish speck
That turned out to be a ladybird.
It looked lifeless;
But on a whim
I dipped a finger into the sun-warmed bucket
And extracted the tiny thing.
Laying it on a mellow brick in the rockery,
I went on down the garden path with the bucket
And filled the bird-bath.
And just now, on my way back,
I stopped to look;
And there was the ladybird
Bustling about the hot, richly grooved brick,
Exploring, interested, totally recovered.

I have saved the life of a ladybird!
And, as I refilled the bucket
For its more sinister purpose,
Suddenly, ridiculously,
In the midst of crashing continents,
I felt for a moment
Extraordinarily happy.

PATRICIA LEDWARD

During the summer of 1941 Patricia Ledward visited a friend who was nursing at Ashridge Hospital, an emergency hospital in the grounds of Ashridge Park, near Berkhamsted in Hertfordshire.

Air-raid Casualties: Ashridge Hospital

On Sundays friends arrive with kindly words
To peer at those whom war has crushed;
They bring the roar of health into these hushed
And solemn wards –
The summer wind blows through the doors and cools
The sweating forehead; it revives
Memories of other lives
Spent lying in the fields, or by sea-pools;
And ears that can discern
Only the whistling of a bomb it soothes
With tales of water splashing into smooth
Deep rivers fringed with ferns.
Nurses with level eyes, and chaste
In long starched dresses, move
Amongst the maimed, giving love
To strengthen bodies gone to waste.
The convalescents have been wheeled outside,
The sunshine strikes their cheeks and idle fingers,
Bringing to each a sensuous languor
And sentimental sorrow for the dead.

Over the human scene stands the old castle, its stone
Now tender in the sun; even the gargoyles seem to find
Some humour in the vision of mankind
Lying relaxed and helplessly alone.
Only the Tudor Roses view with grief
The passing of a kingly age,
The dwindling of a history page,
False-faced religion, sham belief.

Six – the clock chimes for the visitors to go:
The widow reading to her son shuts up the book,
The lover takes his final look

At the mutilated face, so bravely gay;
The young wife, with husband full of shot,
Kisses his brow and quickly walks away,
Her eyes on the stalwart boughs that sway
Still seeing the flatness of his sheets;
The child with dark curls, beloved of all the others,
Jingles his coins and waves bare feet,
Like lily petals, to entreat
One penny more from his departing brother.

One by one the wards empty, happiness goes,
The hospital routine, the usual work
Return for another week;
The patients turn upon themselves, a hundred foes
Imagined swell their suffering;
Fretfully hands pick at sheets
And voices meet
Discussing symptoms and the chance of living.
Only the soldier lies remote and resolutely sane,
Remembering how, a boy, he dreamt of folk
With footballs. Maturity dispelled the dream – he woke
To know that he would never walk again.

PHYLLIS SHAND ALLFREY

Phyllis Shand Allfrey's family were early white settlers in the Caribbean and she was born in Dominica. During most of the war she lived in London but was nostalgic for Dominica and concerned about young West Indian men dying for a distant ideal.

Colonial Soldiers

We who were born and breathed in open spaces,
who warm the blood of the restless in our veins,
are now companion to those shut-in faces
making their cautious way through narrow lanes.

Sometimes, arrested in the greying crowd
to study careful newsprint, see us stand
transfixed to learn that arrogant and loud
evil has dropped upon our guiltless land.

That brown face lifted to the argent sky
to watch the birdlike swoop, with flowering mouth
parted in wonder, spatters out to die
for things uncomprehended in his youth.

Uncomprehending, too, we move confined
by the strict gestures of the modern state,
and bearing arms march with the willing blind
towards some goal as yet undesignate.

VITA SACKVILLE-WEST

The Wines of France

Wine has gone from my table long, long since.
That loveliest harvest of the slopes and sun;
That strangest harvest, wayward incidence,
Unwilling and unamenable to be transplanted
From acre to neighbouring acre, though the soil
Be lifted and transferred to next-door same conditions,
Refusing to reproduce the self-same wine;
Something we cannot control, something beyond our science,
Something more natural than all our expertise,
Something more curious than what we understand,
Something old, something primitive, something of nature,
Something which had to do with the sun and the season,
Something eluding our cleverness, our brain-working.
– For we always get back, at last, in the last resort,
To the things we have not explained, but recognise
As an awkward block in the smooth, the rational path, –
And so with wine, it is a particular thing,
It has its moods and its years; grows old, decays
Even as the human body decays with advancing years;
Up to a point it increases in fermentation
So long as it is alive, as a young man grows
In the strength of his body and intensity of his mind,
But after a point declines till it peters out
As the vintner's number of years will peter out
When he ought to die, and the wine he made will die.

And the connoisseurs will say, as they swirl their glass
With delicate motion, nearly reaching the rim,
'This wine is too old, it is past its peak of time;
It can only be poured away, and the giving earth
Shall be the receiving earth as the wheel comes round.'

Wine has gone from my table long, long since.
The cobwebbed bottle in its wicker cradle
Preciously carried, not to disturb the lees,
Or the rough cheap daily wine in red or yellow
Decanters carelessly poured, that stood on the table
Like Chinese vases of red or yellow amber

In the light of a sunset window, making reflections,
– For if you love wine at all, as it should be loved,
For the beauty of its appearance and the romance of its growing,
You will love it both dear and cheap, both fine and rough,
The great wines and the little, *vins fins* or *pour la soif*,

Aged or young, as one loves human nature
For different qualities or at different stages, –
The exquisite Montrachet, the rare Chateauneuf,
Whose names are of the oldest aristocracy,
An Almanach de Gotha with its princes,
With its eccentrics too, as every ancient strain;
But you will love the workman-wines as well,
The heart, and not the intellect, of France.

But stay. We had forgot. The hideous
Science of men has triumphed over beauty.
Vanished, the strange, the coloured grace. The Boche
Is making petrol from the wines of France.

SHEILA STEEN

True France

DÉDIÉ AUX 'CAHIERS DU SILENCE'

True France! – of hissing grape-vats – of vine and green fig-tree –
With head in hilltop heaven and white feet in the sea;
France of our youth of longing . . . where walnut sabots swing
Festooned round country doorways, and dark-eyed children bring
Little round sugar-cakes to the Feast of Kings, and dance
To the praise of God on the cobbles . . . beloved, lovely France!
We remember and hear you: faith, hope are not in vain.

    Along your shadowed rivers, by Dordogne, Loire and Seine,
    Through your taken cities – despite the sniper Death –
    You smuggle to us the contraband of intellect and breath.
    Scribbled in dark cellars – despite the sentries, come
    Your blood-sealed letters somehow, out of martyrdom.

Soul speaks to soul: and soul surpasses shame.
True France cries out '*I Live!*' Her voice is still the same.

PATRICIA LEDWARD

The poet Timothy Corsellis served as a second officer in the Air Transport Auxilliary.
He was killed on 10 October 1941, aged twenty.

In Memoriam
(TIMOTHY CORSELLIS, KILLED FLYING)

You wished to be a lark, and, as the lark, mount singing
To the highest peak of solitude your soul had found,
You wished to fly between the stars and let your song
Shower down to earth in gleaming falls of sound.

A century ago you might have done all this:
Flowers at your music would have set the earth on
    fire,
Mountains retained it in their hearts of rock,
In poplar boughs winds paused at your wild lyre.

World chaos coiled about you, and each upward flight
Meant struggling with the deep morass of history:
Luck was against you, poet, that you lived when guns
And tramping feet was all that mankind knew of poetry.

But solitude still called – you became an eagle.
Beneath your wings you held the slanting clouds of gold,
The earth seemed now a comic tune, for mighty
    orchestras
Drew you towards the sun, unblinded, bold.

A letter tells us you are dead – at twenty years.
From shocked and nerveless hands the paper slips.
We see it all – the failing engine, the numb fingers
    clutching,
The instantaneous fear, distorted lips,

The starting eyes, the whirling, humming sky,
The sweat of agony, the bleeding fist, the flash
Of life and panoramic view before your mind,
The whistling, screaming, downward rush, the crash.

The grass, the lonely hills, are weeping tears of green,
The sky bends low, embracing in a gentle shroud of air
Your shattered body; and the wind that sweeps the
     waves
Is mourning for your lively eyes and thick locks of your
     hair.

We, your friends, will not give way to alien tears,
But shall think in firelight of your grave voice reading
     verse,
Remember all your wit, your poses, and your heart
Far kinder than you'd ever have us guess.

Come! let us dance in nightclubs you frequented,
Covet with envious eyes half-breeds you wished to gain,
Thrust our hands deep in golden hair you loved to touch,
Drink till your memory ferments within our brain.

The band is changing tune to the century's Blues:
Go on, yes, dance, I'll come when I am needed —
On a far hill a youth lies dead, his mouth towards the mud,
And, like the blood, his song dissolves in earth,
     unheeded.

Play on, O Harlem band, O swing your blues!
Rend every stone with your terrible, lamenting cry:
Those who would sing of life, and hope, and joy,
Are driven out to hunt, to kill, to die.

MYFANWY HAYCOCK

Embarkation Leave

[October 1941]

So short a while to stay – so much to see,
　　To say and hear and do, so much to know,
So many unrelenting tasks to fill
　　The tantalising hours before you go.

So short a while – so much we dare not say,
　　Or even dare think, lest one quick tear
Break down our brave but clumsy barricades,
And leave us naked in a world of fear.

How can I tell you while the hours speed by,
　　Of love as strong as oak trees in their prime,
Of heart that calls unceasingly to heart –
　　How can I tell you in so brief a time?

How can you tell me of the lovely things
　　That hold us close as streams that meet and flow
For ever, ever, ever to the sea –
How can you tell me, love, before you go?

Before you go, dear heart, there's much to know,
　　There's much to say and hear and do and see,
If we poor fools would trap in these brief hours
　　The splendour of our love's eternity.

MARIE CARMICHAEL STOPES

Shouts of 'The Navy's here' came as a boarding party from the destroyer HMS Cossack
set free merchant seamen prisoners in the German supply ship Altmark *in a Norwegian
fjord in February 1940. The men had been captured by the German pocket battleship*
Admiral Graf Spee *during her 1939 exploits in sinking nine ships in the Indian
Ocean and South Atlantic. The following year HMS* Cossack *was one of the ships
involved in sinking the German battleship* Bismarck. *On 23 October 1941 she herself
was torpedoed and sunk by the German submarine* U-563 *in the Atlantic. The poet
H. William Rose, the First Lieutenant of HMS* Cossack, *went down with the ship.*

From Instead of Tears

In Memoriam for Officers and Men
Who went down in HMS *Cossack*
– 'The Navy is Here' –
and especially for Lieut. H. William Rose, RN

I

You have no foothold now on solid earth
 The sky, the sea, the beating sea of tides
  Sway with your multitudinous appeal,
   And you escape the earth-bound common rule
    Of earth to earth playing an earth-warmed part.
     No flowers will spring from any clay you've used,
      The dark sea holds what her cold fires have fused.
     Earth burial means flowers spring from the heart
      But the sea pastures are more strange and cool
      Her phosphorescent ripples in life's wheel
 Show beauty's irridescent changing sides
Darting from death to sensuous new birth.

II

Brown berried sea-wrack tangles round your throat
 In festive chaplets where no fresh wreathed flowers
  Will reach you, and your resolute white limbs
   Are draped with laminaria's crinkled strands
    Swaying about the stillness of your thighs.
     Your eyes are closed to all the hurrying fleet
      Of fin-borne flocks darting between your feet.
     Your breath gives no response to wave-swept sighs.
     The pearl-sailed Nautilus curves to your hands.
    Lucent green water takes the light and dims

Your lips now fading with the passing hours
That sang and laughed with an Elysian note.

III

Our grief for you, poignant, and personal
 But crystallizes woe for all our dead
  In this foul war, that sprang upon the mind
   Like nightmare fiend upon a sleeping man,
    Whose head was pillowed on fair dreaming peace.
    In secret, Evil sharped his horrid claws
     To rend in tatters ancient free men's laws,
    To shackle for all time with no release
    Nations who marched in freedom's gallant van.
   You were on guard, you and your noble kind
  To take the blows on your symbolic head:
We owe to you a song-wreathed pedestal . . .

V

Mothers of sons who that same day went down
 May pride sustain you when your hearts are sore,
  Pride that you mothered men who leaping, said
   'The Navy's here' as *Cossack* grappled to
    In line with Drake. Last visions of the brave
    Upon a sinking deck must be your pride
     Wherein your tears, your grief, not they, have died.
    Your sons spring forward from their watery grave
    To hold our ships that they may win straight through
   The darkest night. Immortalized though dead
  In this world you will meet your sons no more:
Think of the thorns upon the Saviour's crown . . .

IX

In a wild moment all was wrenched in twain
 The *Cossack* murdered, with a broken back,
  Your strength destroyed by instantaneous speed,
   That severed elements, re-crashed and rolled
    Like booming thunder over rearing waves.
    You, our Bill Rose, sucked this vortex down,
    Wearing for ever a rosemary crown.
    Are you now laughing in Nerina's caves
    Herding sleek porpoises to Neptune's fold?
   Or did the impact make your warm heart bleed
  Upon the fringes of the seaweed track
To citadels whence you'll not come again . . .

XIII

I must go to the garden's flower-stocked bed
  Where you had planned to dig the scented earth
   That muscles should be gently harnessed in
    To spirits' service, and from soil to draw
     Soul's nutriment with body's nourishment.
     When of all outward clamour I am rid
     In quiet gardens I will softly bid
    The lily fill her cup with scented thought
   To fling abroad your purest dreams of law
  For all mankind, to close the road to sin.
  Winds from the sea repeat, repeat, give birth
To echoes that your gospel may be spread . . .

XV

We your true friends who loved your radiant glow
  Rippling with laughter, reaching out from strength,
   Who loved your hands grappling with urgent work
    Your eager eyes, piercing the distant light
     Your beating heart, firm in its tenderness,
     Your upright will to serve our country's need,
     The bell of your great voice, its power to plead
    With a contagious valiant happiness;
   You were a magnet drawing towards the right
  Those who, alone, life's harder tasks would shirk;
  We had not known to what a bitter length
Our salt tears on salt waves for you would flow . . .

XIX

You stepped through matter, but you have not gone
  Your imprint on too many hearts was set
  For you to vanish like a morning cloud;
   True love in motion cannot thus be checked.
   As the Immortals fought upon the plain
    With power enhanced by spirits freer guise
    Unfurl new wings of love across our skies.
   Like Homer's heroes, fight for us again.
   What happens when a gallant ship is wrecked
  And moving water is her winding-shroud?
  In seeming chaos life does not forget.
You stepped through matter, sweep our spirits on!

CONSTANCE RENSHAW

Although Hitler claimed to have 'sunk' the aircraft carrier HMS Ark Royal on several occasions early in the war, it was not until 13 November 1941 that the German submarine U-81 succeeded in torpedoing her off Gibraltar. She sank the next day.

Ark Royal the Third
(TORPEDOED IN THE MEDITERRANEAN, 3.45 P.M., NOVEMBER 13TH, 1941)

Ark Royal here, Ark Royal there! – The
   rats could not escape!
She hounded them from sea to sea, from
   Iceland to the Cape.
She loosed her thunders on the deep, and
   launched her eager wings,
And turned a hundred braggart foes to
   maimed and sprawling things.

What of Taranto? What of Crete? What
   of the proud Graf Spee?
What of the fleeing Bismarck and her brief,
   inglorious day?
– With her Fulmars and her Swordfish and
   her turret spitting steel,
The great Ark Royal cracked the leash and
   brought the dogs to heel!

Her name was terror to the foe in every sea
   and clime;
They bombed, torpedoed, mined her, shelled
   her, 'sank' her many a time;
But up she bobbed, with jaunty air, to keep
   a merry date
With every skulking raider from the North
   Sea to the Plate.

. . . A dazzling sea beneath her prow, a
   blue sky overhead
– A sneak shot by a coward foe who hurled
   his bolt and fled

– A shuddering crash – a tilted deck – a
   painful limp to shore
– A hiss of steam – a smudge – a blank! . . .
   Ark Royal was no more!

She will not put to sea again; she will not
   home to port
On any day, on any tide, in battle or in
   sport;
But though she flounders fathoms deep, with
   all her thunders dumb
Her ghost will ride the waters for a thousand
   years to come.

Ark Royal One will hail her in the mighty
   voice of Drake,
And from Ark Royal Two, the 'Hail' of
   Jellicoe will break;
And loud across the years between, in
   ringing, clarion notes,
Ark Royal Three will answer them, from
   sixteen hundred throats!

JOAN POMFRET

War Weddings

Words unforgetting, urgent,
White ecstasy, pale fears;
Confetti in the east wind
Like pink and silver tears;
Living, crammed into moments,
That should have asked for years.

Some hostelry dark-curtained
Through the black muted night,
Kisses made keen by danger,
Stars soaring out of sight,
Red wine and radio music,
Then shaking candlelight.

A grey ship slipping seawards,
A bomber's dying drone,
A khaki column marching,
A live heart turned to stone;
A little time together –
A long, long while alone.

Knitting

My love is on patrol tonight,
The Channel Race is tipped with white,
The wind shouts down the starless sky,
The fire burns red – and here am I
Sitting knitting.

His sleeves bear shabby golden bands,
A pair of mitts for frozen hands,
Mine-sweeper stockings, Navy shade,
A helmet and a scarf I made
Sitting knitting.

And as my needles clicked and flew
I'd time to see a dream or two –

(A dark ship pitching through the foam,
The fun we had when he was home!)
Sitting knitting.

Mine-sweeper stockings, scarf of blue
I knit, and know he will be true!
Sometime – to-night – next week – next year
He will roll home and find me here
Sitting knitting.

MOLLY HOLDEN

Seaman, 1941

This was not to be expected.

Waves, wind, and tide brought him again
to Barra. Clinging to driftwood many hours
the night before, he had not recognised
the current far off-shore his own nor
known he drifted home. He gave up, anyway,
some time before the smell of land reached out
or dawn outlined the morning gulls.

                    They found him
on the white sand southward of the ness,
not long enough in the sea to be
disfigured, cheek sideways as in sleep,
old men who had fished with his father
and grandfather and knew him at once,
before they even turned him on his back, by the set
of the dead shoulders, and were shocked.

This was not to be expected.

His mother, with hot eyes, preparing the parlour
for his corpse, would have preferred, she thought
to have been told by telegram rather
than so to know that convoy, ship, and son
had only been a hundred miles north-west
of home when the torpedoes struck.
She could have gone on thinking that
he'd had no chance; but to die offshore,
in Hebridean tides, as if he'd stayed
a fisherman for life and never gone to war
was not to be expected.

1942

INTRODUCTION

During the first months of 1942 the Allies suffered a series of humiliating defeats. The Japanese continued their successful conquest of South East Asia and on 11 January captured Kuala Lumpur, the capital of Malaya. Allied forces withdrew to the British colony of Singapore, an island base at the tip of the Malayan Peninsula. Within two weeks Singapore had surrendered and 60,000 Australian, British and Indian troops became prisoners and over 4,000 civilians were interned. Many prisoners of war captured in South East Asia during the war years were put to work in constructing the notorious Burma Railway, under appalling conditions of cruelty, starvation and privation. On 27 February a hastily organised force of Allied surface ships was almost totally destroyed leaving Java open to a Japanese invasion. In May United States troops were forced to surrender in the Philippines and British troops commanded by General Alexander were driven out of Burma. However, in the Pacific the Japanese suffered defeat at the battles of the Coral Sea and Midway.

Fierce fighting persisted on the Eastern Front. The German Army advanced towards the Caucasus and Stalingrad. In September German troops entered part of Stalingrad but met strong resistance from the Russians. As the defenders prepared for a counter-offensive, hungry and exhausted soldiers on both sides faced a second bitterly cold winter. In 1942 the Soviet Union was the first country to allow women to fight in the Armed Forces.

In North Africa Rommel's army advanced towards the Egyptian border. On 20 June German tanks entered Tobruk and 30,000 Allied troops surrendered. The Allies were then forced further back to El Alamein, an Egyptian town about 60 miles west of Alexandria. Here the British and Commonwealth Eighth Army made a stand during the first four days of July. With Rommel's supply lines stretched and harried, Lieutenant-General Montgomery, now in command of the Eighth Army, had the opportunity to build up a superior force. Between 23 October and 4 November the second Battle of El Alamein was fought and a decisive victory achieved. Rommel was forced to retreat.

On 8 November a combined force of British and American troops landed in French Morocco and Algeria. 'Operation Torch' was commanded by the United States General Eisenhower. His orders were to gain complete control of North Africa.

On 26 January the first American troops to reach British soil landed in Northern Ireland. They became affectionately known as GIs (Galvanised Iron, as in garbage cans – General or Government Issue). Between April and June, in retaliation for RAF area bombing raids over their cities, the Germans selected medieval buildings from Baedeker guides as targets and launched 'Baedeker' air raids on Bath, Canterbury, Exeter, York and Norwich. On 30 May RAF Bomber Command caused massive damage to Cologne in the first of their thousand-bomber raids against major cities. In September, the US 8th Air Force, which was based in Britain, started attacking German cities in daylight using Flying Fortresses and Liberators; the RAF continued its night bombing campaign.

Meanwhile, the Battle of the Atlantic was still in the balance. The U-boat sought to prevent the transport of troops, essential raw materials and food supplies to Britain. Both sides recognised the campaign was vital. U-boat building was given the highest priority; the Allies sought to improve their equipment and anti-submarine warfare tactics, and to increase their merchant ship and escort building programme.

In October, after three years of war, as British casualty figures continued to mount, the male call-up age was lowered to eighteen. In Britain, shortages became more acute. Soap was rationed in February; shortage of paper affected the production of books; glass was scarce; lack of petrol forced private owners to put cars up on blocks in garages; in July sweets and chocolate were rationed. Inevitably there was an extensive black market in a range of goods, but this did not become seriously out of control. However great their hardships, difficulties and restrictions, the people of the United Kingdom, making good use of self-help and their own resources, remained resolute and undefeated.

Sylvia Townsend Warner, nursing Valentine Ackland at their home in Dorset, was conscious of the starving and oppressed millions in Europe. Six days before Christmas 1942 she wrote to a friend: '. . . I am haunted with the companionship of the innumerable people in Europe who also nurse some loved one dependent on them, and have nothing for them, nothing beyond the barest coarsest husks . . .'.

PAMELA KING

'1942 was a very cold and severe winter and the war news seemed very bleak.' (From a letter from the poet.)

Winter, 1942

The dawn we would not, like a somnambulist
Lurches against our anxious hope.
The night draws to its magnetic day
And down the half-obscured road
There is snow.

Over dying Europe the snow is falling
Blurring and obliterating
Despair's last town and suburb
Where only the clock's indifference stands to remember
This second death in the cardboard cemeteries.

The peasant watching the denying whiteness
Flattening his loins against its silken flanks
While his hand is continually straying
Into the white smoke steaming from its soft side
Notices only the feathers falling like kisses across his cheek
And the vertical map of whiteness lies between
His stationary eye and the last red field
Obscuring his ice-blue islands of the north
Ringed round with stars.

PRISCILLA NAPIER

In the notes at the beginning of Plymouth in War *Priscilla Napier wrote:*

> *This could not be printed when it was written, (over the years 1939 to 1945 and soon after) because too much of it is reporting of what was said at the time by real people under great stress . . .*
>
> *During these war years 27 Plymouth-manned warships were lost at sea by enemy action. The civilian population of Plymouth suffered heavy casualties from German air raids; occasional day-light ones in the early days and many night bombings over the whole five years until April 1944. 1,200 people were killed and many thousands had terrible injuries. One third of the total population of Plymouth, that is about seventy thousand out of two hundred thousand, were driven from their homes by the bombing . . .*

The cruiser HMS Exeter *was sunk in the Java Sea battle on 1 March 1942.*

From Plymouth in War

A Plymouth night,
       a strained and silent hour;
Night, and the burnt-out shell of the civic buildings
Gaunt under fitful moon; St Andrew's tower
Hollowed by flame, the roofless empty choir
A-roost with starlings, and the rubble fields
Trodden with hopeful paths, where once were streets;
Late motors creeping by, their headlights shrouded
From the continuing menace of the air.
And people hurrying home,
Drawing the black-out closer, wondering
What the full moonlight yields.

And the moon riding, slowly, cloudily,
Over the sleeping patterns of the town,
Broken or whole; over the sea's quiet breath,
And all that sighing slumber rising up.
And in an office, under a naked bulb,
The heads at work; the hearts that dare not feel
All that they know; the busy hands at work
Wearily sorting lists of life and death.

EXETER now. REPULSE and PRINCE OF WALES
Are sorrows past; and still a thousand names,
A thousand tragedies, the bitter tales
That must be told till midnight and next day,
Of battle, and the sea's unwearied claims . . .

HELEN WADDELL

Helen Waddell's nephew Major George Frederick Waddell Martin, Royal Engineers, fought at Tobruk in 1941; he was killed on 17 March 1942 aged twenty-three and is buried near Tripoli (Lebanon). Helen Waddell commemorated him in her translation from the Latin of Milton's eulogy Epitaphium Damonis *and wrote in her introductory note: 'It is the first movement of grief to cover the face of the dead, and then to cover its own. The countrywoman's apron flung over her head, the Greek pastoral of lament, serve the same instinct: the privacy of grief . . .'*

From Lament for Damon

O nymphs that haunt the old Sicilian stream,
Himera's stream, you that do still remember
Daphnis and Hylas, and the death of Bion
Lamented these long years,
Sing dirge beside these English river towns,
Sing by the Thames, as once in Sicily,
The low lament, the ceaseless bitter weeping
That broke the quiet of the caves,
River and forest ride and fleeting water,
Where Thyrsis went, bewailing his lost Damon,
Walking at dead of night in the silent places
Uncomforted, alone . . .

. . . No tears, no tears for thee, and no more wailing.
I'll weep no more. He hath his dwelling place
In that pure heaven,
He hath the power of the air, himself as pure.
His foot hath spurned the rainbow.
Among the souls of the heroes, the gods everlasting,
He drinks deep draughts of joy . . .

JANET HILLS

To a Friend

Sliding by river roots,
Or reading by the petal-light of the tall double cherry,
I never thought
We could be so unequal in sorrow.
Now, your brother is dead.

What hand from my sorrow to yours?
I stand outside in numb impersonal mourning.
There is nothing to say.

But I make this vow, as a reaching out of my sorrow
To yours, a vow of vigilant grief:
In my utmost weariness never to lean on hate.
Nor be shocked by the blood on my hands into facile repentance,
Which insults the sober dead,
Nor ever to betray my honesty,
Though it fan the conflagration of this hell.

This is all I can offer you,
Whose brother was younger than us, and is killed.

MAUD CHERRILL

Maud Cherrill was headmistress of St Petroc's School in Bude, North Cornwall.

Easter 1942

{Easter Sunday – 5 April 1942}

Our ears are deaf with War: we only mark
The scream of shells, bombs, curses, threatenings.
And yet – above the new-ploughed field, the lark
    Soars up and sings.

Our eyes are blind with War: there only seem
Scars, gaping wounds, lands where man hates and kills.
And yet – in woods still bare and brown, the gleam
    Of daffodils.

Our hearts are cold with fear and numb with pain
For what may even now our loved befall.
And yet – Spring's here and the warm sun again
    Shines over all.

O God, O God, through all the blood and strife,
To broken hearts and tired eyes dull with tears
Grant but to catch one glimpse of a new life
    Beyond these years.

PAMELA HOLMES

Pamela Holmes was first married to Frederick Claude (Peter) Hall who served as a lieutenant in the Rifle Brigade, attached to the 1st Battalion East Surrey Regiment.

Parting in April
(1942)

Now like my tears these April blossoms fall,
Borne on the wind, as fragile as a breath;
These days are not for keeping after all,
And we must make quick compromise with death.

The little death we die on this fair day
Points to that parting of a later spring;
No wonder then the faltering heart can say
Nothing, for fear of this foreshadowing.

Only – remember me, when other loves
And other Aprils crowd this one we knew:
When touched by a green breeze the bright earth moves,
Surprising tears within the heart of you.

ELIZABETH WHITE

The Parting

I remember now, most clearly,
Your hands! Lean, brown nervous hands
Tired with the deep pain of parting;
Strong hands, twisting
Ceaselessly . . . expressing some inexpressible
Emotion.

Your eyes! Your sick, bewildered eyes
And the thin line of your mouth,
More eloquent than sad sonnets
Or ill-held tears, were
Your strong hands and your suffering eyes
And your mouth . . .

And then, your swift, tortured going,
And nothing of tears to numb
The senses with opium. And after,
Only . . . the memory . . . your eyes, and your mouth,
And your hands.

SHEILA SHANNON

Soldier and Girl Sleeping
ON A PAINTING BY WILLIAM SCOTT

It is late, already it is night,
But still they wait, still spin the moments out:
There is time yet and they rest
Side by side on the hard station bench:
For the train will come, will break
These two apart and bear the half away.

Parting in love is not so hard a thing
(Leaving a bright and crystal certitude
Wrapping within the pain a kernel joy)
As parting in love's echo:
For outgoing love bears on its tide
All things away and is more sure
In its finality than Death.

These two are sleeping now:
She sleeps so lightly,
Wavering on the further verge of waking,
While his stillness holds her firm
In the fixed circle of his dream;
She lies within the cavities of his being,
The bright imagination of his heart,
And through his darkened eyes sees not
The falling hand of Time,
Nor through his sleeping ears can hear
The tiger trains prowl in and out.

They sleep.

And parting has no time for them
Nor place to hurt them in.

FRANCES CORNFORD

From a Letter to America
on a Visit to Sussex: Spring 1942

How simply violent things
Happen, is strange.
How strange it was to see
In the soft Cambridge sky our Squadron's wings,
And hear the huge hum in the familiar grey.
And it was odd today
On Ashdown Forest that will never change,
To find a gunner in the gorse, flung down,
Well-camouflaged (and bored and lion-brown).
A little further by those twisted trees
(As if it rose on humped preposterous seas
Out of a Book of Hours) up a bank
Like a large dragon, purposeful though drunk,
Heavily lolloped, swayed and sunk,
A tank.
All this because manoeuvres had begun.
But now, but soon,
At home on any usual afternoon,
High overhead
May come the Erinyes winging.
Or here the boy may lie beside his gun,
His mud-brown tunic gently staining red,
While larks get on with their old job of singing.

PHOEBE HESKETH

Spring in Wartime

Yesterday
Stark Winter crossed the fields with death,
And paralysed the stirring trees
With cruel breath.
And Spring was in an iron tower
Upon the hill when snow came down
With silent power,
In secrecy, to bury all
The mounds of shovelled earth by night;
And cover all the wounds of war
In stainless white.
The waiting moon
Stared down upon the captive land,
Upon the dark and troubled sea
That washed the sand with waves of blood
Till Spring arose from bitterness.
Now each grim wood
Is loud with song, and branched with light,
And men grown fearless in the sun
Forget the night.

CAMILLA DOYLE

This poem was written at the time of the 'Baedecker' raids on Norwich. The first raids were on 27/28 April and 29/30 April 1942; 131 people were killed and almost 700 injured in the two attacks.

A Game of Bowls
(WRITTEN DURING AN AIR RAID)

My body's crouched beneath a 'Table Shelter',
　　But my unhampered mind is far away;
My hands may quiver and my breathing falter
　　But still my memory watches men at play;
They played at bowls – I see the 'woods' still rolling,
　　And hear the gentle clinking when they touch;
I see the friendly smiles that greet good bowling;
　　My shelter shakes, but I shan't mind too much
If only I can keep those bowlers playing
　　Just as they played last month, beside a wall
Of sunlit yellow stone – yes, they are staying;
　　I hear soft chimes, I hear a ring dove call,
And all the pleasure of the men who played
　　Reaches me still and keeps me unafraid.

ANGELA BOLTON

Angela Bolton was a young nursing sister in the Queen Alexandra's Imperial Military Nursing Service at the 65th Combined Military Hospital in Asansol, West Bengal. During the retreat from Burma in May 1942, thousands of casualties suffering from exhaustion, starvation and sun stroke arrived at the hospital.

Bengal Summer

Egrets haunt the memory,
    Large snow-white birds with green stick legs
Whose delicate feather crests
    Rise and fall like Geishas' fans
Cormorants too abound,
    Black as night, advertising their presence
With a powerful odour of fish
    And a carpet of ivory bones.

The frangipani trees
    Swoon in the heat, shedding waxen petals,
Fragrant as the silken saris
    The high-caste women wear.
Sharp against the sky
    A gibbet tree hangs with strange blossom,
The ragged frames of fruit-bats
    Awaiting the coming of night.

BARBARA LEA

Barrage Balloon

In trains there is a lot of time to think.
We stop, and shunt,
And jolt, and move again. I shut my eyes
And estimate
Our future chances on a second front.

In trains there is a lot of time to dream;
And, half awake,
I ponder on the melancholy state
The world is in,
And feel (quite pleasantly) my heart will break.

In trains there is a lot of time to learn.
Barrage balloon,
Your lot it is to shock my dozing soul
With truth: for here,
Close-hauled among the May trees lies the Moon.

MARY E. HARRISON

Mary Harrison was a WAAF topographical model maker in the Allied Central Interpretation Unit (Photographic Intelligence) at RAF Medmenham, Buckinghamshire. She worked with a team making models for the air attacks on the dams, the Ploesti oil fields, Peenemünde and Cologne and on flying-bomb launch sites.

My Hands

Do you know what it is like to have death in your hands
when you haven't a murderer's mind?
Do you know how it feels when you could be the cause
of a child being blind?
How many people have died through me
From the skill in my finger tips?
For I fashion the clay and portray the landscape
As the fliers are briefed for their trips.

Do those young men in blue feel as I do
The destruction
The pain.
Let me cover my eyes as you cover the skies
Let me pray it can't happen again.
Don't show me the pictures you take as you fly,
They're ruins and scape – little more.

Is all this part
Of the madness we choose to call War?
If there is a God up above who listens at all
Does he know why this has to be.
Did he give me my hands just to fashion the plans
That my own land may always be free?

ALEXANDRA ETHELDREDA GRANTHAM

Alexandra Etheldreda Grantham's son Pilot Officer Godfrey Grantham, RAFVR was killed on 21 June 1942.

Crashed

An hour ago or less this piteous tangled heap
Made up of metal bits whose scattered fragments
    show
Black trace of flames attacking it with deadly leap
  An hour ago,

Soared in the blue, triumphant like a star, sheer
    glow
Of silver on great wings spread wide in spirals
    steep
To rise and climb o'er midnight clouds of ice and
    snow,

And he who swept it upwards – slain, never to
    reap
The harvest of his dreams, nor wondrous joys to
    know
Of coming home, nor wake again. He laughed
    at sleep
  An hour ago.

SAGITTARIUS

The Passionate Profiteer to his Love
(AFTER CHRISTOPHER MARLOW)

Come feed with me and be my love,
And pleasures of the table prove,
Where *Prunier* and *The Ivy* yield
Choice dainties of the stream and field.

At *Claridge* thou shalt duckling eat,
Sip vintages both dry and sweet,
And thou shalt squeeze between thy lips
Asparagus with buttered tips.

On caviare my love shall graze,
And plump on salmon mayonnaise,
And browse at *Scott*'s beside thy swain
On lobster Newburg with champagne.

Between hors d'oeuvres and canapés
I'll feast thee on *poularde soufflé*
And every day within thy reach
Pile melon, nectarine and peach.

Come share at the *Savoy* with me
The menu of austerity;
If in these pastures thou wouldst rove
Then feed with me and be my love.

ADRIENNE GALE

Nostalgia

The meadowsweet with bright and creamy flame
Lights up the rain-dulled country as we pass,
And roses crowd the cottage doors and frame
The windows with their heavy rain-wet mass
Of red and white. But we approach at last
The grey-wet suburbs of a Northern town:
Grey steps, grey walls, grey people hurrying past,
Grey children playing, fighting, tumbling down,
Grey once-white paper slimed with wet footmarks,
The stink of smoky air, the stuffy smell
Of restaurants, rationed petrol and car-parks,
The empty war-time shops, the queues – all tell
Of other days. The roses count no more;
Lost times and places knock upon memory's door.

The monochrome of London haunts my days:
Its roofs against the pallid, smoke-crossed skyline
Peering through lamp-posts to a clanking tramline,
Its grey, tumultuous, seething life which strays
Forever from East End to West and stays
With those who love it. Flower barrows shine
At pale street corners, grey-white houses line
The parks, turning their backs on slums' dark maze
Of grey-black brick. Red buses link them up,
Link dawn to dusk – from when the first footfall
Echoes in empty streets, through clamorous day
To taxi-hooting night when lighting-up
Excites the shops and cabs – uniting all:
The sordid, glamorous, dull, tragic and gay.

NAOMI MITCHISON

Naomi Mitchison farmed on the Carradale estate and spent much of her time in the fields. On 21 May 1942 she wrote in her wartime diary: 'In the afternoon sowing out; we managed about three acres, but it is pretty tough; with this heavy fertiliser one can't cast nearly so far, at least I can't, not really much more than nine or ten feet, and it kept on blowing back into one's eyes and stinging . . . Friday 31 July 1942. A lovely day, with a mild breeze. We picked fruit in the morning, put up the rest of the hay in the afternoon . . .'

The Farm Woman: 1942

Why the blue bruises high up on your thigh,
On your right breast and both knees?
Did you get them in the hay in a sweet smother of cries,
Did he tease you and at last please,
With all he had to show?
Oh no, oh no,
Said the farm woman:
But I bruise easy.

Why the scratched hand, was it too sharp a grip,
Buckle or badge or maybe nail,
From one coming quick from camp or ship,
Kissing as hard as hail
That pits deep the soft snow?
Oh no, oh no,
Said the farm woman:
But I bruise easy.

There was nothing, my sorrow, nothing that need be hidden,
But the heavy dung fork slipped in my hand,
I fell against the half-filled cart at the midden;
We were going out to the land.
Nobody had to know.
And so, and so,
Said the farm woman:
For I bruise easy.

The tractor is ill to start, a great heaving and jerking,
The gear lever jars through palm and bone,

But I saw in a film the Russian women working
On the land they had made their own,
And so, and so,
Said the farm woman:
And I bruise easy.

Never tell the men, they will only laugh and say
What use would a woman be!
But I read the war news through, every day;
It means my honour to me,
Making the crops to grow.
And so, and so,
Said the farm woman:
But I bruise easy.

VERA BAX

Vera Bax's son Pilot Officer Richard Filson-Young was killed during air operations over El Alamein.

To Richard
(KILLED IN ACTION, 17TH AUGUST, 1942)

I hide my grief throughout the weary days,
And gather up the threads of life again,
Remembering you ever gave your praise
To those for whom fate's hardest thrust was vain.
Now, when I feel my courage flicker low,
Your spirit comes to breathe it into flame,
Until I lift my head, and smiling go,
Whispering softly your beloved name.
And yet to me it seems but yesterday
You were a child, and full of childish fears;
Then I would run to you and soothe away
The loneliness of night, and dry your tears;
But now you are the comforter, and keep,
From out the shadows, watch, lest I should weep.

JOYCE ROWE

In August 1942 a joint British-Canadian commando force raided the German-occupied French port of Dieppe. It met strong resistance and had to withdraw under heavy fire. Three men were awarded the Victoria Cross but Allied casualties, particularly Canadian, were high.

Dieppe

19 AUGUST, 1942

It started early, the attacking trek
by sea and sky. Early
and quietly, like a well-told lie.

   His hair was very crisp and curly.
I ran my fingers through his hair while he expressed his views
on this and that and my new hat and the length of movie queues.
Nothing dramatic. And now he's – there. And I tune-in to the
   News.

The barge-like boats, packed panting tight,
eat up the narrow strip of water,
and in the sky the grey wings wait
poised on the edge of a well-planned slaughter.

I wait as well and see it right
in my mind's eye.
                    Then suddenly a white
smoky curtain covers the beach where the forsaken promenade
   winds its course,
and men charge up from the sea, hoarse
with excitement, afraid to swallow lest they miss a sound.
Then everywhere
the carefully planned attacks mass in their place
and hundreds, hundreds falling in the race
for shelter from the stuttering guns; falling face-
downwards, just a mile or two of sea between
them and us and all that might have been,
the trampled sand blinding already sightless eyes.

Yet, when all's said and done, who'd have it otherwise?
Not they.

Women wait long enough for paradise
and if it's now – or in a million years –
it makes no odds. Their blood flows, and my tears
If I could shed them.

There's the pips
and news again of men and planes and ships.
But I already know, and feel my lips
grow cold and my heart a hot, hard ball
wedged in my throat. I knew they could not all
come back.

HONOR ARUNDEL

Paris 1942

In every café they make smoke and swear,
Swilling champagne and bad French beer;
They bribe the women with cigarettes,
And keep one hand on their bayonets,
And in every café that suits their will
FOR GERMANS ONLY is hung on the wall.

Along the boulevard, the park, the pub,
The cinema, theatre, the gay night-club,
Wherever the field-grey dares to haunt,
Cabaret, dance-hall and restaurant,
Wherever the jack-boot dares to fall,
FOR GERMANS ONLY is hung on the wall.

For the swastika sign with its white, red and black
Has often led to a stab in the back.
The storm-trooper's badge has been sought in vain,
And the field-grey floats down the sullen Seine.
The Fascists prefer to be safe and lonely,
And they label the city FOR GERMANS ONLY.

But one day the General slopes down the street
And the soldiers follow on wary feet,
And on every lamp-post that is in sight
FOR GERMANS ONLY is painted white.
On every lamp-post exclusive space
Where the swastika'd rats can swing in their place.

The General bellows, the soldiers falter,
And every collar seems tight as a halter,
And whoever they torture, however they rave,
The city will still be a conqueror's grave.
The people of Paris have plainly spoken –
The Fascist neck shall be bent and broken.

MARGERY LEA

Bomb Story (Manchester, 1942)

For a year we lived like troglodytes,
Then a landmine, a near miss,
Blew in the cellar-door.
It flattened my mother's camp-bed.
She rolled under the next one
Murmured, 'How noisy',
And slept peacefully on.

The rectangle of the skeleton doorway
Framed a crimson furnace – the city on fire,
Under the lowering weight of an endless heavy roar
Of the bombers circling – 'theirs', of course;
And over that the booming racket of the ack-ack guns –
'Ours', thank heaven!

Our neighbour descended two floors in her bed
Unhurt; two others were buried.
Another, away for the night,
Rushed home and found it a steaming ruin.
Her mother's Chippendale sideboard –
A few charred fragments – was what
Caused her abandon to helpless tears.

Our windows were all shattered, every one;
The curtains shredded into long vertical strips,
Like the tattered colour of the regiment
After honourable battle.
Our neighbour's garden had a crater that would hold two buses.
He said the rich soil thrown up was most productive,
And round the perimeter he grew excellent lettuces
The next spring of the war.
Meanwhile his wife's lace corselet and her mended red jumper
Hung forty feet up in an elm
Whose leaves were scorched off.

Next morning a Pompeiian pall of dust and smoke
Loomed over all, with hosepipes snaking
Slimily in black mud across the thoroughfares.

One errant spray
Trespassing into our too, too-open windows
Unkindly moistened our National bread and marge,
Our ersatz coffee, and soya-porridge
And straw-pale tea.

But everywhere you could hear the cheerful tinkling
Of broken glass, as housewives swept it up
Into neat heaps on their garden paths;
One bemoaning her Persian carpet's ruin;
Another the grit on her drawing-room settee.
But at seven sharp the milk was on the step,
And at seven-thirty the news boy came cycling,
Zigzagging among the firemen;
Whistling, surprisingly, an air from a Nocturne of Chopin –
The most beautiful sound in the world.

MARGERY LAWRENCE

Wild Flowers in London

('The strange sight, in London's traffic-crowded streets, of wild flowers, self-sown, growing in the heaped rubble of bombed-out houses . . .' *Daily Paper*)

[The poem was written in September 1942.]

I have seen meadow-sweet at Hyde Park Corner
    And red valerian in Berkeley Square
Daisies in Down Street, ferns in Piccadilly
    Decking the ruins of the houses there.
        Over the life that German bombs laid low
        Brave in the wind the gallant wildflowers blow.

To right and left the crowding traffic bustles
    Busy, intent, the people hurry by
And never stop to mark the wonder growing
    Life conq'ring death, Beauty brutality!
        I've seen strange sights. Yet in these flowers small
        I see the sweetest, strangest sight of all.

So may it be, Lord! When this horror passes
    Beauty and kindness will return again
To heal our souls, and hide the wounds of memory
    As these flowers hide the scars of London's pain.
        Rooted in death, they live. So may it be
        That from our death may rise a people – free.

AGNES GROZIER HERBERTSON

The Return to the Cottage

She enters . . . shuts the door . . . confronts the bare
Intolerable loneness of the room;
Her thoughts turn enemy in that chill gloom . . .
He has but left her . . . back to duty . . . where?
To what stern task, what hazard of the air?
Almost she hears the guns roar crack and boom
In the dead stillness voiceless as a tomb
And feels the creeping anguish of despair . . .

Only for one dark instant . . . then breaks free,
Recovers, lights the lamp, is strong once more . . .
She tends the fire: a-kneel on the stone floor
Lays bough on bough from some old sturdy tree . . .
And sees the bonfires blaze along the shore
To welcome Peace and him and such as he.

JO WESTREN

Jo Westren was a nurse attached to Anti-Aircraft Command at Colchester Military Hospital.

Brief Sanctuary

You from the guns
and I from tending
made love at an inn;
deep-dusked
in a narrow room
were freed from war,
from fear of our fear,
made of our smooth limbs
our sweet love
sanctuary
each for the other.

In the empty saloon
drank then cool wine
and sang as you
strummed the piano.
When time moved from us
and we must go,
we drew our glasses close
on the bare table,
their shadows one.
Look, we said,
they will stand here
together
when we have gone,
images of ourselves,
witnesses to our love.
As we left
you smiled at me
lifting the latch,
then the bombs came . . .

Behind the Screens

Meticulously
I dress your wound
knowing you cannot live.
In ten swift rivers
from my finger-tips
compassion runs
into your pale body
that is so hurt
it is no more
than the keeper
of your being.
Behind these screens,
soldier,
we two are steeped
in a peace deeper
than life gives,
you with closed eyes
and I moving quietly
as though you could wake,
all my senses aware
that your other self
is here,
waiting to begin
life without end.

MYFANWY HAYCOCK

'Killed in Action'

[Autumn 1942]

It's strange to think you will not come again
To watch for Springtime in this quiet lane;

A thousand fleeting, perfumed Springs will go
Back into Time, but you will never know;

Each tree will be a harp with green, green strings
Where birds will sing for joy of lovely things;

But you who loved warm birdsong best of all,
You will not heed the rapture of their call;

Nor will you hear grey larks when days grow long,
Splashing the billowed clouds with cool, clear song;

A million leaves will fall and snow lie deep
In silver folds, but you will be asleep;

Yes, sleeping, you who were so young and brave,
In a far land – in some uncharted grave;

And we who wait and mark each sorrowing year
Will hold your youth and courage very dear –

We know you died that we might see again
A host of Springtimes in this quiet lane.

DOROTHY WELLESLEY

During the war years Dorothy Wellesley lived at her home Penns-in-the-Rocks, Withyham, Sussex. Both her husband and son were serving overseas; Lord Gerald Wellesley in Egypt, and their son in the Household Cavalry in the Middle East, Italy and North West Europe. Later she wrote in her autobiography: '. . . during the war no one could see the wood for the trees; there was great noise, the sound of it shook the world; sometimes at night it came close to my bed, shaking the windows of this peaceful hidden house, vibrating tingling along the finger tips, flashing a light through the dark curtains; then gone with a great sound, to circle again round the rent, unhappy world . . .'.

Milk Boy

There are no more tears for the body to weep with.

Early this morning at the break of day,
A boy of sixteen went out for the milking
Up on the white farm alone on the hill,
With a single white candle upheld by his hand,
Carrying his pail through the air so still.

Then came the Nazi, knowing the white farm there,
The hour of milking white heifers of morning.

There lay the red pools, with the milk pools mingling
O there in the sun – in the red sun arising,
The white boy, the white candle, the white heifer
Dying . . .

PHYLLIS REID

Fireworks
(REFLECTIONS AFTER NOVEMBER 5TH, 1942)

Long ago, November
Was lit by fireworks, and I remember
Still, the thrill of spending three long-hoarded shillings
In a little shop that used to sell only stationery.
The week before the fifth – behold
A magic change
Would enfold it. The window was bright
With coloured sticks and gaily paper-flowered Roman candles,
And tight crinkled crackers.
And there was a smell inside –
The sharp perilous smell of gunpowder –
How to decide
The best outlay of three shillings?. . .
We must have rockets, of course, and again
Golden Rain was safer than Catherine Wheels,
(These sometimes refused to turn, wouldn't burn,
If the nail was too close to the ladder-end holding them.)
But always the crackers –
(Backarappers they were called)
Meant the fearful joy of jumping aside, as they sprang
Zig-zag after girl, after boy –
Oh, fireworks were fun!
And the mystery of the dank dark garden, unlit
Till the sudden flare of a squib
Showed the mysterious boxes where
Fairy fires waited – we had to be brave
To save squibs to the very end, they would bend,
Nearly (but seldom quite) burning our fingers.
The dark-light pattern lingers
Making an unforgettable design
On a child's heart – that was November.

Will children ever again love fireworks?
November colours remain,
Red poppies for Armistice Day,
Red ruin of war – but no more
the gay gunpowder toys. A glare

Sinister instead
Tinges the air overhead.
I shall never hear
Even in a peaceful year
The rocket's swift swishing sigh falling
Without recalling those seconds of time
Before the bombs landed – never again
The coloured stars, the Golden Rain
Will mean anything but enemy flares
Lighting our land to death.
The pattering rat-tat-tatting of the crackers
Are sticks of incendiaries,
Their mutter on pavement, in gutter –
And the sparkling Catherine Wheel
becomes a martyrdom of more
Than a saint of yore –
Fireworks are fun
No longer. November's feast is over and done.

BRENDA CHAMBERLAIN

During the early part of the war Brenda Chamberlain lived primitively in a cottage in Snowdonia, high above the village of Rachub, near Llanllechid, Caernarfonshire, Wales. On behalf of the Red Cross she worked as a mountain guide searching for lost aircraft.

Dead Ponies

There is death enough in Europe without these
dead horses on the mountain.
(They are the underlining, the emphasis of death).
It is not wonderful that when they live
their eyes are shadowed under mats of hair.
Despair and famine do not gripe so hard
when the bound earth and sky are kept remote
behind clogged hairs.

The snows engulfed them, pressed their withered
    haunches flat,
filled up their nostrils, burdened the cage of their ribs.

The snow retreated. Their bodies stink to heaven,
potently crying out to raven, hawk, and dog,
Come pick us clean, cleanse our fine bones of blood.

They were never lovely save as foals
before their necks grew long, uncrested;
but the wildness of the mountain was in their
    stepping,
the pride of Spring burnt in their haunches;
they were tawny as the rushes of the marsh.

The prey-birds have had their fill and preen their
    feathers:
soft entrails have gone to make the hawk arrogant.

MARGARET CROSLAND

Margaret Crosland, a civil servant in London, and a man friend walked to their office each day from Victoria station passing Westminster Cathedral 'in a cloud of hopeless romance'.

December 1942

This autumn at least was ours;
with what hopelessness or joy remember
this gusty-with-rain-November
and radiant in the dark December
days the short flutter of hours
like pigeons on a sunny roof;
passing the Cathedral every day
slowly we learnt its guardian austerity;
the gathered shapes of solemn things
darken, yet dare not speak of pain.

In December with you, discovered this world
so peopled with thoughtful beat
of rain on the empty street,
and the rush of invisible feet
suddenly under the trees,
or the fingers careless on window or wall –
nobody came through our hidden monotone gate
and only you walked with me to hear
the rain speak its maudlin autumn tale,
while the last leaves in Vincent Square were ours.

This autumn done, what strange nostalgia
will come with the elusive spring again,
broken to blossom through the long-lain
secrecy of solemn rain . . .
easy with sunshine or shower-tangled,
how soon we may not know this ghost
companion of our starless walks, compassionate
in the long grief that we cannot lose,
for through the smouldering end of another year
we cannot see the comfort or the close.

PAMELA HOLMES

Pamela Holmes' first husband, Lieutenant Peter Hall, The Rifle Brigade, attached to the 1st Battalion The East Surrey Regiment, was killed during the operations in Algeria and Tunisia on 3 December 1942.

Missing, Presumed Killed

There is no cross to mark
The place he lies,
And no man shared his dark Gethsemane,
Or, witnessing that simple sacrifice,
Brought word to me.

There is no grave for him;
The mourning heart
Knows not the destination of its prayer,
Save that he is anonymous, apart,
Sleeping out there.

But though strict earth may keep
Her secret well
She cannot claim his immortality;
Safe from that darkness whence he sometime fell,
He comes to me.

ANNE RIDLER

Anne Ridler joined her husband in the Orkneys until he was suddenly ordered overseas to an unknown destination. It was popularly supposed that the men were routinely given an anaphrodisiac in their tea to quell their cravings.

Remember Him

Remember him when the wind speaks over a still bed
   In restless report; remember
   Him faring afar in danger –
Neutral stars and enemy sea – sped
By the will unwilling, steaming against the heart, against the
     blood,
   Faring for ever, and unimaginably far.

       And this is foolishness, for
        No parting is for ever,
     And all divergence meets in a round world.
        Yet it is now more vivid
        Than hope of ultimate good
      From this evil; while our dearest, filed
        Numbered inoculated comforted
        By a drug to dampen love, are forwarded
      To endure the life-giving sun, or to be killed.

Tropic of Cancer: yet even this we willed, though not fore-
     seeing.
   It is now to remember
   The glory even there
Where boredom, heartache and discomfort are.
Not in the News, where hills are plains and battles plain in
     meaning,
   The risk all past – but a senseless, timeless war.

       O all you lovers, listeners, when
       The strange sea flings him back again
       Into your arms, these histories hear
       Only as a wind that shakes the door
       And makes more grateful the good fire.
       I pray that comes: but now remember

Him in loneliness and danger,
And let the wind fill your ears.
For if imagination shares
His pain, he bears only
A divided burden, and a grief less lonely.

PATRICIA LEDWARD

Patricia Ledward joined the ATS in 1942 and trained as a driver near Gresford, North Wales.

Evening in Camp

Mist and cold descend from the hills of Wales,
Relentless as a flood they cover
Deep valley, wood and town,
They creep into our hut,
We cough and shiver:
The oak leaves fall against the door
And somebody murmurs: 'It feels like snow.'
The work is done, the violence of the day
Goes westward with the sun:
To weary senses all things are
The tone of khaki, hair and eyes and skin,
And girls relaxed on chairs and floor are still
With the stillness of saints;
The light is dim and voices
So slow it seems they dream.

At this hour of quietness we wonder:
Where are we? What are we doing?
Perhaps we are players in a Russian scene,
Crouching around the stove discussing
Love and death and the dusty path of time:
Or it may be that we pause
In one of life's vacant places
Where nothing happens,
Where we wait for evolution wondering
What are we doing?

Somebody pokes the fire; the sparks
Rush up the old tin chimney, the coal
Scatters in blue and crimson light.
We remember the pit lads who we saw
Going for lunch through country lanes
To poor cramped homes,
This jet of flame is like the laughter
On their grimy faces.

Some of us think – our thoughts are soft
Because our life is harsh;
Some of us scan the tender, drifting faces
Of our friends to stanch our fear;
We are all so much the same, it is only the weak
Who believe they are different,
Who give themselves airs;
Peace has elusive qualities we do not understand,
We do not turn our minds in that direction,
Nor do we seek for joys not worth the seeking,
But sometimes features shrivel with a lonely pain,
Calling for help we cannot give.

Rest, rest, do not speak. It is right
That the dying year should fill you with dark grief,
Give yourself up to the coming and going of life
Let the leaves and the snow drift over your heart
If you would rise to the sun like a phoenix.

E.J. SCOVELL

An Elegy

In early winter before the first snow
When the earth shows in garden beds
(for the foam is blown of flower-heads
And the gardener has cut low
Or tied in place the stock and green)
When the world wears an inward mien
Of mourning and of deprivation,
The appearance fits this time and nation.

In early winter before the first snow,
The child whose steps began in June
In the short misty afternoon
Walks in the mournful park below
Branches of trees, and standing stretches
Her arms and sings her wordless catches.
Like light her play and happiness
Flicker on the world's distress.

In this city still unraided
Where the queues stretch round the corners
It befits us to be mourners
Who read of other lands invaded,
Who have heard at night death pass
To northern cities over us.
It befits us who live on
To consider and to mourn.

The quiet days before the snow,
The child's feet on the yellowing grass –
How can I make a rite of these
To mourn the pang I do not know,
Death fastened on the life of man?
Sorrow uses what it can.
Take as my rite this winter tune:
The child's walk in the darkening afternoon.

JILL FURSE

This poem was written in Devon in 1942.

Carol

Beyond this room
Daylight is brief.
Frost with no harm
Burns in white flame
The green holly leaf.
Cold on the wind's arm
Is ermine of snow.

Child with the sad name
Your time is come
Quiet as moss.
You journey now
For our belief
Between the rich womb
And the poor cross.

MAUD CHERRILL

Christmas 1942

Christmas Day this year in the West!
Not the Christmas of carol or story.
No snow on the hills, no frost outlining the hedges,
No gale driving down from the moors or in from the sea,
No keen breeze crisping the pools,
No sunshine sparkling on waves with spray blown radiantly
    backward.
This Christmas is different.
The sea is grey, tranquil and smooth;
Only the broad white foam-edge betrays the Atlantic swell.
The indeterminate sky is grey, tranquil and soft,
Tenderly soft,
So soft one scarcely misses the sunshine.
Peewits in hundreds over the marshy field all day have been
    wheeling and circling;
Voices of children at play come clearly across the valley;
A thrush is singing – a thin little winter tune, it is true –
But the blackbird who follows me up the field,
Flying from tree to tree, has forgotten it's winter
And is trying out songs for the spring –
Full-throated, joyous.

Black-out already in London,
But here in the West daylight still lingers.
I linger too in the fields –
I do not want to go in to the fun and the firelight,
To the rooms that are gay with decorations and glistening holly.
They have finished tea, the Christmas cake is bereft of its red
    paper trimmings;
They are drawing their chairs round the fire,
Smoking and talking,
Laughing and talking,
Endlessly talking,
Gathering up the threads of the year's separation.
It has all happened before, year after year;
It is part of Christmas Day.

But somehow this year Christmas seems to me nearer, more real
  in the fields,
In the grey mysterious twilight.
The blackbird has finished its song,
The peewits have flown inland,
The children are going home and their voices fade in the distance.
There is silence,
Silence hushed but expectant.
I am waiting, I know not why,
Waiting and wondering.
Was it an evening like this in a village in Jewry?. . .

Suddenly over the sea in the West a red streak gashes the sky,
Broadens and deepens,
Blood-red.
Was it for this I was waiting?
Blood-red, sinister, strange – reminding of War.
(But why should we need reminding, we who never forget?)
It holds me gazing and gazing, with dread fascination;
It fills me with anguished foreboding.
Then slowly it narrows again to a streak,
Blood-red.
And now it is gone.
Night falls
And the soft grey stillness enfolds me.

1943

INTRODUCTION

The first months of 1943 brought a slow reversal of fortunes for the Allies in the various theatres of the war. At the end of January, Rommel withdrew from Tripoli into Tunisia. After a further four months of fierce fighting the German-Italian forces capitulated in Tunisia at the beginning of May. The Allies suffered 76,000 casualties during the North African campaign but took more than 200,000 Axis prisoners of war.

On 2 February the beseiged German forces in Stalingrad surrendered and 110,000 German troops were taken prisoner. Months of bitter fighting followed until the end of the year when the German Army was forced into a long and costly retreat. They fought with determination until the Russians eventually reached Berlin two years later.

General Wavell's troops in India were halted in their first attempts to recapture Burma from the Japanese and re-open a supply route to China. General William Slim was appointed to regroup and renew the attack. Brigadier Orde Wingate commanded a group of men known as Chindits (from the Burmese word 'chinthe', the winged stone lions guarding Buddhist temples). These British and Gurkha soldiers were highly trained in long-range penetration guerrilla warfare. On 13 February 1943, 3,000 Chindits set out on their first operation, a 500-mile journey into Burma, through jungle, over mountains and across wide rivers. Their surprise attack from behind the Japanese lines inflicted much damage but by the time they returned to Burma some 800 men had died in the mission.

The 'Final Solution' continued to take its appalling toll as Jews were rounded up and sent to various extermination camps. They arrived in trainloads at Auschwitz-Birkenau death camp from every region in Europe under German rule. Children, the elderly and the sick were then sent to the gas chambers; those who were fit became slave labourers. On 19 April 1943, the remaining 60,000 Jews in the Warsaw ghetto rose against their oppressors believing the Russians would liberate the city within a few days. This was a brave and symbolic gesture. The Russians did not come and the Germans organised a special force to destroy the ghetto and its defenders. Few Polish Jews survived.

On 10 July Allied forces landed in Sicily. There were severe casualties on both sides but on 17 August the Germans withdrew to the mainland. Italy surrendered on 8 September; eight days later the Allies landed at Salerno and after hard fighting established a bridgehead from which they broke out and started the long advance northwards up the Italian mainland.

On 14 January Winston Churchill and the United States President Roosevelt met at Casablanca to discuss the next stage of their war policy. One of the points agreed was that massive bombing raids on Germany should be intensified. A few days later RAF bombers raided Berlin; in retaliation, the Luftwaffe renewed air raids over Britain. Gradually the devastating Allied air raids slowed up the German war machine: production of aviation fuel was so badly hit that the Luftwaffe was brought almost to a standstill.

On the night of 16/17 May, 617 Squadron, an elite unit of the RAF, led by Wing Commander Guy Gibson, dropped a canister-shaped bomb designed by Barnes Wallis on the Mohne, Eder and Sorpe dams in the main industrial area of the Ruhr; only the Mohne and Eder were breached. Eight of the nineteen 'Dam Busters' were lost. Wing Commander Gibson was awarded the Victoria Cross for this mission. On the nights of 24, 27, 29 July and 2 August the RAF bombed the German city of Hamburg. The initial raid, which caused the first ever man-made firestorm, killed over 42,000 civilians. On the night of 17/18 August 596 bombers from RAF Bomber Command launched a precision bombing operation against Peenemunde, the German V-weapons research station on the Baltic coast. They met formidable opposition from the Luftwaffe and lost forty-four aircraft, but the damage resulted in a delay in production of the rocket.

On 22 September 1943 three British midget submarines, each with a four-man crew, succeeded in crippling the German battleship *Tirpitz* in Kaafjord, north Norway. The submarines were towed over 1,000 miles to within striking distance of their target and after negotiating minefields, gun defence hazards and nets they placed explosive charges underneath the battleship. Six survivors were captured and spent the rest of the war as prisoners. Lieutenant Donald Cameron, commanding

Midget Submarine *X.6*, and Lieutenant Godfrey Place, commanding Midget Submarine *X.7*, were awarded the Victoria Cross.

Meanwhile, throughout the year the Battle of the Atlantic continued, turning slowly in favour of the Allies as the German submarine building programme was no longer offsetting losses; new technology including radar, used in the detection of submarines was paying dividends, and by the end of December the U-boat was no longer considered a threat in the Atlantic.

News of Allied successes boosted morale at home, but casualty lists were high, and families were anxious and war-weary. Enlistment meant that the dangerous and vital work in coal mines was being carried out by older men. From December 1943 one in ten of all men between the ages of eighteen and twenty-five were chosen by ballot to serve as coalminers instead of in the armed services. They were known as the Bevin Boys, named after Ernest Bevin, the war-time Minister of Labour. Because of the increasing shortage of man-power, the age of conscription for women was lowered to nineteen and extended to fifty. Mothers with a child of under fourteen were exempt and the great majority of women remained in the home caring for their families. By the end of September 1943 over a million women worked with the Women's Voluntary Service. Nearly 8 million women were in paid employment, almost half a million serving in the Armed Forces and nursing services. They served in the Women's Royal Naval Service (WRNS), known affectionately as the Wrens; the Auxiliary Territorial Service (ATS); the Women's Auxiliary Air Force (WAAF); the First Aid Nursing Yeomanry (FANY), many of whom worked as cypher clerks in the SOE (some seventy-three were trained as Agents); and as nurses in the Queen Alexandra's Royal Naval Nursing Service (QARNNS); the Queen Alexandra's Imperial Nursing Service (QAINS); the Territorial Nursing Service (TANS); and Princess Mary's Royal Air Force Nursing Service (PMRAFNS); and in the NAAFI. Some 2 million women were employed in munitions industries and 400,000 in civil defence. Over 80,000 women were working in the Women's Land Army; 6,000 joined the Timber Corps. It was a physically tough existence for the land girl; one-third of the girls came from towns and cities and were away from home for the first time. They worked long hours in all weathers. They were paid less than £3 per week and had one week's holiday a year, but the majority enjoyed the out-of-doors way of life.

Working for Army Education, Sylvia Read – a young actress from RADA – performed with Doris Hibbert, a distinguished concert pianist, in a series of recitals of music and poetry to troops throughout Britain. In October 1943 they toured the Islands of Orkney, playing to camps and military hospitals. In her *Orkney Diary*, Sylvia Read describes a performance at a hospital in Kirkwall:

They were all so kind and provided us with mirrors and tables and places to wash our hands and all the things that make our life easier. We gave our performance in a long ward which was warmed by two stout stoves at either end. Behind us was a backcloth of scarlet screens. Some of the men looked pale and very ill. Others were bandaged. All were cheerful and they all listened greedily to everything we did. They loved it all and saw jokes everywhere. If only audiences knew how we loved to hear them laughing . . .

We hoped that the laughter made them forget their sufferings for a while. They looked spick and span in their hospital blue, and their white shirts and red ties were a part of the colourful day. The sun came into the ward and shone in competition with the firelight till there was such a feeling of warmth and happiness that even the pale ones looked joyful.

There are some occasions in life when a window is opened to us, a time when suddenly a new meaning is flashed across our consciousness – a sense that questions we didn't know we had asked were being answered in an unknown language. Suddenly I knew why we were there and why the way to Orkney had been opened out for us. This morning and these men were the answer, and yet I couldn't put anything into words . . . !

WRENNE JARMAN

On 3 September 1940, during the Battle of Britain, Flight Lieutenant Richard Hillary was shot down in his Spitfire over the North Sea and suffered appalling burns and injuries. At Queen Victoria Hospital, East Grinstead, Sussex, Hillary received treatment from Archibald McIndoe, who with his cousin Harold Gillies was a pioneer in plastic surgery. Hillary was then sent to the United States on special duties. His book The Last Enemy, *published in 1942, became a classic of the Second World War. He returned to flying at an Operational Training Unit in Berwickshire and died in an air accident on 8 January 1943, aged twenty-three.*

In Memoriam: Richard Hillary, R.A.F.V.R.

Dazed, with the trumpets sounding in his ears,
He felt, reluctantly, Life's staying hand:
Saw fade the splendour of the ardent years,
And waited what, so late, life should command.
Mute mourning shadows mocked him while he slept
Within his broken manhood – as a spark
Glowed, flickered, paled to ash again, and crept
Back from the day into forgetting dark.

But resolution paced beside his pain
And love brought light again to quenched young
        eyes,
And tongues of courage lit and leapt again,
Arching like rainbows over shaken skies.
Sunlight moved on him – and then in him
Memory of flight in windy caverns of air:
The lift of eagle, soar of seraphim,
And fields where only he and planets were.

Steeled and remote, the grafted man arose
And knew he must inhabit once again
The lucent realm that had been his, espouse
Anew the bride who had desired his pain.
This time, the high exacting gods approved
His gift made perfect in the passioned clay,
And took the clean oblation, which they loved . . .
And Life was dumb, and turned her head away.

He had known evil; seen the vampire Thing,
Waxed swollen on the treason in man's heart,
Stronger than man, than nation, battening, –
But from the mortal clinch he was apart:
He has no politics who only draws
A shining pattern on the startled night
In careless glory, like a meteor's
Ardent signature in lovely light.

Harold Gillies was born in Dunedin, New Zealand, in 1882. He became a plastic surgeon at Queen's Hospital for Facial Injuries in Sidcup, Kent, and was later a consultant plastic surgeon to the Admiralty .

Plastic Airman

(FOR SIR HAROLD GILLIES)

His face is smooth as sculptured faces are,
His features fair enough to draw a girl's
Arch backward glance, his disciplined blond curls
Swept from a grafted brow without a scar.

But this young mottled face does not betray,
As other faces do, the moods behind –
If he has secrets, they are locked away:
He looks out at the world from a drawn blind
Screening the man he was. And who was he?
Only the grave eyes know, and do not tell . . .

Be gentle with him, World, who has foregone
His unique pattern, his identity:
Be tender, lest the frozen mask should melt
Abruptly, and surprise us with its scorn.

LISBETH DAVID

Lisbeth David was a wireless operator ('Sparks' or 'Sparker' in naval slang) in the WRNS, stationed at Holyhead. HMS Torch, *the naval base, was a large, isolated house close to the shore. Aircraft from RAF Valley occasionally went down in the sea and motor launches were sent to find survivors. The author wrote 'it was the only time we worked in Plain Language and knew what was happening, which made it all very immediate'. Before going off watch in the morning the duty wireless operator had to scrub the floor of the small wireless room.*

Air Sea Rescue

{11 January 1943}

Twenty-three hundred – and Skerries light is steady
Coming through the rain and the night:
MLs* are in harbour lined and silent lying ready
And Sparks is dozing in the light.

Telephone . . . Duty Officer? . . . Telephone: Warning
Plane believed down in sea.
Broadcast. IMMEDIATE. Operator yawning
Switches on and reaches for the key.

'All British ships in area quoted
Keep a good lookout for plane . . .
All British ships . . . position to be noted . . .
Sending message through again . . .'

Enter Commander, magnificent and swearing,
Gentleman, vague to the hair,
Clutching the warm British sack* he's wearing
Over crimson Gent's Night Wear.

'Send this to SOUTHERN SPRAY – IMMEDIATE. No,
    cancel,
Send what I gave you before.'

---

* Motor Launches, used as part of the coastal forces for patrols and for air-sea rescue.
* 'Since I had never seen a duffel coat before, I described it as it seemed to me, a cross between a sack and a British Warm.'

The Duty Officer, distractedly wielding her pencil
Scribbles and smiles to the floor.

'Message coming in, Sir. Object sighted,
Believed rubber dinghy.' 'Go ahead –
Phone through to Valley and get some flares lighted –'
'One picked up, believed dead.'

Feet on the stairs, to the SDO and back again . . .
Telephone . . . 'Anything new?'
Drifting Commander in his warm British sack again . . .
Messages . . . the long watch through.

O Five Double O – and Skerries light is steady
Coming through the rain once more.
MLs are in harbour lined and silent lying ready
And Sparks is scrubbing the floor.

DAPHNE NIXON

During the First World War men of the Royal Naval Division trained at Blandford Camp. Among the young sub-lieutenants who marched from the camp at the end of February 1915 to sail for Gallipoli were the poet Rupert Brooke, who died two months later, and Bernard Freyberg, who became a distinguished general during the Second World War. By 1943 the camp had become a transit and battle-training camp for large numbers of units. Daphne Nixon served in the ATS.

Blandford Camp 1943

Once in the other war to end all wars,
There marched out of the camp upon the hill
More than a thousand men, to fight their way
On to the shores of blood-red Gallipoli,
More than a thousand men . . . and two came back.

Again the bugle call upon the hill,
And sentries stand to watch the men march by
A monument, that rises white and still
Out of the sun against the winter sky,
A stone built by two men in memory.

And never a Flander's day shall pass but they
Will lay the wreaths of their remembrance
Against that place, where former ideals lie,
And flames burnt out, what are their thoughts when they
Must watch another sacrament go by.

BRENDA CHAMBERLAIN

Early in the 1930s Brenda Chamberlain met Karl von Laer, a young German. Their long years of correspondence were broken by the war when he fought on the Russian Front. During the war she re-read his old letters and started to weave them into her poem The Green Heart.

From The Green Heart

Part II
IX

Someday,
In near or distant time,
You shall in your land,
I in mine, lie dumb,
Dead, dug-under,
Mixed with clay.

O dear Lord!
Grant that my poems
May grow as trees
Over our graves;
That they may give cool shade
To men of both our nations,
For so long bitter enemies.

Part III
IV

Greenland heart, magic lamp,
Comfort me; take the taste
Of nightmare from my tongue.
Lift the weight from eyelids
Sealed in long German nights.

O the coldness of a rifle
At dawn in Siberia
A thousand miles from home.
Battalions of soldiers,
Armies of snowflakes;

Nowhere a path, only wounds
Rain has inflicted on the earth
Of the desolate plains
Where no tree or hovel stands.

It is always twilight
Or midnight: expectant
Or seared with gunfire.

I have a horse that can run
Like an elk in snow. Tomorrow
There will be a battle.

Having drunk wine
And visited past time
With its bivouacks,
Sorties, ambushes,
And dawn attacks,
I think I could
Write a poem about you.

V

We being darkened
More than moon sevenfold
Crave hearth's cheer or the sun to free
The breath of pine for these hours spent
Together: grace-time
By God lent

Lie close to me
And comforted be
By touch of hands. Let my fingers heal
Your wounds of war.

MARY DOREEN SPENDER

The poet Richard Spender served as a captain in the 2nd Battalion Parachute Regiment, AAC. He was killed during the night of 28/29 March 1943 while leading his men against German machine-gun positions at Sedjenana, Tunisia.

For Richard Spender

Gone in an instant
Like a light, when fingers touch the switch,
In the last second of his consciousness,
Leading his men in Tunis.
Gone, like the light.
And yet, not like the light. He suffered and he sang.
And in his growth he rooted in our hearts,
Until he seems the fabric of our lives.
So in the Spring we stand, our eyes still gazing,
For all the thousand tints of green and myriad flowers
Seem just for him – not wreaths spread on a grave,
But little brother buds that blow and glow beside him.
Our ears, too, listen to the song of birds,
Which fall felicitous from green hedge and tree,
Voices as sweet and piercing as his own.

That grey-haired age should weep with mordant sorrow
For lovely golden youth in glorious Spring,
– A sad reversal of accustomed ways!
And yet – who knows?
A comet on the low horizon
Shines in the dark before the break of day.
A mystery to us, what path it follows hidden,
And what, beyond our sight, its secret orbit shows.

TERESA HOOLEY

The Singing Heart
(IN MEMORIAM, RICHARD SPENDER)

His poem was a blossoming thorn,
Pricking like a Christ-crown upon the brow –
White flowers of beauty, alight upon a wounding black
   stem,
Intolerable,
Not to be endured.

To the April fields I fled for hope and solace.

There were lambs under the hedgerow,
Sheltering from the soft warm quickening rain,
(Be happy, you little lambs, did he not love you?)
There was a nightingale in the green coppice,
(Sing, you nightingale, true and clear and sweet as the
   songs he made!)
There were buds of cowslip and clover,
(Clover-stem and cowslip he forbore to remember,
Out of his love and yearning, on the cross of his exile)

Yet the fields brought comfort –
They were full of singing,
The singing of his heart:
One with blossom and bird and little lamb,
Born of an English spring, for whose sake he died.

PATRICIA LEDWARD

The poet Bertram Warr, a sergeant navigator (bomber), RAFVR, serving with 158 Squadron, was shot down in a night bombing raid over Germany on 3 April 1943.

The Dead
(FOR BERTRAM WARR)

Back from a raid on Germany you said:
'You're wrong to let the physical death
Fill you with such dread;
Believe me when I say
Only the tragedy is large, each death is small.
In a bomber one is not alone,
Courage is met with quietness and all
The members of the crew are strong,
And all for one another,
And that is how the end would come.'

So many go it wasn't strange to hear
You'd not returned when Essen blazed
That April night last year.
Although I wished a man with Owen's feeling
And the satire of Sassoon could write
Your epitaph – how you hated war,
How kind you were with the overwrought,
The refugee, the maimed, the old,
Could tell the irony and pity in your eyes
When German boys bombed London.

You had a bitterness I never understood,
Did not believe in 'afterwards,'
When people planned in happy mood
You keep your silence although once you said:
'The dead have all the luck, you see.'

PAMELA HOLMES

Four months after Pamela Holmes' first husband Lieutenant Peter Hall was killed their daughter Jacqueline Peta was born.

War Baby

He has not even seen you, he
Who gave you your mortality;
And you, so small, how can you guess
His courage or his loveliness?

Yet in my quiet mind I pray
He passed you on the darkling way –
His death, your birth, so much the same –
And holding you, breathed once your name.

Valentine Ackland

From 'War in Progress'

*This running commentary on the present war was started in Spring, 1940 and
continued until Spring, 1943 when, for reasons given, it ended.*

April 1943

Stalingrad did not fall. This poem perhaps
Would have finished if that had ended, but Oh, instead
It began, by its lasting, an agony in the head,
A sickness, some said, of the brain, a teasing impulse to lapse
Into the commonplace, into the worst kind of war, the Offense.

Some said that, but this diary of war
Cannot continue because the war has begun,
Now there is nothing to say not said before
Each time that outnumbered Man fought back with pen and gun:
No broadcast to listeners now – there's no one left on the fence.

BEATRICE MAYOR

The Young Actress and Munitions

Bear with me, I am bewildered,
I am aghast this evening
At what my life holds for me,
And at the world.

To-morrow I bind bombers' pipes with a blue liquid paste.
For ten hours I shall bind them.
On Tuesday I bind bombers' pipes with a blue liquid paste.
For ten hours I shall bind them.
On Wednesday . . .
On Thursday . . .
I know, I know, there is a war.
Yet bear with me.
I have known a joy, an agony, an intensity, a need . . .
I am an actress.

Have you ever waited breathless for the heavy curtain to ride up?
Have you listened for the last soft murmur as it steadies itself
And there is stillness?
Have you then strolled on,
Passed through a door,
Or risen from a chair,
And found yourself . . . not you, but Elizabeth Jones,
Or Rosa Smith,
The Queen,
The Parlourmaid,
Weeping old woman from the crowd?
With voice, limbs, gesture, thought and heart,
Have you lived that other being,
And loved her,
For so only shall you have given her life?
Have you listened to your own cry – another's –
And felt the air throb
With the quick sympathy of a thousand hearts?
And have you uttered quiet words,
O so quietly,
With a sly gesture,
And heard the great sea roar,

And half seen, through the black mist, enjoyment, a tide,
Sweep over the grey tired faces?
And have you failed too,
Felt the air thicken with the wide straying thoughts
Of that huge sedentary mass?
And that night wept,
And cursed your so brazen conceit:
And later – after what travail! –
Found that so, so, you may fix minds,
And wake in them the sympathy you yourself feel.
O, and have you met your friends – your lover perhaps – in cafés
    or at street corners,
Or in minute enchanting flats?
Have you slipped through hours in an easy intoxication?
Knowing: to-night we shall hear the heavy curtain stir.
Joy! Agony! We shall step into those other beings, live other lives,
Our one aim to delight, thrill, or touch with a live breathless
    sympathy . . .

To-morrow I shall bind bombers' pipes with a blue liquid paste,
For ten hours I shall bind them.
On Tuesday I shall bind bombers' pipes.
On Wednesday, Thursday . . . That so more men shall die,
Houses and huge ships will be hurled through the air:
Homes, all in them, explode – splutter, be as a spent match.

I am bewildered.
There is a war, I know,
And I am aghast.

FRANCES MAYO

Lament

We knelt on the rocks by the dark green pools
The sailor boy and I,
And we dabbled our hands in the weed-veined water
Under a primrose sky.
And we laughed together to hide the sorrow
Of words we left unsaid;
Then he went back to his dirty minesweeper
And I to a lonely bed.
O the anguish of tears unshed.

And never again on this earth shall we meet,
The sailor boy and I,
And never again shall I see his face
Framed in a primrose sky,
For the sea has taken his laughter and loving
And buried him dark and deep
And another lad sleeps on the dirty minesweeper
A sleep that I cannot sleep.
O that I could forget and weep.

ADA JACKSON

From 'Behold the Jew'

Dedicated For Walter and Anni Landau

I

. . . Jew, I say – and in my heart
it rhymes with all the hunted things
that cower in brakes or die in reeds
of shattered breasts and broken wings,
so that upon the selfsame breath
I pray for Jews and driven birds
and badgers baited to their deaths,
and bulls that, with nor wit nor words,
must bleed for strutting matadors –
beseeching God for such as press
all night against the trap's steel teeth,
for others slain for wantonness,
for foxes and for hounded deer
and all the creatures man pursues,
the blinded and the lamed, the scourged
and prison-fast – but most for Jews.

But most for Jews – for lo, the fox
has yet his lair, the bird her nest;
the hare can leap and love and play,
the coney is not dispossessed;
the hart hath sanctuary and shade;
only among them all the Jew
must run and run without surcease
by day and night the long year thro',
the baying ever in his ears,
the dogs forever at his throat,
and hard upon his heaving flanks
the Huntsman, thirsty as a stoat.

No pause, no refuge for the Jew;
no truce, no hope beneath the sky;
only the shambling flight that wins
nor space to breathe, nor room to die;
only a wilderness of grief
where come no rains, nor healing dues –

Wherefore of all earth's harried hosts
I beg God hardest for the Jews . . .

IV

But Jew, I say – and lo, the word
lifts haggard eyes and looks at me,
great hollow eyes where sorrow drowns,
dark crystals in whose depths I see
the age-old shapes, the cursèd shapes
of gaberdine and ghetto wall;
of rack and stake and gallows tree;
of whips and knives; and, with them, all
a newer hate can frame and bring –
the water cure, the firing squad,
the slaughter camps; the piteous vans
where souls must choke their way to God.

Jew, I say. The very word
falls slow and heavy as a tear,
as all the woe in all the world
were heaped and pressed and fashioned here
into a space three letters long.

Jew – It has the sound of breath
blown from a million whitened mouths
of men tormented unto death;
the shape and seeming of the grown
that splits the bursting heart in two;
the muted wail of winds that thread
the bared skull's sockets thro' and thro' –

V

Behold the Jew – from ancient time
a wanderer, an Ishmael;
scapegoat and man acquaint with grief –
these be thy names, O Israel.
The Chosen People, set apart;
chosen of God to breathe and dwell
forever in His Shadow – this
hath been thy portion, Israel.

But now and in this hour is come
a colder death, a sharper cup,

a heavier curse than any one
thy patient shoulders lifted up.

A Voice hath said, 'The Jew shall die!
In his own blood his name shall be
wiped from the earth for ever more.
The Jew shall perish utterly'. . .

HEBE JERROLD

Hebe Jerrold served in the Timber Corps of the Women's Land Army.

War, which has brought to others fear

War, which has brought to others fear,
Pain, sorrow, slavery and death;
To me has brought what I held dear
And longed for but could not possess.
Has given me wide stretch of sky,
The sailing clouds, the wind's sharp breath,
A roof of leaves, the wild flower's eye,
Bird song, all woodland loveliness,
Health, vigour, deep content, and faith
That at its source our stream runs clear.
What have I done? I never meant
To be a war-time profiteer!

PAMELA HOLMES

The poem was written in memory of Flying Officer William Torrens Hinds, Royal Air Force Volunteer Reserve, who was killed on 7 September 1943.

Once

Do you remember how,
Once, when we were children,
We lay under the apple trees
All anyhow, and all the day,
Flung down in the long grass
Below the swinging hammock?

Do you remember how we used to say
'How far do you think the sky is?
How deep down go the daisies?'
And how we laughed and rolled
Beneath the sun, at such absurdities?

Now, oh my childhood love,
Now you have gone:
It's a strange tryst I keep.
You know
Just how far the sky,
How deep the daisies go.

And only I,
Here, where the hammock used to swing,
Keep wondering.

SHEILA SHANNON

On Pentire Head
SEPTEMBER 1943
FOR *P.D.*

I
Only the earth bears scars
that will not wear away
    for generations;
the stones of Carthage
mark Aeneas' stay,
    Dido's betrayal.

Dungeons and prisons stand
whose walls still bar
    innocent prisoners
from day's long beauty
and night's darker star,
    Diana's splendour.

The carrion flesh and bone
of ordinary men
    ruined in battle
(whose dying semen
golden pastures sicken)
    poison the fountain.

II
Westward from Pentire Head
the wide Atlantics reach
    to the Americas;
the waters finger
rock and shell-moled beach
    like tender lover.

No one could guess for sure
what ships and roving sailors
    lie on the sea-bed,
where darkness filches
all tone from colour,
    echo from whisper.

In the abyssal seas'
monotonous cold,
   spin the sea-spiders;
among the sea ferns
stilted crabs behold
   man's dissolution.

Under the sloping sun
the waters tenderly spread
   innocent surfaces,
at heart rejoicing
rich in earth's dead
   no more returning.

III

Only the sky casts out
the tragic defeated
   from its element;
bears only the living
young and exalted
   victor and joyous.

There, men like dying stars
burn to extinction
   in night's dark cavern,
like meteors falling
in expectation
   of death's delivery:

No scar reveals their fall,
no wound, no weeping
   mars the serenity
of heaven, innocent,
as child who, sleeping,
   sleeps undreaming.

Olguita Queeny Berington

Where is Everybody?

Isn't it odd
How the price of cod
Has risen
Since June forty-two?

The sole and the turbot
And dear Uncle Herbert
Have vanished
Like most of 'Who's Who'.

Their social birthright
Has been lost overnight;
Now the cod and the mob
Are 'in lieu'.

No relation of 'Bertie's'
Would wait, (in the 'thirties)
With the mob – for some cod –
Now they do!

Lieutenant Charles Graham Tanner, RNVR was awarded the George Medal for his part in an underwater mine disposal operation in the River Thames, off Margaret Ness, Woolwich. This took five weeks, between 6 October and 9 November 1942. He was killed on 27 September 1943 defusing a mine and was buried near his family home in Tilford Church Cemetery, Surrey.

Someone I Know

(In Memory of C.G. Tanner, G.M., R.N.V.R.)

She couldn't bear red roses,
And looked the other way;
Some said she was eccentric,
Some hadn't time to say.

And when she passed a florist shop
Where roses pierced the glass,
She jerked the collar of her coat
And quickly hurried past.

Few saw her as her gallant son
Was lowered in the land,
But when they tucked the earth around,
A red rose left her hand.

MARGERY SMITH

Margery Smith wrote this poem in the autumn of 1943: 'encouraged by a beautifully clear rainbow and the announcement of the Allied landings in Italy given at a Drumhead Service while on a course at the S.M.E. (School of Military Engineering) at Ripon.'

Poets in Uniform

Morning creeps towards the Nissen Huts.

Daily the ruin of the breakfast table
Straggles across our vision.
Winds of song
Weave their magic
Among the clattering of plates
And idle chattering.

Only the ice and fire of thought
By music rarefied
Can bring us to the brink of song.

Daily we march to work,
Casting our shadows
Into the puddles,
Casting the shadows of our thoughts
Along the avenues of dream.
Will they find a pathway rich with leaves?

Have we learnt
To value each day
As the first that we shall live?
To welcome suffering
As necessity for song?
To open all our doors
On every wind of feeling?
And begun
To render up the beauty we have found?

We look constantly
Out of the window;
Smoke from the Disinfestor Station
Muffles the sky.

Our ink and books
Lie on our desks,
But walls and weeds
Measure their strength
Against the light.

A mist obscures
Where our own rivers flood
Into the universal sea of thought.
The tide returning brings
Treasures among the flotsam.
What is beyond?

Noon hovers above the Nissen Huts.

A coming storm
Ruffles the silences,
Rustles the poplar leaves,
Unbends the ivy round the window sill.
All moving things become
Part of the sky,
And birds fold in their wings.

Can ice and fire
Give back their song?

Mists of fern
Fall on the shadows of grass.
Hand and shadow travel over the page
Weaving their patterns
Of music and echo.
Shadows of song
Curve over each other
In the sky.

Where does the singing lead?

Lapwings pierce the day with song
Sharply, as the bare boughs
Strike the air.
The last high-waving leaves
Remind us Autumn has not gone,
Spring is to come.

Evening crawls towards the Nissen Huts.

MARY WINTER WERE

To Saint Francis of Assisi
OCTOBER 4TH, 1943

You walked the fields of Italy
Your naked feet with peace were shod;
You carried wild flowers in your hands
And in your heart you carried God.

Your bed was tangled leaves and grass,
At times a thorn would pierce your side;
And with you for companion
Walked Poverty, your Lady-Bride.

Through the wide golden Umbrian plains
You sought the Timeless and the still,
And in your timeless, mystic world
You found and loved the Perfect Will . . .

Come back great Saint to Italy,
Your land to-day in ashes lies;
Not ashes of humility
That claimed you 'neath Assisian skies.

Ashes of lust and greed and hate
A traitor-hand to-day has flung
About your paths, and where you sang
Your canticles a dirge is sung.

Come back O Little Saint of Love
With Holy Michael wield the sword
Of God, till Satan be cast down
To hell; till reigns the Living Word –

Come, Francis of the burning heart
The burning feet, the burning hand;
Burn clean through sacrificial fires
Your own incomparable land.

Editor's note. Francis of Assisi was born in 1181. In his mid-twenties he renounced war and his inheritance, founded the Franciscan Order and became a roving preacher. His vocation was dedicated to God, the sufferings of Christ and to his love of all Creation. Francis died in 1226 and was canonised two years later; his feast day is 4 October.

SYLVIA READ

During Sylvia Read's two-week tour of the Orkneys in October 1943 an old friend, Richard Bishop, Director of the Council for the Encouragement of Music and the Arts, arrived to give lectures on the theatre.

Second Meeting

Meeting in summer was the warm green
And curtain of gold tissue, the long evening
Slipping to rest as arm slides into water,
The road winding easily as hand or fingers
Playing upon the surface of the water.

Meeting you then, and words between us limpid,
Slow rings on the lake of conversation;
Our easy sentences that ran with smiles
Lights on the hills, fast as the light of eyes
And over bridges between the strangers' smiles.

And now this meeting here, the flat security
Of handshake in a crowd; the monotone
Of talk that should be weaving gold in trees
Now flat against the background of the guns;
Guns are more physical, more intent than trees.

And meeting here noise gongs the evening air;
As spent bullets fugitive our time:
Now hand in hand we make our conversation,
The talk is guns, their tongues more rare than mine,
I meet them here; theirs is the conversation.

JOAN MARY AND J. MITFORD VARCOE

Neighbours

In days of yore before the war,
  With all its devastation,
Smith used to live, like many more,
  In glorious isolation.
The garden wall was his defence and being non-
  gregarious,
Relations with his neighbours were decidedly
  precarious.
The Whites were 'not the sort of folk with whom
  the Smiths could mingle'
And 'Mrs White was far too old to wear her hair
  in shingle.'
Besides she went 'out shopping'
  Whilst the Smiths, they used the 'phone
And disturbances were 'shocking'
  When the 'White kids' were at home!

And though the Ricks at Number Six
  Had friendly aspiration,
Smith circumvented all their tricks
  Of peaceful penetration!
Whilst as for Jones of 'Briar Lodge,' who borrowed
  Garden rollers –
The very thought of such a man made Smithy grind
  his molars!
The Robinsons were socially acceptable, but foolish
To send their boys to high school when their Dad
  was Public Schoolish!
Besides, they carried banners
  And went marching with the Scouts
Whilst they sadly lacked in manners . . .
  And in fact were little louts.

Then (what a bore!) there came the war
  And with it dislocation
Of Auction Bridge and Social Score –
  Just cause for irritation!

Smith felt that he *must* do his bit, but being hard
   to please,
Debated if to firewatch or take evacuees
Or desecrate the garden lawn – his pride and his˜
   ambition –
In order that the family might wallow in nutrition.
At last in desperation –
   Yes, a Warden he became,
A gesture to the Nation . . .
   Inscribed on roll of fame!

He came to mix with Jones and Ricks
   (Albeit by compulsion)
And prejudices came to nix,
   Without undue repulsion,
He'd drink a pint and throw a dart, and although not
   a Newman,
Would play a game of Snooker – and in fact was
   almost human!
No more black looks for Mrs Jones
   Inferring 'Keep your mug out!'
But smilingly the ladies meet and share the same
   old dug-out.
It's 'Mary dear' . . . and 'Elinore'
   And 'Jane and Meg and Heather.'
A pity that it takes a war
   To bring us all together!

RUTH TOMALIN

Hunting Song

We from whom otters swam wild-eyed,
who drove the backward-glancing hare,
who dug the spent fox from his lair
and watched, complacent, as he died –
now it's our turn to crouch and hide.

The guns, a clamorous pack, give tongue;
the keen bomb whimpers on our trail:
the little tattered hare was flung
to pacify that hungry wail.
Are we as innocent, as frail?

To-night they sleep beyond the storm,
careless of thunder and strange stars –
in willow holt, in earth and form,
lap't round with peace, while under Mars
we expiate their crying scars.

JOYCE ROWE

Point of View

War has a terrifying, nullifying slant
    on women.
Men are part and parcel of it. They, the fighters,
    they the plant
machinery, politicians, journalists,
all have their day and say in it, all have their fists
in every martial pie.
But women – you, my sisters, you and I,
we do our share, it's true, our mansize job
day in, day out, and gladly. But the stifled sob
at nights, the ache that absence brings
in small familiar things,
these prove that muted strings perform our symphony –
not the loud brasses of a man-made band.
We have our music too, but please to understand
our chords are quieter now, though every omened
    orange envelope
turns them staccato. Hope,
fortitude and an inborn, still despair,
these mould our busy days and form our share
in war.

E.J. SCOVELL

A War-time Story

Florence, her husband two years overseas,
In summer knew herself pregnant by another,
Her passing lover, an airman, and at Christmas
Alone one morning before light gave birth.
This is the story she told the police:
'It was born alive. I wrapped it in a blanket.
I laid it under the bed. At half past nine
I went down and made breakfast for the children.
When I came up it was dead. I left it
For two days in the blanket out of sight,
Then late at night made up the fire and poured
Paraffin on and burnt it.'

                Agent of fate:
Large head and feeble neck and fakir limbs;
Blind eyes once opened on blood and closed in night,
And faint life, mere sentience of pain, soon ended:
Still you played your part, accuser, evidence
To be destroyed; and when all was uncovered
Lived on as trouble and sorrow to the living.

Did she act in pain? Did she love the baby at all
Alive or dead? Did she draw the incurable lightning-
Pang of pity? Did she remember the spring
And think of the father? Or was there only fear,
Anxiety and her body's sick exhaustion?
We have not seen her face.

                But we can imagine
The baby's face, haggard with birth; the head
Cast in the womb and flattened in the cervix;
And the shadow of the womb lingering, the shadow
Of sleep, the haunting of non-existence still
On the flower of the body, perfect in every part.
Beauty, life, infinite infolding; soul
Nameless, sex unrecorded, agent of fate
Like a stone dropped in the pool of grosser lives

That leaves its stir and itself sinks out of sight,
Deep, one-way, plumb-straight, heavy from hand of God:
In your whirlpool you draw our hearts down after,
But we do not find you.

Sarah Churchill

1943

The roll of glory reaps another name,
The mounting toll of grief goes on,
How gay and crowded is the house of fame,
How still the house from which you've gone.

It's all been said and felt before
But repetition does not ease the pain;
The battered heart that thought it felt no more
Learns it can break as bitterly again.

Christmas 1943

There was a clink of glass
Friends grown thoughtful in the mellow gloom
Thought awhile on the years ahead
As the firelight leapt through the dim-lit room
And prayed that when those years were dead
And we'd reached the years that would come after
That revenge and hatred,
As our tears, would pass
And some of us would be left for laughter
After – after

Chequers

VERA BAX

Christmas 1943

Now Christmas comes again, to find my heart
Still as the frozen landscape: cold and still.
Like an automatum I play my part,
To noisy merriment must bend my will;
Yet how can I be glad, remembering,
Though all my tears so long ago were shed?
I would, in solitude, let fancy wing
Back through the past to that poor manger-bed,
Where gladness shone in such a night as this,
And holy peace descended for a while;
No laughter, loud and mirthless, marred its bliss,
No grief was there to hide behind a smile;
Only an innocence, a hope, a gleam:
A star that beckoned, and a woman's dream.

1944

INTRODUCTION

On 6 January 1944 the Red Army crossed the 1939 Polish–Soviet border. This was followed by a new offensive in the Leningrad region to relieve the city of the German grip. By the end of January the Soviets were liberating Polish towns almost daily in their relentless westward progress towards Berlin.

In the Italian campaign between January and May 1944 four bitter battles were fought around Cassino, some 75 miles south-east of Rome. A hill crowned with a sixth-century Benedictine monastery dominated the town and its successful defence prevented the Allies from reaching Rome. The first battle, fought between 17 January and 11 February in appalling winter conditions, ended in deadlock. The second battle started three days later. After dropping leaflets warning of the impending attack, the Allies bombed the medieval monastery. The Germans evacuated most of the monks and the priceless art treasures but 250 civilian refugees were killed and the monastery was reduced to ruins. The huge craters, piles of masonry and deep cellars provided the Germans with a virtually impregnable fortress against General Freyberg's New Zealand Corps, which included British, Maori, Indian and Gurkha troops, and their assault failed. Meanwhile, in an effort to hasten the fall of Rome, a second seaborne landing on the west coast of Italy at Anzio was achieved with total tactical surprise. The Germans reacted with great vigour and occupied positions overlooking the landing areas before the Allied forces, under the American General Lucas, had struck inland. After heavy fighting the Allies were eventually able to link up their forces. The third battle of Cassino fought between 15 and 27 March, again in atrocious weather, was preceded by a heavy aerial bombardment of the monastery ruins but ended in stalemate. Monte Cassino was finally taken on 18 May by Polish troops after a week of continuous fighting. The casualties on both sides during the four month campaign were very high but the Allies were now able to continue their advance towards Rome which was eventually taken by United States troops in June.

On 2 March the Second Chindit operation was launched into Burma. Large numbers of Allied transport aircraft carried 9,000 men of the Long Range Penetration Group some hundred miles behind the Japanese lines. Later that month their commander, Major-General Orde Wingate, was killed in an air crash in Burma. On 15 March the Japanese Army in Burma attacked General Slim's Fourteenth Army with the aim of pre-empting a British offensive and gaining a toehold in India. They hoped to precipitate a revolt there which would be supported by the anti-British Indian National Army. At the beginning of April Japanese troops reached the Kohima area and later cut the supply route at Imphal. The Fourteenth Army stood their ground and after prolonged and desperate fighting the Japanese were repulsed with devastating casualties.

On the nights of 2 and 3 January a total of almost 800 bombers raided Berlin; 54 aircraft were lost. Over the next months the United States and British air offensive against German cities continued with considerable losses to Allied airmen and aircraft and to the German civilian population, foreign slave labourers and refugees. Germany exacted her revenge on the United Kingdom for the destruction caused by these Allied bombing raids, and 'The Little Blitz' on London and other cities lasted from mid-January until mid-April. The Vergeltunsgwaffen (retaliation weapon), a small pilotless aircraft, called the V-1 flying bomb, or Doodlebug by the British, was launched against London in the early hours of 13 June 1944. Over the next three weeks almost 2,500 doodlebugs were sent over; some 800 reached their target and crashed in and around London. Other cities suffered flying-bomb raids and many Doodlebugs landed off course. After the defences had mastered the technique of shooting down the weapon, most were destroyed by fighters, anti-aircraft guns or balloons. On 8 September the first V-2 bomb reached England and crashed on Chiswick. These larger, faster and more sophisticated rockets were a more deadly threat. Fortunately, they were introduced too late to be effective in numbers and the progress of the invasion forces caught up with the launching sites. However, by the spring of the following year over 6,000 civilians had been killed and almost 18,000 injured by the Doodlebugs and almost 3,000 killed and over 6,000 injured by the V-2 weapons. Edith Sitwell gave a reading of her poem 'Still Falls the Rain' at the Churchill Club in London in the Autumn of 1944. As she started to read, the air-raid warning sounded but she continued unperturbed as the noise of the Doodlebug increased. John Lehmann later wrote in his autobiography: 'Edith merely lifted her eyes to the ceiling for a moment, and, giving her voice a little more volume to counter the racket in the sky, read on. It was a magnificent performance . . .'

Throughout occupied Europe partisans formed groups to carry out guerrilla operations against the occupying forces. Supported and encouraged by the Special Operations Executive (SOE), which was set up in London in 1942, clandestine operations were carried out to disrupt communications on the continent and to collect vital intelligence. On 1 February 1944 the Forces Françaises de l'Intérieur (FFI) was formed to unite most of the French Resistance groups. A precision bombing raid on Amiens prison freed members of the French Resistance who were important for the sabotage plans to the railway system and to hamper German communications for the Normandy landings.

'Overlord' was the code-name for the Allied invasion of occupied north-west Europe. On the night of 5 June 1944, as more than a thousand British bombers attacked German defences on the coast of northern France, over 3,000 Allied ships crossed the Channel. Late that night there were massive US and British airborne assaults which confused and paralysed German defenders. At dawn, American, Canadian and British assault troops went ashore from landing craft on five beaches – Utah, Omaha, Gold, Juno and Sword – and by midnight almost 155,000 Allied troops were in France. They met strong opposition, particularly the Americans on Omaha beach, and suffered over 10,000 casualties. With General Eisenhower as Supreme Commander and General Montgomery as Commander of the land forces, the Allies consolidated and continued to advance into Normandy. The Germans fought desperately to contain the landing but by August they were defeated and after enormous casualties were forced to abandon France. French forces were allocated by the Allies to liberate Paris on 24 August.

On 20 July at Rastenburg, one of his headquarters, Hitler narrowly survived an assassination attempt by Count Claus von Stauffenberg, one of a group of disillusioned aristocrats, diplomats and high-ranking Army officers attempting to seize power. A bomb placed in a briefcase devastated the room in which Hitler was holding a morning conference. Three of his staff died but Hitler was only slightly wounded. The coup failed and the conspirators were rounded up; von Stauffenberg was shot and many others brutally murdered.

On 1 August 1944 the second Warsaw Rising broke out when the Poles attempted to take control of the city before the expected arrival of Russian forces. The Germans reacted viciously, sending in special SS and Police battalions who suppressed the rising with great cruelty, while the German Army held the Russians outside the city. Every street and house was fought over during sixty-three days of bitter engagements. 15,000 Polish resistance fighters were killed, some 10,000 Germans died, and an estimated 200,000 Polish civilians died in savage reprisals during and after the fighting.

The British captured Antwerp on 4 September but the port was unusable, the approaches still occupied by the Germans. On 8 September Major Jack Trefusis, a fluent German speaker on the staff of British 30 Corps, forced sixty German soldiers to surrender in the hôtel de ville in Brussels. He then reinstated the burgomeister to the welcoming crowds in La Grande Place as the remaining German troops retreated. In an attempt to break into Germany via Holland an attack with a large airborne force was made on 17 September. Two United States Airborne Divisions and the 1st British Airborne Division, commanded by Lieutenant General Frederick 'Boy' Browning, landed at Nijmegen, Eindhoven and Arnhem in a bold attempt to seize a bridge over the Rhine. The capacity of the German Army to regroup was underestimated and the attempt failed after an eight-day battle. The Germans retook the bridge and more than 6,000 men of the original force of 35,000 were taken prisoner.

On 7 October the German Army evacuated Greece and two weeks later the Allies captured their first German city when Aachen was taken by United States troops. On 16 December Hitler launched what was to be his final counter-offensive in north-west Europe. The Ardennes campaign – the Battle of the Bulge – aimed at splitting the Allied armies and driving a wedge through to Antwerp. A quarter of a million German troops were thrown into this desperate attack, and initially, helped by fog and surprise, they had some success, penetrating some 60 miles before being halted on Christmas Eve and driven back.

As the year progressed more and more Pacific islands were won back by the United States. Casualty figures in the war against Japan in South East Asia continued to be appallingly high as the Japanese, fighting ferociously, virtually fought to the last man.

On 20 October American forces in the Pacific landed on Leyte Island in the Philippines and eventually overcame the stubborn Japanese garrison. It was evident that the defeat of Japan was now inevitable. The final destruction of the Japanese fleet took place at the battle of Leyte Gulf when thirty-six Japanese warships were sunk for the loss of six US ships.

By the end of the year the Germans in Europe and the Japanese in South East Asia were in a disastrous position. But they were not yet prepared to surrender.

WRENNE JARMAN

On 18 February 1944 three squadrons of Mosquitoes, led by Group Captain Charles (Pick) Pickard, DSO and 2 Bars, DFC, Czech Military Cross, carried out a daylight precision bombing raid on Amiens prison where members of the French Resistance were held by the Gestapo. Fifty Resistance members escaped but Group Captain Pickard and his navigator, Flight Lieutenant Alan Broadley, were killed when their aircraft was shot down.

Target Amiens
(I.M. GROUP CAPTAIN PICKARD, R.A.F.)

Grey walls shadowed, grey yards star-lit,
    Taut at the end of the white road's rope
Men that the dawn would etch in scarlet,
    Breathless for death in the graveyard of hope.

Fighters' swift weaving, over and under,
    Smooth loads falling like drops from a knife,
Stone walls tearing like paper asunder,
    Black mites racing for thickets and life.

Odyssey over, soaring to skyward,
    Nosing to north and the wind from the sea –
Left behind, for a toast and a byword,
    Hearts grown great in the old chivalry.

NANCY CUNARD

During the war Nancy Cunard, an ardent francophile, worked for the Free French in London. The members of the Maquis were a formidabe part of the French Resistance movement.

Relève into Maquis

(February 1944)

The mayors put up the Order on the walls:
'Labour, well paid, in Germany to-day.'
Laval found better with these words: *'France calls*
All men of France . . . Each man who goes will free
One prisoner . . . Duty . . . Brothers . . . Gratitude . . .'
Three generations looked at it, and said:
'Grandfather, father, self – we fought the Boches
Each in his youth, then prime – shall yet, to-day.
It's NO. The Relève, this "changing of the guard"
Is planned for dupes, by Vichy's fear of us;
They want a France unmanned. We shall not go.'

And a mean wind blew doubt – 'Can one claim a son?
If so one takes his place.' But no. Meanwhile
A million and a quarter prisoners stay in the Reich,
In France come hunger and threats between nerve and flesh;
In July of '42 the first prisoner-train,
The barter of the Relève: three hundred, packed
Like a load of curses, sick, and half un-limbed.

Man sits in a fireless kitchen head in hands,
'From under our feet the ground . . . and France is done . . .
Is done? Is *down*. But I live. I'll fight against that.'
Just before dawn he unearthed the rabbit gun
And his old revolver, blessed by Spain, and went –
To the high lands by the goat track, a wind of decision
Blowing dawn into day. 'Wife and life now these two . . .'
Gun and pistol under knee after the four-hour trek he sat
Till a boy surged calling 'Password?' 'Not a hundred miles
                              from Vichy'

'Nor a hundred months from freedom.' So into Maquis,
Hidden camp of partisans, francs-tireurs, guerillas –
'Refractories to law and order' Vichy calls them;
Into the Secret Army the months have made them.

They swore him in: Enlisted until war's end –
Not to see folks or friends again – Don't count on any pay –
Death if your weapon's lost – Total secrecy, death if not –
Tolerance of each man's views, religious, political – and
Obedience to Maquis discipline in its very hard totality.
Marseille, Lorraine, Angoulême, Lille, Savoie, Franche-Comté,
Paris, Bretagne, Languedoc, Normandie – here is all France.
Loam and letters, student, shepherd, mason, agronomist,
Army-captain, priest, mechanic, and a lawyer-poet. To-day
                              comes a veteran
Of Spain and of the other two wars each side of that.

As yet there's a gun for every twentieth man –

'Always you hold your hand till the strategy's ripe.
You time your fuse for success. You hold your hand
Till it finds Death's hand responding as an ally.
This is the start. When we have won we shall build
Not out of *hope*, but out of *strength*,
        Freedom – signed, FRANCE.'

VIRGINIA GRAHAM

Nanny

Where is my Nanny in her long grey coat and skirt,
    and a black straw hat stuck with a pin to her head?
Where has she gone with her creaking petersham belt,
    and the strange, flat, comforting, senseless things she said?

'Cheer up, chicken, you'll soon be hatched!' she would tell me,
    drying my ears in a rough methodical way,
and 'Mark my words, it'll all come out in the wash',
    and 'It's just Sir Garnet Wolseley!' she used to say.

I still don't know what she meant, but oh, it was nice
    to hear that distrait voice so ruggedly tender,
as glimmering starchily she would cross the room
    to hang my liberty bodice on the fender.

Would she were here on this perilous bomb-scarred night,
    as warm and satisfying as a loaf of bread,
to stand like a round shield between me and the world,
    to give me a bath and carry me up to bed.

MYFANWY HAYCOCK

Canary in an Air-Raid

[February 1944]

All suddenly your tiny voice rang shrill
    Among the pandemonium of guns,
Threading their giant thunderstorm of sound
    Obstinately with little trills and runs.

So clear you sang, so daringly and clear
    Above those angry guns' incessant rage,
Spilling brave notes through all the shuddering house
    In cascades from your flimsy prison-cage.

And we, who crouched beneath the basement stairs
    While every thud seemed ominous with doom
And unbreathed fear, grew suddenly ashamed
    To hear you singing in an upper room.

STEVIE SMITH

I Remember

It was my bridal night I remember,
an old man of seventy-three
I lay with my young bride in my arms,
A girl with t.b.
It was war-time, and overhead
The Germans were making a particularly heavy raid on Hampstead.
What rendered the confusion worse, perversely
Our bombers had chosen that moment to set out for Germany.
Harry, do they ever collide?
I do not think it has ever happened,
Oh my bride, my bride.

PAULINE LENDON

Pauline Lendon served in the WAAF.

Returned Airman

Die peacefully brave boy I do not know
O God please hear my prayer and help you now
Morphia calms the pain of but a while ago
And smooths the fear wracked furrows from your brow

The morning star that lately was your guide
That served in place of navigator lost
Is waiting now for you in humble pride
Who saved friends' lives and didn't count the cost

Your blood that stains my battle-dress grows chill
The flames light up the pallor of your lips
Your breath comes fainter pulse is almost still
The hand that clasps my own goes limp and slips

Die peacefully young hero yet unnamed
Neath fading bomber's moon on grass dew wet
We who remain may live to feel ashamed
But even so we never can forget

BEATRICE RUTH GIBBS

The Bomber

White moon setting and red sun rising,
    White as a searchlight, red as a flame,
Through the dawn wind her hard way making,
    Rhythmless, riddled, the bomber came.

Men who had thought their last flight over,
    All hoping gone, came limping back,
Marvelling, looked on bomb-scarred Dover,
    Buttercup fields and white Down track.

Cottage and ploughland, green lanes weaving,
    Working-folk stopping to stare overhead –
Lovely, most lovely, past all believing
    To eyes of men new-raised from the dead.

To a Country Boy

How can it be in vain, your morning sleeping,
You who have died for all you loved so much?
Grassland, and grain that ripened in your keeping,
Slow patient beasts that knew your gentle touch:

The sprawling farm-house, white of wall, thatch-crested,
From which you ran with morning in your eyes,
Hay newly-mown, on which at noon you rested,
Watching white clouds a-drift in Summer skies:

Rain-heavy earth you ploughed in long straight furrows,
Carts, turnip-laden, jolting in the ruts,
Gorse, and the rabbits scuttling to their burrows,
Small winding lanes you searched for Autumn nuts:

Woodland and hill, green-tipped by Spring's returning,
Whiteness of foam upon the cherry trees,
Cold Winter evenings, with the great logs burning,
Your sheep-dog with his head upon your knees:

Sunrise to sunset, sowing, tending, reaping.
Then dreamless resting at the pillow's touch:
You have not died in vain, who died in keeping
Freedom for all the things you loved so much.

ELIZABETH BERRIDGE

Elizabeth Berridge, her husband Reginald Moore and their two small children rented the reputedly haunted fifteenth-century Glanbrogan Hall, near Llanfechain in North Wales. Rats were also tenants; there was running water in the house and an Aga to heat it but no electric light. On a train journey from Gobowen (near Oswestry) to Paddington Elizabeth Berridge listened to the talk among service men. They arrived in London to the sound of air-raid sirens.

Conversation

I sat by a sailor to learn of the sea,
But he swore as he drank,
Then he said to me:
'Leave it alone, lad, the sea's a bitch.
   All smells and bells
   And bo'sun's yells.
   The stokehole a stinkhole,
   The galley a hell-hole.
And we're carrying carrion into Cadiz.'
   'But what of the flying fish,
   White moon and mermen?
   What of the islands –
   Your tropical trips?'
But the sailor swore and laughed as he said,
'The sea would be fine if there weren't any ships.'

I sat by a soldier to learn of the wars,
But he swore as he drank,
Then he said to me:
'Leave it alone, lad, the army's a sod.
   Attention, detention
   And brasshat pretension,
   You spit and you polish,
   You fight and they promise.
And maybe you'll find yourself bound for Cadiz.'
   'But what of the glory,
   The trumpets and singing?
   What of the friendship –
   The nation's applause?'
But the soldier swore and laughed as he said,
'Life would be fine if there weren't any wars.'

I sat by an airman to learn of the sky,
But he sighed as he drank,
Then he said to me:
'Leave it alone, lad, the sky's a witch
    All zooming and booming
    And gunning and bombing,
    The pranging and slanging,
    All drinking, no thinking.
Forgetting the massacre – was it Cadiz?'
    'But what of the power,
    The freedom and stillness?
    How lovely to fly
    High over the town . . .'
But the airman drank and swore as he said,
'To fly would be fine if you never came down.'

In a train to Oswestry Elizabeth Berridge travelled with a young woman who had just said goodbye to her husband who was going overseas.

Speculation on a Beauty

What will she do when her love is gone
When his hands are stone?
When every pebble she walks upon
Is a lost caress and a fleshless bone?

What will she do when her man is dead
His words are silent, yet hang in the air?
When every turn of their firstborn's head
Turns her once more to her ancient fear?

What will she do when her sons are away
When the dust drops softly upon their bed?
When her limbs are old and her head is grey
And all the words in the world are said?

Will she return to the past and weep
For her thick gold hair and passionate hands?
For her tall sons' steps and her heart's gay leap
Blind to the steady drain of the sands?

O spirit dwelling behind the face
O spirit hidden, curled in a cone
Grant her the necessary grace
To gather, to garner, and travel alone.

*German and Italian prisoners of war worked near Llanfechain; the Germans dug
ditches for drains and the Italians worked on farms.*

Letter from an Italian prisoner

I am a barber.
You, Violetta, know this.
You know too that my paunch
Is not meant for farm-work.
You, Violetta, olive wife, soft one
Will you laugh at your husband –
Your Luisi, Luisippi?
They have taught me to plough
And, without boasting,
I can drive two horses
Straight as a parting.
The mayor – remember
The slap of his wet hair,
His beam while I combed him?
But, Violetta, being alone here
A city man, small man; a barber.
I have to remember my craft.
The other day, in the morning
I caught a sheep, shaved him –
Sheep love the ploughed land –
When I had finished he looked like a poodle.
I have learned very slowly
Many things I must tell you.
Animals are better than men, Violetta.
I would need Jaco's tongue
To say why. (Is he dead, Violetta?)
On market days I weep for my friends
Herded together on vans – just like men.
Through this cold mountain valley
The spring shudders – so slowly.
I long for processions, the white

Girls of Easter, and too I remember
Staring at you at our first communion.
I come to love the priests. It is
better to be robbed with a little ceremony.
At evening the soft bellies of calves
Is your softness, oh yielding dark wife.
I think, are you faithful?
I fear, are you living?
O Violetta, the warmth of your loving
Eases my cold days – your eyes hold
Such darkness of giving.
The pain of this poem
Has held me all winter.
I could not enter my countryman's singing
Nothing can defeat this cold, cheerful country.
This poem written,
I look with more hope to the sun, and even
Like a little the flat pink faces of the English.

BRENDA CHAMBERLAIN

The poet Alun Lewis died on 5 March 1944 while serving in India with the South Wales Borderers.

For Alun

'I'll come walking the hills with you in flesh or ghost, surely I will.'
From his last letter to me, dated February 7th, 1944.

Now his sweet singing spirit leaves the orange grove:
The blood-hibiscus and dust-wheeling suns
Burn through tranced leaves above earth-resting body
Of Alun, son of the grey Valleys,
By whose hearths' ash we weep him
In his own land.

Slowly returning on our tidal tears,
The homing spirit smiles through mountain rain,
Throws war's dirt from him
In the barren lake;
Becomes complete.
The dreaming poet,
Lover and soldier
On rock begins promised pilgrimage,
For he said, surely he would come again
In flesh or ghost beside me on the hill.

SHEILA SHANNON

On a Child Asleep in a Tube Shelter
LONDON, MARCH 1944

He sleeps undreaming; all his world
Furled in its winter sheath; green leaves
And pale small buds fast folded lie
As he lies curled as if his mother's arms
    Held him tenderly kept the world away.

His eyelids draw soft shadows down
And ward away the harsh lights' glare;
His parted lips draw breath as though
Breathing grass-scented, cool, hill-country air
    He tasted not this subterranean draught.

Indifferent trains roll in and out;
Indifferent crowds, who stand or stroll
Wearily up and down, who shout
Against the echoing din: yet he sleeps still,
    Deep in oblivion beyond their farthest call

Whose searchlights finger stars but pass
Looking for something else; whose town
Sleeps with its eyes half-closed, its ears
Alert for war's alarms, whose troubled dreams
    Stir the light surface of night's uneasy sleep.

The child is hidden underground
Yet Sleep still lovingly seeks him out
And keeps him tenderly till dawn.
Above, men listen for the roll of guns
    And sighs lie on the lips of drowsy watchers.

OLIVE HALLETT

Good Friday was on 7 April in 1944.

Easter Break
(1944)

'Plenty of fish,' the papers said.
(The good news nearly turned my head.)
So I began this Easter break
And made resolve my way to take
Down to the market place to see
If there were any fish for me.

Once out of doors, I quickened pace;
'Twas not, perhaps, the month for plaice,
Nor did I even hope for hake,
But just a simple salmon steak.
Quite humbly then I took my stand,
With paper ready in my hand.

The queue was long; I had to wait.
I watched the clock, 'twas growing late.
Good gracious – nearly ten to two!
Should I have joined another queue?
Yet hopefully I stood my ground;
My turn must surely soon come round.

Ah, yes, the task was almost done.
Before me there stood only one.
But what sad words now reached my ear?
'We've only one piece left, I fear.
Will that do, Ma'am?' She gave a nod,
And took the last lone piece of cod.

My patience gone, I turned away,
Firmly resolved that come what may,
Such precious time no more I'd spend,
But back my weary way I'd wend.
No fresh Good Friday fish for me;
I'd have the tinned variety.

ANGELA BOLTON

By the end of April 1944 the sick and wounded from the Battle of Kohima, and a little later from the Battle of Imphal, arrived at the 52nd Indian General Hospital at Gauhati in Assam. One night Angela Bolton, a nursing sister with the Queen Alexandra's Imperial Military Nursing Service, cared for a soldier dying alone in a small tent. Although she discovered he was American, she could find no case history and never knew his name as the next morning she woke with Dengue fever.

The Unknown Soldier

All men who die in war are in you, soldier.
Here in this lonely tent
Sunk in a coma,
With the yelp of jackals falling on deaf ears.

The light from the oil lamp bathes you in shadow.
No one has come to call
Bringing you flowers
Nor words of loving hope to calm your fears.

I shed the tears suppressed in crowded wards,
Fall to my knees to mourn
The untimely dead,
Who measured life in giving, not in years.

OLIVIA FITZROY

Olivia FitzRoy served as a fighter direction officer in the WRNS at Yeovilton Royal Naval Air Station in Somerset.

Fleet Fighter

'Good show!' he said, leaned his head back and laughed.
'They're wizard types!' he said, and held his beer
Steadily, looked at it and gulped it down
Out of its jamjar, took a cigarette
And blew a neat smoke-ring into the air.
'After this morning's prang I've got the twitch;
I thought I'd had it in that teased-out kite.'
His eyes were blue and older than his face,
His single stripe had known a lonely war,
But all his talk and movements showed his age,
He had no thought but of the latest mod.
His jargon was of aircraft and of beer.
'And what will you do afterwards?' I said,
Then saw his puzzled face and caught my breath.
There was no afterwards for him, but death.

DIANA JAMES

Presage: 1944

I sometimes feel it but a passing thing,
These walls and pictures and your gentle ways,
And being hand in hand with you and being
Alone with you when stars in darkness blaze.
I sometimes feel that it is past and done
And we shall go no more to Charborough wood
To watch the embers of the dying sun
Litter the hazel with a brighter bud.
For now, it seems, the agony of spring
Has touched my heart, and April is not long,
And time which sheds its loves will shed this thing
Before the thunder of the summer song!
And yet for sleeping in your arms I have
A new eternity, with stones and trees
And street and hills and music that are brave
With youth and love, passions and enmities;
Your voice, your touch remain; in these I find
Beloved fragments of your gentle mind.

The Munition Workers

They sat upon a hill,
They could forget
The dark oppressive roof-tops of the town.
They drank their fill;
The buttercups were wet;
The evening sunlight, webbed and mystical,
Transfused the iron bands that were clamped down
On their bright hair; the fetters of the mill
Became a circlet and a coronet.
The wheels poised and the hammers were laid still.

But now the night is deep,
The caverns burn,
The great machine is grinding in a dream.
They cannot weep,
The coronet is stern,

The fountain of their tears has ceased to gleam:
Somewhere men die; somewhere the waters churn
With flame consumed; somewhere the bullets teem
In this dark night, and wreathe their brows with iron,
With the dread weight of an eternal sleep.

RUTH TOMALIN

'In the approach to D-Day the countryside near the south coast became a vast arsenal, spied on by the enemy from the air. Ancient cornfields were taken over as airfields; woodland rides and roadside verges paved with concrete to hold tanks and army vehicles.' (Note from poet.)

Invasion Spring

Where purple cuckoo-clappers quake
within their green translucent shrine,
and cobra-headed ferns awake,
the sullen mighty tanks recline.

Young shepherds sleep beside their flock,
or watch the stormy skies all night,
where brown owls with soft voices mock
great bands of darker birds in flight.

Like old calm shepherds of the fell
these know and call their lambs by name –
Susannah, Charmer, Cheyenne Belle,
Calamity and Texas Dame.

All Sussex flows with silver blood
from wounded white anemones,
while flowers in dark remembered mud
lie drowned among the waiting trees.

Here light words die as soldiers dream
beneath green hedges in the sun,
and see their twentieth April gleam,
who dare not hope for twenty-one.

VERA ARLETT

War in Sussex (1944)

I passed a tank. It was half dismembered by the road,
And the men slept like dogs, worn out by night
   manoeuvres.
I thought the tank was the ugliest thing I had ever
   seen;
It was so typical of that state of intelligence and
   inspiration
Which six thousand years of civilisation have wrought
   in Man.

Then I saw an unbelievable miracle –
A red rose was stuck in the snout of a tank.
Is it possible, I wondered, in the mechanised inferno
   of modern war,
That any man can survive with a rose in his secret
   self?
O heart of man, I prayed; O spirit, almost of iron,
Save for yourself a rose in the midst of the deadly
   battle!
Bring only one tattered petal to the world after the
   war,
And we shall be saved at last, and the future be born
   in peace!

AILEEN HAWKINS

Aileen Hawkins' husband was in the first wave of troops to land in Normandy. They did not see each other again until the end of November 1945.

End of D-Day Leave

Please, hold back the dawn, dear God
I cannot bear to let him go,
the world's a battle field out there
big distant guns pepper the skies
a wailing siren stabs the air.
This moon-washed room our paradise
where we have had such little time
to share this precious love of ours.
My gentle one – a soldier now –
these years have left their mark on him,
touching his war-wearied face
I almost stare into his dreams.
At day break he must go away
and I know just how it will be.
I'll see that sad-look in his eyes
as I have often seen before,
a trembling smile just for me,
as, handsome in his uniform,
he will stand silently at the door;
Then we will walk hand in hand
through the dew-washed lane,
the Station bleak, the engine steams;
He will hold me close without one word
so much to say – no time to talk.
The clock's long hand will point the hour
the train will rattle from my view
and I will be alone once more
just longing for his love again.
'God', as he sleeps close to my heart,
slowly the end of leave draws near.
I cannot bear the time to part:
'Hold back the dawn another hour'.

LISBETH DAVID

Lisbeth David, a WRNS cypher officer, was at the Naval Control of Shipping Office at Bangor, County Down, on Belfast Lough, as preparations for D-Day gathered momentum. She later wrote: 'As D-Day drew near everyone was kept very busy, and in the last few days the bombardment fleet, heavily armed, but old, French and British warships considered expendable, assembled in Belfast Lough. There was W/T silence, and the night before they sailed all orders had to be taken out "by hand of officer", so I was pressed in to help as postman round the fleet. It was a very moving experience to board these ships, poised, as we all knew, for the assault. "Pray for us," someone said. By the morning they were gone, and we had to wait until the war was over to find out what happened to them . . .'

Sonnet before D-Day

What can we lay before thy mailed feet
Waiting wing-ready for the streaks of dawn?
What hymns, grey-mantled goddess of the fleet,
Sing we to swell the brazen battle horn?
Stern blades of steel that sightless Vulcan wrought
And arrows swifter than the swallow's wing,
Such gifts as these alas we would have brought
But well thou knowest they are not ours to bring.
And so we come, BELLONA; in our hands
These secret petals from the war-thorned rose,*
With hidden truths for him who understands
And all our hearts and happiness for those
Who if unskilled in cyphers still can read
Between each rosy line the words God Speed.

---

* Secret signals were typed on pink paper.

DALLAS KENMARE

'Home Service'
June 6th 1944

7.30 a.m. 'This Week's Composer: Johann Strauss.'
> Lightly, in gay billowing swirls and waves the music floats,
> light-hearted figures float easily on the billowing melody-
>   waves –
gay young innocence, happy in a waltzing world . . .
> 'Voices of Spring', and the light flowing rhythm of the
>   gay river,
> the sparkling Danube, blue in the summer sun –
> young voices of spring, of laughter, of care-free love . . .
> Lightly, lightly the gay music floats.

7.55 a.m. 'Lift up your hearts'
> '. . . and grant, O Lord, that we may walk always in Thy
>   light.'

8 a.m. NEWS.
> 'The Supreme Allied Command has issued a warning
> to the inhabitants of the coastal districts of Northern
> France to be prepared to leave their homes at an
> hour's notice, preferably on foot, taking with them
> only that which can easily be carried.'

'Prepare to leave their homes?' But we go – where?
Listen, my darlings, the great men, les grands soldats say
    we may have to go away;
to-night perhaps you sleep with Maman on a bed of hay,
happy among the animals, just like L'Enfant Jesus . . .

On foot we go, my Jean, my Georges, and la toute petite
    Yvonne –
you I carry, ma petite, and what besides? I have little
    strength
and that I need to feed you, my darling.

But the wise, the great men, say we may have to go –
so we do not question, only I would know – where?

No one tells us where –
only they tell us to be ready to leave our homes.

C'est bien, perhaps, who can say? C'est pour la France –
En effet, mes enfants, c'est la guerre.

WINIFRED DAWES

German Boy, 1938

At fifteen, I remember him:
As he washed at the sink in shorts,
He chatted carelessly to me,
Half turning round with soapy skin,
With soapy, golden, freckled skin;
And from the naked kitchen bulb
Quite unaware he caught the light,
While naturally he cleaned himself,
Foot high and pensive in the bowl:
He was an ode to all that's gold,
To all that's sunburned, ripe and live,
To all that uncorrupted is,
Unconscious elegy of youth:
Does loving vision blind the sight?
Was he as wholesome as his skin?
Could beauty only give delight?
Did he love me as I did him?
For now he lies in Normandy
Though maybe 'Never blows so red—'
I see long fields of rustling corn
Where lies the glinting head.
Poetic vision blinds my sight!
Ripe fields of waving corn?
There dwelt within my kitchen bright,
In million kitchens that same night,
As on the cornfields' burnished height,
Grey masses of the dead.

VIRGINIA GRAHAM

Losing Face

This is my doodle-bug face. Do you like it?
  It's supposed to look dreadfully brave.
Not jolly of course – that would hardly be tactful,
  But . . . well, sort of loving and grave.

You are meant to believe that I simply don't care
  And am filled with a knowledge supernal,
Oh, well . . . about spirtual things, don't you know,
  Such as man being frightfully eternal.

This is my doodle-bug voice. Can you hear it?
  It's thrillingly vibrant, yet calm.
If we weren't in the office, which *isn't* the place,
  I'd read you a suitable psalm.

This is my doodle-bug place. Can you see me?
  It's really amazingly snug
Lying under the desk with my doodle-bug face
  And my doodle-bug voice in the rug.

GRACE GRIFFITHS

Grace Griffiths served in the ATS (Royal Signals, Special Y Section) at Shenley, Hertfordshire.

Doodlebugs

A bomb, last night, fell close by Radlett.
The pulsing engine stopped right overhead.
Four minutes to the crash. Slowly we counted;
One girl cried 'Oh God! Dear God!'
The tension grew to bursting point; the blast
Shattered the windows. We breathed again.
Always the bombs come over in early evening
Just before we go on shift. We talk of rush-hour traffic
But underneath the fear remains. Death can come
From so many angles. Tomorrow, next week, next month
It may not pass us by.

LISBETH DAVID

In July 1944 Lisbeth David was sent from Northern Ireland to General Eisenhower's invasion headquarters at Fort Southwick near Portsmouth. She worked in airless conditions under the ground in Portsdown Hill behind the city. After a night watch she would sometimes take a bus to Winchester and 'breathe in the civilised English air'.

Forty-Eight Hours

Quick, catch the bus from Pompey and the war
And with faint morning eyes begin to find
Green oaks along the road, and hedges twined
With clematis unrecognised before;
Fleet wary foals, carts loaded high with straw,
And sunburnt village houses, while behind
Night watch retreats into a distant mind
And newly woken eyes look on for more.
Then seek this city where the grey stone grows,
A place where peace can never leave unblessed
Dishevelled allies sprawling in the Close
Or cold crusaders in their stately rest;
And as the sands of stand-off swiftly spill
Cling to this ecstasy where time stands still.

DOROTHY WELLESLEY

The artist Rex Whistler was killed by a mortar bomb on 18 July 1944 as the Welsh Guards attempted to break through into eastern France after the Normandy landings. His tank became entangled in telephone wire while crossing a railway cutting in the small village of Giberville.

In Memory of Rex Whistler

Leave him, sweet Eros, give him peace at last.
His long, his great despair, his blood, are cast
In a rough, war-scarred, unforgotten tomb.
Only his friends remember
His gaiety, his merriment, his wit,
His art and his swift mind, pointing warm thought
With satire, learned, elegant, and fit;
The tragic mask, the eyes,
One blue, the other grey. –
As Shelley saw, he saw
Himself, at ghostly four o'clock of the morning,
Standing outside in the street, his lamp still burning,
And he still drawing, drawing.
Resolved, he went the way the heroes went.

Sleep on, dear Rex, whispering 'I am content
With immortal peace, that finds at last a rest
Upon the ultimate Breast'.

RUTH OGIER

Ruth Ogier and her sister Priscilla were interned on Guernsey during the war.

Tomatoes, July 20th, 1944

Tomatoes! tomatoes! tomatoes!
And no one will buy any more.
The growers, through force of the Germans, of course,
Had to grow them, and now they are poor.

Tomatoes! tomatoes! tomatoes!
For breakfast and dinner and tea:
Now all should have health, though they're minus of
    wealth,
If they eat just as many as me.

Tomatoes! tomatoes! tomatoes!
Are had for the taking away;
So no one must grumble, the Island's a jumble;
It's only Black-Market will pay!

Tomatoes! tomatoes! tomatoes!
Now the growers are apt to see red!
They were told they'd be shipped; but tomatoes are
    tipped,
For the Tommies have reached France instead!

Clothes, 1944!

Our clothes are a worry,
They're looking so sorry,
For over four years they've been worn;
We patch and we darn
With just all sorts of yarn,
Yet repeatedly they become torn.

Rubber boots are in holes
In their tops and their soles,
So we paddle around with wet feet;
But the Nazis are here,

And what do they care
If the feeling is not very sweet?

Then there are our macks;
If still on our backs,
They will let in the rain like a sieve;
But we cannot buy new,
So what can we do? –
This is a poor life that we live!

When our Allies arrive
If we are still alive!
They will stare at the sights that they see;
And will think of the Ark –
We have been in the dark
As to what latest fashions can be.

For everything sags;
We are dressed all in rags;
And I think at times every one grieves:
If this goes on much longer,
Clothes will not grow stronger,
So we may end by dressing in leaves!

Substitutes

Substitutes for everything –
Bramble leaves for tea;
Parsnips turned to coffee now,
Or acorns, it may be.
A custard, and a jelly, made
From sea-weed of the beach;
Oh, what a lot of things there are
Necessity will teach!

Our daily bread, so small a share,
Is substitute as well;
From what ingredients it is made,
The doctors cannot tell!

For fuel, to take the place of coal,
is rubbish mixed with tar;

To find a dirtier mess about,
You'd have to travel far.

To wash, we get a substitute –
But it is sold as soap;
And those who think of clean results,
Have certainly a hope!

To get more salt, we boil and boil
A saucepan full of sea;
It needs, of course, a lot of fuel
And patience, all agree.

And now we have a substitute
For our late radio set;
A little crystal we can hide –
And many turns we get!

Oh, substitutes, oh, substitutes,
Their praises we will sing;
But who would choose a substitute
Before the real thing?

CAMILLA DOYLE

Damage by Enemy Action

I went to see the house where I was born,
That earliest home I always love the best;
Windows were splintered, ceilings cracked, the lawn
Covered with flowers as tall and thick as corn,
Springing as weeds, looking their loveliest;

Delphiniums, poppies at their greatest height,
Laughing at desolation, all untended –
Like poems made in prisons, planes that fight
Outnumbered, knowing this is their last flight,
Radiant and doomed, unreasonably splendid.

JOY CORFIELD

Joy Corfield joined the ATS in Guildford during 1944.

I Didn't Believe It . . .

Two weeks in uniform
Strangers now friends.
Rosa teaching us to polish shoes;
Senga, the expert, pressing skirts.
Every morning
Jacky rushes to help me make my bed:
Three biscuits, neatly stacked.
On top, sheets and pillows wrapped
In one big grey blanket.

Two weeks confined to barracks
Then let free.
Best-dressed, checked in the guardroom,
Then off to town.
Self-conscious, shy,
We glanced in darkened windows
At our familiar faces in unfamiliar clothes,
Straightening our hats and shoulders,
Laughing when caught.
We shared chocolate, fish and chips,
And returned sober and properly dressed
In good time.

But three girls stayed out.
They'd been seen in a pub
With some Americans.
'They're fast,' someone whispered.
I couldn't believe it.
Seemed nice and friendly.

They were brought back by M.P.s
At lunchtime next day.
Dirty, untidy, defiant;
One wearing a U.S. army jacket.
They collected their things and left.
Never saw them again.

Someone shocked me saying,
'They boasted they'd each had thirty men.'
I didn't think it possible
So I didn't believe it, then.

Soldiers' Pets

Those dogs
Scavenging the ruined shells of former homes,
Abandoned by dead or scattered families,
Bewildered and frightened.
Soldiers, grieved by their suffering,
Coax them out,
Smuggle them on advancing trucks,
Sharing their rations
And, maybe their affection.

But soldiers die, are wounded, posted away,
A lucky dog is adopted by a friend,
Then another, and another,
Most of them, like most of the women,
Fail to find a permanent home.

FRYNIWYD TENNYSON JESSE

A Tale of St. Peter's Gate
ARNHEM 1586–1944

St. Peter stood at his gleaming Gate
Wondering what should be the fate
Of those muddy men who laughed like sin
And crowded the Gate and peered within;
Bloodstained men who had fought their best
And now stormed heaven with careless jest.
'Oh Peter, we didn't win – we died . . .
But when cocks crowed no man denied
The cause for which we all of us fought . . .
So open the Gate – you damn well ought.'
Then out came a man with a song on his lip
And a wound that shone like a star on his hip;
In his hand he carried a soldier's cup
And he stayed his singing and he spoke up.
'Let them in, Oh Peter, for these are my men,
Like me they fought and died at Arnhem!'
And then the voice of Hollanders said:
'They fought for us, we too are dead.
We also perished in farms and dykes,
Not only when Sidney's men held pikes,
But we true Dutch – men, women and children
Helped – and died with these Englishmen.'
Sir Philip lifted his cup and said:
'These men will live, though they be dead!
They came from heaven in newest fashion
But just as mine were their pain and passion.'
So Peter opened the Gate and bowed,
And Sir Philip Sidney sang aloud:
'They came from the skies and they're here again
Oh men of Arnhem, be free from pain!'

September 25, 1944

MARGARET CROSLAND

Margaret Crosland took the train from Euston, often travelling at night, when she returned to Cumberland for brief holidays.

Reverie at a Main Line Station

We have all written of these,
the stations at night,
of the endless parting and the last embracing,
the sweaty soldiers and the distant shouting,
the droop of eyes and mouth and the lifted hands.
We have all seen the world-farewell
in our myriad broken kisses,
but nothing saves the raw Prometheus
from the iron eagle of our loneliness
when the wheels darken our separate lives.

Behind the great blank mist of eyes
what treacherous tortuous seas of grief,
boiling and coiling and curling inwards,
like the whirl and whorl of the smoke in the dark rush of tunnels.
While those we love, whose bodies are warm to ours,
whose thoughts and words build up the soul in our flesh,
they fade immeasurably far away,
a few stars in a cloudy sky of faces,
and soon to be buried in the storm.

Yet can we push this darkness back,
lean on the wind and grasp the thunder,
taking our strength from love
and our will from the hatred of hate –
no other way is the clean world sped
and our own gigantic living stars
fired in the hollow furnace of our hearts;
then are the scrap-heaps of our younger lives,
Guernica, Arnhem, Buchenweld,
illumined with a richer sun,
while in our grey immediate night
the bursts of steam unloose a flight of gulls
and the shouts are a hundred larks singing on gorsey moors.

MYFANWY HAYCOCK

Myfanwy Haycock, who was working in London for the BBC in 1944, returned to her home in Pontnewynydd, near Pontypool, Gwent, whenever possible.

Going Back to London
(IN THE TIME OF FLYING BOMBS)

[October 1944]

Lord, give me courage to go back
    To face the horror and the pain,
And in that gallant city's streets
    To walk with eager Death again.
It would be easy, Lord, to stay
    Here where ecstatic skylarks sing,
Where city streets are vague as dreams
    And war a strange and far-off thing.

I am afraid, Lord, so afraid!
    Almost my sanity takes wings;
Lord, You Who chose to give me songs
    And tears for all unhappy things,
Give me the courage to go back,
    Help me to walk the Darkened Way,
Where I, who die with each man's death,
    Must die a hundred times a day.

Here in the quietness of hills
    Where lark-song patterns every day,
Here in the blessed peace of hills
    It would be easy, Lord, to stay.
So, You Who know I am afraid
    Because I feel, because I see,
Grant me the numbness that is faith,
    The blindness that is bravery.

I am not steadfast, Lord, I know;
    Give me the hardness that I lack.
It would be easy, Lord, to stay –
    Grant me the courage to go back.

SYLVIA READ

For the War-Children

Out of the fire they come, headlong from heart's desire,
The children, leaping and laughing, and breaking from the
    womb;
Bursting aside the foliage of flesh, as through a bush
Plunges a swift racer, or tumbles the wind's rush.

From the white world of the spirit, from the patter of light on
    leaves,
The spiralling fall of motes, the gold discs in the ether,
They come, they are born to us. They lie on the sunflaked
    grass
Cradled in fiery green. They kick, they scatter a mass

Of laughter and leaping fury, the thrust of bud, the push
Of light like a hand carrying a candle, a hand with a torch,
Daring its way out of night, from the worm's earth, from under
Thought and dream and desire, to the acknowledgement of the
    tender

Of these, the inarticulate, like angels whose tongues of fire
Speak only of Heaven; like these, the dumb children
Play on our bare earth, our back yards, our floors,
Grow in our soil like plants, like puzzled beautiful flowers.

Who remember the tides of Heavenly light, and the salutation
Of waving in the fields on the celestial day.
These are the flowers we gather, that our desire grows,
Springing from the stars to the soil our love allows.

In the broken house they play; In the garden among the ruins
They coo like doves or pigeons for pieces of snapped brick;
They crawl among wreckage on the sands, at the sea's edge
They sprawl where wind and wave make smooth the bright
    pillage.

Familiar are the black wings that come between them and the
    sun;
The black hand that explodes, that is stronger than a mother's
    arm;

Familiar the monstrous crow, big as a tar barrel.
These children are rocked out of sleep by their father's quarrel.

Out of our desire they come, from the hands of lovers
Stretching towards Heaven to pluck a growing blessing;
Out of the world's desire to feel the blood in its veins,
To spring as the corn springs, to clamber as the vines

With outspread arms for the sun across the breast of the earth;
To feel to the roots, to suck, to imbibe the full draught;
Declaring to its mountains, 'I am world that survives,
In them I acknowledge myself. I acknowledge that man lives.'

Out of our desire they come, from the fire that forces us
Out of our loves, the flowers, that we must gather and nourish.
And for them the world must be woman; hearts turn to
   the Heavenly Mother,
Who sets us in a cradle of peace, whose hand is a firm rocker.

1945

INTRODUCTION

Ferocious fighting continued in South East Asia. On 19 February United States marines landed on Iwo Jima, a small island airbase in the Pacific Ocean. From there American bombers launched regular bombing missions on the Japanese home islands. Three days later Manila was taken by United States troops after the city was reduced to ruins and nearly 100,000 Filipino civilians had been murdered by Japanese troops. On 9 March the Japanese seized control of French Indo-China.

On 17 January the ruined city of Warsaw was liberated by the Soviet Army. When the Russian troops arrived at the concentration camps at Auschwitz eight days later they discovered horrendous scenes of mass murder and more than 7,000 survivors close to death from starvation. During the first months of 1945 the Soviet Army continued its advance into East Prussia and by 1 February they were close to Berlin.

Between 4 and 11 February, Churchill, Roosevelt, Stalin and their advisers met at Yalta in the Crimea to discuss future strategy and the division of post-war Germany. To assist the advance of the Soviet Army, an air-raid on the medieval city of Dresden was planned for the night of 13 February. Air Chief Marshal Arthur ('Bomber') Harris dispatched over 700 British bombers which attacked Dresden in two waves and created a firestorm. On the two following days United States bombers raided the burning city. It was estimated that almost 60,000 citizens of Dresden, including many refugees, were burnt to death or buried beneath the ruins of the city. This raid, with its uncertain military value, was considered by many to be unjustified.

In February and March a number of Latin American and Middle Eastern countries declared war on Germany and Japan. On 26 February United States troops reached the Rhine south of Dusseldorf and over the next weeks crossed the Rhine in a number of places and enveloped the Ruhr. On 11 April the Americans reached the concentration camp Buchenwald and four days later British tanks entered Bergen-Belsen, the concentration camp near Hanover. Only a few weeks earlier the diarist, Anne Frank, a fifteen-year-old German Jewess, had died from the typhus epidemic that swept the camp. Thousands of the 'walking skeletons' who were liberated died over the following weeks.

In the space of eighteen days three of the war leaders died. President Roosevelt, who died on 12 April, was succeeded by President Truman; on 28 April Mussolini was executed by Italian partisans; and two days later Hitler committed suicide in his Berlin bunker. On 7 May at Reims the Germans signed an unconditional surrender. The war in Europe was over but an estimated 30 million men, women and children were homeless and destitute refugees.

VE Day – Victory in Europe Day – was celebrated in the United Kingdom on 8 May with a national holiday. There were parties and thanksgiving church services throughout the country. The Prime Minister broadcast to the nation that afternoon. The following day crowds still thronged the Mall cheering and singing as the King, the Queen, the two Princesses and the Prime Minister appeared on the balcony of Buckingham Palace. Winston Churchill led the crowd in singing 'Rule Britannia'. A twenty-three-year-old clerk serving in the ATS wrote in her diary for Mass-Observation:

May 8th . . . All through the East End the battered little streets are gay with bunting – recent V2 damage, barely tidied up, borders the bravest shows of all . . . VE-day was very quiet at home. My father came home from Liverpool, and we stayed in listening to the radio, and had a family party at teatime. In the centre of the table was a dish of canned pineapple, which Mother had saved through all the long years for this day. We went to the village church for a short service; it was full, and everyone sang 'Onward Christian Soldiers' with might and main. Back home to hear the King's speech and the news. The children have built a bonfire, and, unable to wait for darkness, have a lovely blaze at dusk, under the watchful eye of an NFS man . . .

Between 17 July and 2 August the Big Three Conference was held at Potsdam to discuss post-war Europe and the war which still raged in South East Asia. At home during the Conference the Conservative Party was defeated in the general election and Winston Churchill resigned.

The Labour Party came to power and Clement Attlee, the new Prime Minister, took part in the final negotiations at Potsdam.

At 8.15 a.m. on 6 August American bombers dropped an atomic bomb on the Japanese city of Hiroshima; 80,000 people were killed instantly and a further 70,000 had died within the year. Three days later, having heard nothing about a Japanese surrender, the Americans dropped a second, much more powerful, atomic bomb on the city of Nagasaki. This did less damage than at Hiroshima but some 40,000 people were killed. With the terrible results of long-term radiation, the final death toll for the two cities has been given in the region of 300,000. On 14 August 1945 Emperor Hirohito of Japan announced his country's unconditional surrender.

The fighting was over but a large proportion of the world's population had suffered physically and emotionally. The scale of death and destruction was immeasurable. Tens of millions of men, women and children died during the six years of war. The Soviet Union lost an estimated 20,000,000 soldiers and civilians; Germany lost almost 7,000,000; Japan some 3,000,000; 6,000,000 Polish citizens were killed under German occupation and 3 million of these were Jews. A further 3 million Jews were murdered in other parts of Europe. Over 1 million Yugoslavs died. The United States lost over 362,000 combatants and the British Commonwealth lost over 129,000 men in action.

Almost 265,000 British soldiers, sailors and airmen and over 30,000 merchant navy seamen were killed in action; over 60,000 civilians had been killed. Members of the armed forces returned home from war zones and prisoners-of-war were repatriated. Women's lives had been revolutionised. There was the huge aftermath of war damage to be dealt with. The country was impoverished and the population exhausted. Years of rebuilding, readjustment and reconciliation lay ahead.

JOY CORFIELD

This poem was written on the Isle of Man at the beginning of 1945.

Morse Lesson

A cold, cold room with cold, cold girls
In buttoned greatcoats, scarves and mitts;
Frozen fingers try to write
The letters for the dah-dah-dits.

'Faster, faster,' says the sergeant;
Slower, slower work our brains.
Feet are numb, our blood is frozen,
Every movement causing pains.

Yet – four of us swam in the sea
Just last week, on Christmas Day,
Through frosty foam and fringe of ice,
Warmer than we are today.

E.J. SCOVELL

Early in 1945, Breslau, the chief city of Silesia, became a fortress defended by 35,000 German troops as the Soviet Army advanced on Berlin. Most of the civilian population was forcibly evacuated by the Nazi authorities.

A Refugee

My heart had learnt the habit of earthly life
In an accustomed place.
My voice had learnt the habit of maternal
Sharpness and gentleness.

My thighs had learnt the speech of love. The house
And market tasks that show
So small a flower, rooting in hands and feet
Had matted my flesh through.

My husband died in the mercy of Russian snow.
My child died in the train,
In three days in the weeping cattle truck
From Breslau to Berlin.

I was not taught the song of extremity,
The dancing of duress.
All that I know of infinite is the intensity
Of finite tenderness.

All that I have of goodness is through love –
Their love my only worth.
My rigid arms set in the shape of their love
Have no more use on earth.

OLIVIA FITZROY

Olivia FitzRoy served in the WRNS as a fighter direction officer. She was in Ceylon between the summer of 1944 and late 1945. This poem was written in January 1945.

Piayagala

And in the day, we said, we'll watch the sea
From the warm beach
Or swim between the waves
Among the bright fish and starry shells
We'll lie
Upon the sand
Under the nodding palms,
While beautiful brown children bring us fruit,
Cool from the hills
And listen to the melody of waves
And the sweet sudden song of magic birds.
Our house will be upon a little rise,
Soft skins upon the floor and the wide couch,
And ever-open windows to the stars.
We shall not want for eggs nor fish nor cream
Nor gentle music nor a host of books
And in each other find a deep content.
Nor shall we care
For anything forgotten from this world
Nor left behind.
And in the dawns,
While the air is cool,
Or by the light of the great silver moon
By the wave's edge
We shall ride furiously
And feel the wind stream through our hair
And see the flashing sand
Under the winged feet of our immortal horses.

Olivia FitzRoy's pilot boy-friend was killed near Singapore two months later on
20 March 1945.

Sonnet Experiment

I

They do not know, who have not tasted tears
The magic ecstasy that love can bring
For love that's known no sorrow seldom bears
Complete perfection on its flaming wing.
Thus we that shared together for a year
Laughter and joy and sorrow, rapture and peace
Cannot now be apart, nor ever fear
That all the strength we gained, being one, shall cease.
We knew, in that short spring, more than our share
Of perfect inexplicable content
And gained possession of a something rare,
Ours forever, neither shared nor lent.
  So, dearest, though I know that you have gone
  Without me, still I shall not be alone.

II

And now they say there is an end of war,
That all the fabric of our adult life
Will change and there will be a cease of strife
And hideous sudden death shall come no more.
The gentle arts of peace will grow again,
There will be time to stand aside and know
Quietness of evening and the winter's snow,
Slow village cricket and soft summer rain.
And now that this has come to me I find
These years of war have left an empty heart
And you have gone and left me far behind,
Alone in life of which you were a part.
  Too late the end that we were longing for,
  Peace cannot touch my heart nor end of war.

ANNE BULLEY

Anne Bulley served in the WRNS in HMS Highflyer *in Trincomalee, Ceylon. She wrote 'Leave Poem' at Diyetalawa in Ceylon where the Navy had rest camps. Lieutenant Michael James, for whom these two poems were written, was waiting for his ship to sail for the Pacific but was killed in a car crash on Sydney bridge.*

Leave Poem

O let the days spin out
In leisure, as the clouds pass;
Weave webs of shadow
Across the grass.

Let nothing touch me now,
But the minty mountain air,
Sun, wind and your fingers
Through my hair.

And when the hills grow cold
Outside, lock out the night,
Tell me long tales and stir
The fire bright.

For I would be bastioned here
Against the constant hum
Of streets and men and ships
Whence we have come.

So let the days spin out
In magic hours and laughter
That I may hold the thought
Long, long after.

Poem

I loved but once.
He was more fair
Than sunrise.
The lovely rare
Exquisite things
We knew are gone.
The sun is set,
The day done.

NORAH K. CRUICKSHANK

Norah Cruickshank served in the ATS attached to the Royal Army Service Corps.

Farewell to X Platoon

Once more, the train; the wet,
Grey, hauled-on, flying fields,
The sadness, the cold. This year
For the second time I set
Behind me the far from dear
Place with a strange regret.

A tale as hard to begin
And finish as *War and Peace*
A system of people, ends.
For a breathing-space, within,
You walk and speak, my friends,
Before the loud others win.

I see a leaf that grips
A twig lodged in a stream,
Tugged at, as good as gone,
When I think of these years' friendships:
The straggling tide sweeps on;
The face from fond-thoughts slips.

The time is salt with farewells.
But, calling the better years,
But, tuned to the rushing train,
My stumbling verse tells:
In this body of death and pain
Were green, rebellious cells:

Were cells of kindness, whose sum
Worked softly to lift the whole,
To leaven this doughy lump
Our sighing world, this numb
Sin-tip, devil's dump,
And make the good kingdom come.

Hate thickens. But who will take
Back the same feckless heart,
Having seen in many places
The dull, cold, sealed crowd make
Way for names, for faces,
And liking and laughter break?

Good luck! A safe return
To city or glen or vale
At no distant day.
Heaven bless your return.
May tides be gentle, may
The tide of the world turn.

FRANCES CORNFORD

For M.S.
Singing Frühlingsglaube in 1945

Nun muss sich alles, alles wenden

Here are the Schubert Lieder. Now begin.

First the accompaniment,
Heart-known and heaven-sent
And so divinely right
The inmost spirit laughs with sure delight.

And now the fountain of the melody.

To your forgiven fields I am entered in,
Spring of my adolescence, Spring of the world,
Where every secret lime-leaf is unfurled,
Where all's made well again, yet more's to be –

Then why this misery?

Because, O enemy alien heart! we fear
That you are lost on your demoniac shore,
Whilst we deny that in your music – here
Is your unchanged, unchanging innocent core.

Joy W. Trindles

The concentration camp Bergen-Belsen was liberated by the British on 15 April 1945. On arrival they found mass graves, 10,000 unburied bodies and over 30,000 sick and dying men, women and children. Joy Trindles served as a sister in the Queen Alexandra's Imperial Military Nursing Service. She spent nine weeks in Belsen with the 29th British General Hospital and later wrote: 'We took over from the front line medical staff and set up the first hospital at the camp. We arrived on a day when they were burning some of the camp, after moving the people from there into the German SS barracks. We were under canvas two miles away and trucked in every day. We were not allowed to stay overnight in the camp. We were sprayed with DDT regularly because of lice. Typhus eventually spread through Europe . . .'

Until Belsen

We thought we had seen it all.

Our cheeks bloomed like peaches,
Bright eyes, Quick light movement.
Flashes of scarlet, snow white caps,

We thought we had seen it all.

The London Blitz, bombs, fires, headless corpses,
Screaming children: Yankee Doodle Dandy!

We thought we had seen it all.

Scabies, Lice, and Impetigo, T.B., Polio
and unmentionable V.D.

We thought we had seen it all.

Then France.
Day followed night and then another day
Of mangled broken boys.
Irish, Welsh and Scots
Jerries, Poles and French –
They cried in many tongues as needles long and sharp
Advanced.
Their blood ran very red and so they died.

We thought we had seen it all.

Our souls shrank deep and deeper still,
Until with nowhere else to go, soft hearts
Hardened and cocooned themselves.
Laughter broke like glass over fields and orchards
And from tent to tent.
We tried; we really tried, but some they died.

We thought we had seen it all.

Until Belsen

There are no words to speak.
We hid within our souls, deep and silent.
We clung together trying to understand,
The smell pervaded the mind and the sights and sounds
Reached those souls buried deep within and for so long
Encased in rock.
Bitter, scalding tears melted the rock
Our hearts were broken.

We had seen it all.

CHLORIS HEATON ROSS

Spring in Russell Square
(LAST SUMMER A FLYING-BOMB FELL IN THE SQUARE)

The stricken tree puts out small flags of green,
Brave bunting strung to fete the Spring again;
Torn bush and broken bench are sweet with rain,
New lit with colours pastoral and clean.

Roll Winter's stone away! Recharged the air
Is urgent like a rush of joyous feet,
As if God's trumpets blazed above the street
A sign. The grey old houses seem aware,

And shabby folk make pause before they pass
To see the all-forgiving green unfold,
The Word fulfilled: O mortal man, behold
The resurrection in each blade of grass!

MARION COLEMAN

From 1944 Marion Coleman, a doctor, worked with the Catholic Committee for Relief Abroad in a camp near Bari, southern Italy.

Monte Cassino 1945

The old, snow-summitted mountains
stand back in the spring light,
sheltering wide plains.
Here white almond flower shakes on the wind,
pruned vines and figs swell knotty buds,
green corn presses under the olives,
willow canes spring yellow from pollard trunks.
The road steps among fields and villages,
twists round little hills,
runs up and down through high towns
built in dangerous days
when life was hunted by death.

The houses are broken, wasted,
fields and trees wounded, killed.
Crosses crowd where corn grew,
sprouted from bodies hurriedly buried,
sown deep and thick in the raked soil.
Warm air distils
a scent, not of flowers and young leaves,
but of putrid decay,
heavy as magnolia, horribly rotten.
Pools shine among splintered stones,
life remaking in their scum.
Behind fragmented buildings, the grey mountain
leans scored, and split, and shaken.

Where light shone, order and praise sang softly,
years of learning were stored
like honey gold in the comb,
now is only bomb-struck desolation.
Death has leapt upon life,
and the shriek of the encounter
echoes on and on through silence
for ever.

MARGARET WILLY

The Reprieved
(9TH MAY, 1,945: VICTORY IN EUROPE)

We, who six springs were wrung by the world's sorrow,
Snatched each frail, threatened joy from war's red
    spite,
Nor dared to hope, or build some brave tomorrow,
Seeing love's sun eclipsed in starless night —
We live, reprieved, to day-dream in the heather,
and watch May's antic wind leap through the wood.
    Today, full heart and heightened sense together
Exultantly affirm that earth is good.

Yet other youth which praised this kindly sunlight
Encountered the bomb's searing splinter; died
In icy seas; far in the parching desert
Moaned at the last for some green countryside . . .
    Wondering, O soul who weathered this blind strife,
Bow for your precious privilege of life!

VERA BAX

A week after V-E Day Vera Bax lost a second son serving in the Royal Air Force. Wing Commander William David Loraine Filson-Young, DFC and Bar, was killed near Singapore, aged twenty-five.

To Billy, my son
(KILLED IN ACTION, MAY 15, 1945)

Now comes, indeed, the end of all delight,
The end of forward-looking on life's way,
The end of all desire to pierce the night
For gleam of hope, the end of all things gay;
The end of any promise Spring might hold,
The end of praying and, O God, the end
Of love that waited to be shared and told;
Now, evermore, shall life with sorrow blend;
That sorrow whose dark shape the months had fought,
And strictly kept in confines of the will;
Had held quiescent while each conscious thought
Searched far horizons where joy lingered still;
But, my beloved, fearless, gallant, true,
Here is fair end of sorrow, now, for you.

ALICE FRANCES BARRY

A Prisoner Returns – 1945

I had forgotten how the lacey foam
Edges the floating garment of the sea,
Grey fluted folds, green shot, and spangle sewn,
Seem lit in lavish generosity.
I had forgotten how beneath those waves
The careless bells of youth are ringing still,
And thunder from a thousand hidden caves
Wakes gentle echoes from each placid hill.
I had forgotten how the scent of thyme
Lures to the pink-flowered margin of the peak;
Thyme and the free salt air of Northern clime
Can purify all taint of city reek.
Watching, with face uplifted to the sky,
The weaving of white wings across the blue,
I had forgotten how the shrill sweet cry
From those wild throats has power to pierce me through.
Now I may tread again the sandy shore
Where my tired heart belongs; the past dead years
Are buried, and, with these dear loves once more,
I have forgotten all their sad arrears.

WRENNE JARMAN

Threnody for Berlin – 1945

Was there no mute to mourn this crumpled city,
No funeral drape, no stern bell left to toll? –
Does it pass unattended, without pity,
No requiem said for its delinquent soul?

There where the wind plays through the broken copings
And toppled keystones mark the death of streets,
Her veins lie open to the vultures' droppings;
The blood coagulates, and no heart beats.

Go barehead, even her slaves, in this quenched hour –
No Sodom raked to ash five thousand years
Is deader than this mortuum of power,
Watched, in its final rigor, without tears.

MARGARET CROSLAND

Margaret Crosland corresponded with a man she had met while working as a voluntary part-timer in the National Fire Service. In 1945 a letter was returned to her with a message scribbled on the envelope.

Reported Missing
(For G.H.)

Over our blue and idle trees
came refugee clouds from France
in the complacent summer wind.

The torn land sagging at the knees,
the fountains die in the broken towns
and the men rot, till the fires come.

Four years since you died with these,
without hope or thought of heroics
gone out from time to silence.

There was time to take our reckoning,
all Europe dulled with racing guns,
and each day was a heavy knife.

Now, with the new earth-stirring
a living spring breeds in the village
and banners blossom in the town.

You will not know this quickening,
will not exist for these who march –
but your life is a chord in their song.

EDITH SITWELL

The atomic bomb dropped by an American bomber on the city of Hiroshima killed 80,000 instantly. An area of 5 square miles was reduced to ashes and about 60,000 buildings were destroyed.

From 'Dirge for the New Sunrise'

(FIFTEEN MINUTES PAST EIGHT O'CLOCK, ON THE MORNING OF MONDAY THE 6TH AUGUST 1945)

. . . There was a morning when the holy Light
Was young. The beautiful First Creature came
To our water-springs, and thought us without blame.

Our hearts seemed safe in our breasts and sang to the
   Light –
The marrow in the bone
We dreamed was safe . . . the blood in the veins, the
   sap in the tree
   Were springs of Deity.

But I saw the little Ant-men as they ran
Carrying the world's weight of the world's filth
And the filth in the heart of Man –
Compressed till those lusts and greeds had a greater
   heat than that of the Sun.

And the ray from that heat came soundless, shook the sky
As if in search of food, and squeezed the stems
Of all that grows on the earth till they were dry
– And drank the marrow of the bone:
The eyes that saw, the lips that kissed, are gone
Or black as thunder lie and grin at the murdered Sun.

The living blind and seeing Dead together lie
As if in love . . . There was no more hating then.
And no more love: Gone is the heart of Man . . .

VERA BAX

The Fallen
(V.J. DAY, AUGUST 15, 1945)

Have no self-pity now for loneliness;
Permit no tear, no sad, recalling sigh
For these, the dead, who counted all things less
Than honour, and the courage so to die;
Remembering that age too seldom gives
What youth has dreamed: our hopes are mostly vain
And fortunate indeed is he who lives
Forever young, beyond the reach of pain.
Yours is the sorrow, heart that still must beat,
Yours is the heavy burden of the day,
Yours the long battle now against defeat,
Be not less steadfast in the fight than they;
Nor shun the throng: their spirits linger there,
Whose laughter rang so gaily on the air.

ANGELA BOLTON

In June 1945 Angela Bolton was posted to the Combined Military Hospital in Dibrugarh in the north-east of Assam. Three weeks after Japan surrendered she went on short leave to Calcutta. She flew in a decrepit Dakota thick with dried mud and observed a scene which filled her 'with a sense of the utter futility of war': '. . . I became aware of a row of elderly men in crushed khaki with pale weary faces staring blankly into space, their bodies slumped into attitudes of despondency . . . They were high-ranking British officers who had been taken prisoner in the Far East early in 1942 . . . They looked so weak and thin.'

The Generals

Generals seven* from Singapore
   Netted in the tide of war,
Left to rot in Nippon's jails
   Four long years, like stranded whales.

Pale of eye and grey of face,
   Staring blankly into space,
Slumped in attitudes of care
   Each wrapped in his own despair.

Travel-stained but wearing still
   Crushed and threadbare khaki drill.
Here at last they join the quota
   In the battered old Dakota.

Generals of advancing years,
   Prey to memories and fears,
Cheated of post-mortem glory.
   I at least shall tell your story.

Loving you across the plane
   As you face the world again.
Generals seven from Singapore
   Netted in the tide of war.

* Major General Callaghan, Major General Key, Major General Macrae, Major General Maltby, Lieutenant General Sir Louis Heath, Major General Keith Simmonds and Major General Stilwell.

Angela Bolton sailed from Bombay on the troopship Franconia *on 1 November 1945. She wrote in her diary: 'We lined the ship's rail looking back on the "Gateway to India" in silence, each coping with his or her emotional response: some glad to escape from a country where they had felt completely alienated; some with nostalgic memories of people and places; others oblivious to everything but the longing for home and family. A sadness as with the close of some great epic drama settled on my heart . . .'*

Return from India by Way of the Suez Canal

Blue haze over the sandstone hills
Of barren Arabia's Bible land.
   Drab are the garments its people wear,
   Dazzled and drugged in the sun's mad stare,
Shimmering light through the dust-laden air
Separates camels from sand.

Remember the comrades who rounded the Cape,
Four long years and a war ago.
   (Over Egypt the orange sky
   Flickers and fades as our ship goes by)
The dreams of the dead are our dreams now
Through us they must flourish and grow.

We sailed out East with the freedom of youth,
Came back with a focused view.
   Cheered by the vessels on either side,
   Out of the barbarous port we glide,
Into the arms of the West once more,
Into the Mediterranean's blue.

IDA PROCTER

The One

In the mass is the one.
In the thousand drowned,
In the hundred shot,
In the five crashed,
Is the one.
Over the news
Falls the shadow
Of the one.

We cannot weep
At tragedy for millions
But for one.
In the mind
For the mind's life
The one lives on.

Propaganda

This thought
I think I think
Is not my thought
But the thought
Of one
Who thought
I ought
To think his thought.

SARAH STAFFORD

The Unborn

Will the tree bloom again, and the red field
Suffer the soft invasion of the wheat?
Will the bomb-crater be a standing pool
Where little boys catch minnows? Will the town
Cover its scars and ring its bells again?
Shall we have peace at morning, and at noon
No gun to shake the quiet of the hills?
And in the dusty lane, no bullets' hail,
Only the small, sweet clamour of the birds?
All this shall come, and we have peace again,
A haunted peace, for we have done a thing
The ancient gods, in all their wrath, had wept for.
We have robbed the world of a myriad human faces
And twice a myriad beauty-making hands.
For in the bodies of the slain in battle
And in the dark wombs of the mourning women
Lie lovely nations, never to be born.
Some, it may be, better unborn, but some
Irreparable losses, and for these,
Not in eternity can we atone.
Not in eternity can we remember
The song unsung, nor read the word unwritten,
Nor see the coloured landscape through the eyes
And the warm minds of artists never born.
So, when a man lays down his lusty life
To save his land, he says with dying breath,
'Here, people, since you need it, is my life
And my son's life, yes, and my son's son's life,
And my wife's joy, and all our sums of joy
And God knows what of richness and delight
That might have flowed from me. You make me now,
In death, a sad, perpetual Abraham –
Slaying my son, slaying my son forever.
You know there is no thicket and no ram
And no reprieving angel at my side.'

DAPHNE NIXON

In These Five Years

In these five years
we grew,
out of the mire of ease,
into the rhythm of reality;
we came alive,
and part of this new world,
in which the fact of life and death
discarded frill and fantasy.
We saw our lovers,
and our brothers go to war,
heard their defeats with fear,
their gains with adulation,
but outside the circle of their lives,
the whole was lost
to the small infinities of our minds.

So the years have wandered,
winding us into the pattern,
until we learnt the meaning
of our life and theirs.
The anchor of our homes
lie far behind,
we are, as we can make ourselves,
without surrounding prejudice.

To be a woman now
it is expected that you live
like men,
and work like men,
yet struggle always to remain
fundamentally feminine.
But in our new born hearts,
has grown the urge to act
in equal part of fight and fear,
we want no time to weep,
only the wasted hours bring despair.

And we have learnt
submission,
to have our lives laid out
not by personality,
but by position,
with undefeated soul
we have our minds,
and they are still ours
to control.

Out of the chrysalis we came,
young and foolish,
eager and undecided,
if we have hardened,
fought to brush aside
the heartache and the fear,
should we be blamed?
learning endurance even men have changed,
and these five years have been strong stuff
to give these women.

PHOEBE HESKETH

Post-War Christmas

Lean forward Spring and touch these iron trees
And they will come to life!
Unchain the fettered stream, bring warmth to ease
The wounds of Winter's knife.
Lean forward Spring, and I will learn your art
Which out of love has grown.
(War, my life's Winter took my living heart,
And left a heart of stone.)
And though the bright drops on the holly tree
For ageless Christmas shine,
And though the world was saved through agony,
I faint through mine.
For he whose love once bore my grief away,
And made his joy my own,
Sleeps this cold Christmas in a colder clay,
And I must wake alone.
But if a new design for those who mourn
Is shaped through pain,
O Spring, lean forward with creative hands,
And hew this stone again!

Biographical Notes

ACKLAND, VALENTINE (1906–69)
Born Mary Kathleen Macrory Ackland in London. Daughter of a London dentist. Educated at Queen's College, London and in Paris. She became Sylvia Townsend Warner's lover in 1930 and they lived most of their years together in Dorset. In 1935 she became a member of the Communist Party of Great Britain until her resignation in 1953; a few years later she returned to the Roman Catholic Church. During the war she was a clerk with the Territorial Army, Secretary to the Controller of the Civil Defence Unit in Dorchester and worked in a local doctor's dispensary. She became a Quaker shortly before her death from breast cancer.

ALLAN, MABEL ESTHER (b. 1915)
Born in Wallasey, Cheshire. Privately educated. During the war she served in the Women's Land Army in Cheshire and then became warden of the nursery in a Liverpool slum school. She wrote thrillers and novels for children.

ALLFREY, PHYLLIS SHAND (1908–86)
Born on the Caribbean island of Dominica where her father Francis Shand was Crown Attorney. Left the island in 1927. Married Robert Allfrey in 1930. They lived between the USA and Great Britain. She was a member of the Labour Party and Fabian Colonial Bureau. She worked for the London County Council as a welfare adviser to those bombed out of their homes during the war. Returned to Dominica in 1954. Founded the Dominica Labour Party which came to power in 1958. She became the West Indian Federation's only white woman minister. Wrote poetry, novels and short stories.

ANDERSON, MARY DÉSIRÉE (1902–73)
Born in Great Shelford, Cambridgeshire. Daughter of Sir Hugh Anderson, Master of Gonville and Caius College, Cambridge. Wrote poetry from an early age. Married Trenchard Cox in 1935. Lived in London during war and then in Birmingham between 1944 and 1955, when her husband was Director of Birmingham Museum and Art Gallery. He was Director of the Victoria and Albert Museum between 1956 and 1966 and was knighted in 1961.

ARLETT, VERA ISABEL (b. 1896)
Born in Wolverhampton. Playwright and poet. Contributor to magazines. Received the Medal for Lyric Poetry at Liverpool University in 1931. She lived in Worthing, Sussex.

ARUNDEL, HONOR (1919–73)
Born in Llanarmon, Gwynedd, North Wales. Educated at Hayes Court, Kent and Somerville College, Oxford. On staff of *Daily Worker* for a year before being called up. Worked as a fitter in an engineering factory. Married Alex McCrindle in 1952. Journalist and film, radio and theatre critic.

BARRY, ALICE FRANCES (1861–1951)
Granddaughter of Sir Charles Barry who designed the Houses of Parliament. Her grandmother laid the foundation stone of the new buildings in 1850. Lived in Worthing, Sussex and was a friend of Vera Arlett (q.v.).

BARTON, JOAN (1908–*c.* 1986)
Born in Bristol and educated at Colston's Girls School, and Bristol University. Between 1936 and 1947 worked with the BBC in Bristol; county secretary for the Women's Land Army in Hampshire and worked for the British Council. In 1947 she started the White Horse Bookshop in Marlborough in partnership with Barbara Watson. In 1967 she moved to Salisbury and continued bookselling until her death. Poems read on BBC television and Radio 3 and published in many periodicals; one poem included in *The Oxford Book of Twentieth Century English Verse*.

BAX, VERA (1890–1974)
Daughter of Colonel Claud Rawnsley. Studied at Royal College of Art. First married to the artist Stanley North and had one son. Divorced and married Alexander Bell Filson-Young in 1918, a journalist and editor of the *Saturday Review* and advisor to John Reith, Director of BBC. Their two sons were killed during the Second World War. In 1936 she married the writer Clifford Bax. She was a member of the Poets' Club and a portrait painter. Her work was exhibited by the Royal Society of Portrait Painters and at many London galleries.

BEECHAM, AUDREY (1915–89)
Educated at Wycombe Abbey and Somerville College, Oxford. Briefly involved with the Catalonian anarchists in Spain during the summer vacation of 1936. Taught and worked as a researcher at Oxford University between 1940 and 1950. Active in Women's Home Defence in Oxford during the war. Between 1950 and 1980 she was at the University of Nottingham until her retirement in Oxford.

BELLERBY, FRANCES (1899–1975)
Born in Bristol. Daughter of the Reverend F. Talbot Parker. Educated at Mortimer House School, Clifton. Her brother was killed in France in August

1915. She worked as a kennel-maid and later became tutor to the Fry family in Bristol. In 1927 she worked on the staff of the *Bristol Times and Mirror* in London. In 1929 she married an economist, John Rotherford Bellerby. She injured her spine in an accident in 1930 and was crippled for the rest of her life. Frances Bellerby and her husband became pacifists in the early 1930s and she became a Quaker in 1934. She parted from her husband in 1948 and lived on her own in Cornwall. She recovered from an operation and treatment for cancer in both breasts and in 1955 moved to Goveton, near Kingsbridge in Devon where she lived until her death. She wrote one novel, several volumes of short stories and six books of poetry.

BERINGTON, OLGUITA QUEENY (1899–1981)
Née Queeny. Born in St Louis, Missouri. Married Thomas Patrick Berington of Little Malvern Court, near Malvern, Worcestershire. During the war she lived at Whitmead, Tilford in Surrey which became a home for Canadian airmen and where she wrote her poetry. She and her husband returned to the family seat at the end of the 1950s and restored much of Little Malvern Court to its original medieval condition.

BERRIDGE, ELIZABETH (b. 1921)
Born in London. Spent the war years in London and Wales raising a family, writing and helping her husband Reginald Moore publish his literary magazines, of which *Modern Reading* was the most important. Her husband died in 1990. She has written nine novels, the latest *Touch and Go*, 1995; four have been re-issued in paperback; she has also produced two collections of short stories. Fiction reviewer for the *Daily Telegraph* from 1964 to 1989. Contributor to BBC Radio 3 and 4. Her short stories from the 1940s are to be reprinted by Persephone Books in the near future. She was elected a Fellow of the Royal Society of Literature in 1999.

BOLTON, ANGELA (b. 1918)
Née Noblet. Born in Preston, Lancashire. Educated at Winckley Square Convent, Preston. Trained as a nurse at hospitals on Merseyside and Manchester; spent a year as a staff nurse in a hospital in Surrey. In 1942 she was commissioned in the Queen Alexandra's Imperial Military Nursing Service (Reserve) and posted to India. She nursed British, Indian, West African, American, Chinese and Japanese casualties in military hospitals and hospital river steamers in Bengal and Assam. She met her husband Captain James Bolton not long before she left India, when he was serving in the Royal Artillery. She spent most of her married life in Oxford where she worked as a

nursing sister at Balliol College; her husband taught classics at Queen's College, Oxford; he died in 1981. She has four children, twelve grandchildren and four great-grandsons.

BOWES LYON, LILIAN (1895–1949)
Born in Northumberland. A granddaughter of the 13th Earl of Strathmore and cousin of Queen Elizabeth the Queen Mother. Served as a VAD in the First World War. Farmed in Dorset and lived abroad. During the Second World War she helped in rehousing the bombed, worked in canteens and shelters and in the evacuation of children from the East End of London. She was nicknamed 'the Angel of Stepney' for her work during the Blitz. After the war she was severely crippled and had both her legs amputated. She wrote several volumes of poetry.

BRIGGS, GRETA
Lived in Clacton-on-Sea, Essex, with her two sisters. Greta wrote poetry; one sister wrote girls' books under her own name, Phyllis, and books for boys under the name Philip Briggs; the other sister worked for the BBC.

BRITTAIN, VERA (1893–1970)
Born in Newcastle under Lyme, Staffordshire. Family owned a paper mill. Spent most of her childhood in Buxton. Educated at St Monica's, Kingswood, and Somerville College, Oxford. She served as a VAD during the First World War. Returned to Oxford at the end of the war. She became a pacifist and a prolific writer. Married George Catlin, Professor of Politics at Cornell University in 1925. Two children; their daughter Shirley Williams became a politician and was created Baroness Williams of Crosby.

BRYAN, SARAH
No biographical information.

BRYHER (PSEUDONYM OF WINIFRED ELLERMAN) (1894–1983)
Daughter of a wealthy shipping magnate. Her pseudonym comes from the name of one of the Scilly Islands where she spent many holidays. She spent the war years in London. After the American poet Hilda Doolittle (H.D.) parted from the poet Richard Aldington in 1918, Bryher became her companion; they travelled widely and lived together until H.D.'s death in 1961; Bryher was twice married; first to Robert McAlmon, the American writer and publisher, and then to H.D.'s lover Kenneth Macpherson; they lived in a ménage à trois and the Macphersons adopted Perdita, H.D.'s daughter by Cecil Gray. Novelist, poet and patron of the arts.

BULLEY, ANNE (b. 1922)
Educated at St Swithun's, Winchester. Trained as a VAD; worked in the War Office. Served in the WRNS in Ceylon. After the war she went up to Oxford. Married Alan Maier in 1948. Became a potter and latterly a history researcher. Her *Selected Poems* were published by The Lomond Press in 1980, *Free Mariner* was published in 1993 and *Bombay Country Ships 1790–1833* is to be published in autumn 1999. She has four children and twelve grandchildren.

BURTON, DORIS (b. 1894)
Born in Bishop's Stortford, Essex. Educated privately and in Switzerland. Writer on Catholic subjects.

CARTLAND, BARBARA (b. 1901)
Father, Major Bertram Cartland, killed in First World War. Her first novel published in 1923. Member of the WVS, Chief Lady Welfare Officer to the Services and a county cadet officer for the St John Ambulance Brigade in Bedfordshire during the war. Tireless social and charity worker in many parts of the world. Married twice; to Alexander McCorquodale in 1927, marriage dissolved in 1933; and to Hugh McCorquodale in 1936. Author of over 600 books; 650 million sold worldwide; books translated in 23 languages; won the world record in 1994, for the 21st year, for an average of 23 books published annually. Created a Dame of the British Empire in 1991 for her contribution to literature and her work for humanitarian and charitable causes.

CAWDOR, WILMA (1906–82)
Daughter of Vincent Vickers. Married The Earl Cawdor in 1929. He commanded a battalion of The Queen's Own Cameron Highlanders in France until June 1940. Wilma Cawdor was an ardent Francophile during and after the war.

CHAMBERLAIN, BRENDA (1912–71)
Born in Bangor, North Wales. A distant relative of Neville Chamberlain. Educated Bangor County School for Girls and Royal Academy of Art. Married the artist John Petts in 1935. They ran the Caseg Press from their primitive cottage in Snowdonia. John Petts became a conscientious objector at the beginning of the war. They separated in 1943. Three years later she went to live with a young Frenchman on Ynys Enlli, Bardsey Island, 6 miles off the Llyn Peninsular where her work as a writer and artist flourished. In 1962 her book *Tide-Race* based on her eighteen years on Bardsey was

published. From 1962 she lived on the Greek island Ydra for five years. She spent the last four years of her life in Bangor.

CHERRILL, MAUD (1877–1947)
Born in Hampstead. Daughter of the Reverend A.K. Cherrill. Taught English at Hoe Preparatory School in Plymouth. In 1912 she and her colleague Ann Vivian founded St Petroc's Preparatory School at Bude, North Cornwall, on an initial capital of £5. They continued as co-principals until 1944 when they retired to a little stone house at Gentle Jane overlooking the Camel Estuary near Rock, Cornwall.

CHURCHILL, SARAH (1914–82)
Daughter of Winston Churchill. Became a dancer and an actress. Served in the WAAF as an aircraftwoman and then an officer during the war. Resumed her acting career in 1946. Married three times: the actor Vic Oliver, Antony Beauchamp, who died in 1957, and Lord Audley who died in 1963.

COATS, ALICE (1905–78)
Born in Birmingham. Educated at Edgbaston High School for Girls, Birmingham College of Art, the Slade School and in Paris. Served in the Women's Land Army in Warwickshire during the war. Artist and writer on horticulture.

COLEMAN, MARION (b. 1898)
Educated at Derby High School and Cheltenham Ladies' College. Became a doctor and worked in the East End of London and in Hull. In 1944 she joined the Catholic Committee for Relief Abroad and was sent to a camp near Bari in southern Italy. Later worked with Save the Children Fund in Germany and Poland. After the war she became a psychologist and worked in Gloucester and London.

CORFIELD, JOY (b. 1925)
Born in Manchester. Joined the ATS in 1944. Married in 1947. Disabled by polio in 1950.

CORNFORD, FRANCES (1886–1960)
Born in Cambridge. Daughter of Sir Francis Darwin and granddaughter of Charles Darwin. Privately educated. Married in 1909 to Francis Cornford, Fellow of Trinity College, Cambridge. Their son John fought for the Spanish Republicans and was killed in 1936. Apart from travelling occasionally she spent her life in Cambridge. Published several volumes of poetry.

CROSLAND, MARGARET
Born in Shropshire. Moved to Cumbria when her father became a senior mathematics teacher and writer of mathematical text books. A student at the Royal Holloway College, London University between 1938 and 1941; wrote poetry while working for her BA in French. Civil servant and volunteer with the National Fire Service during the war. Became a freelance writer and translator. Wrote first biographies in English of Colette and Jean Cocteau; biographies of Edith Piaf and Simone de Beauvoir; poetry has been published in the *Spectator*, the *Observer*, the *New Statesman* and the *Evening Standard*.

CRUIKSHANK, NORAH K.
Driver in the ATS attached to the Royal Army Service Corps in Norfolk between 1941–45. German scholar.

CUNARD, NANCY (1896–1965)
Daughter of Sir Bache Cunard, the shipping magnate. Married briefly in 1916. Lived in Paris during the 1920s and 1930s. In 1928 she founded the Hours Press at her home in Normandy and published many prominent writers of the time including Richard Aldington, Samuel Beckett and Ezra Pound. She worked for the Associated Negro Press of the United States; love affair with Henry Crowder, a black pianist. She compiled a Negro anthology in 1934. During the Spanish Civil war she was a reporter on the Republican side. Worked for the Free French in London during the Second World War.

DANE, CLEMENCE (PSEUDONYM OF WINIFRED ASHTON) (1888–1965)
Born in Greenwich, London. Educated in England, Germany and Switzerland. Studied art in Dresden and at the Slade School. In 1913 started a career on the stage under the name of Diana Cortis. After the First World War she became a novelist, her pseudonym taken from St Clement Dane's Church which symbolised her love for London. After initial success her reputation as a playwright dwindled but she continued to write novels and to paint. She was appointed CBE in 1953.

DAVID, LISBETH (b. 1923)
Born in Wales. Educated at Howell's School. Joined WRNS in 1942. Based in Dundee as a trainee wireless telegraphy operator. Commissioned 1943. Cypher officer on staff of NCSO, at Bangor, County Down, and C-in-C Portsmouth and C-in-C East Indies; stationed in Colombo, Ceylon, between April and December 1945. After the war gained MA in Theology at St Hugh's College,

Oxford. Worked in industry and government service. Since retirement in 1983 many activities including Chairman of the Llandaff Society and a Welcomer at Llandaff Cathedral.

DAWES, WINIFRED
No biographical information.

DE BAIRACLI-LEVY, JULIETTE
Born in Manchester. Father Turkish and mother Egyptian. Educated at Withington Girls' High School, Manchester, and Lowther College, North Wales. Studied biology and veterinary medicine at Manchester and Liverpool Universities. Served in the Forestry Section of the Women's Land Army during the war. Her brother and childhood sweetheart were killed during the war and many French relatives died in the holocaust. She became a farmer, botanist, tree physician, practising herbalist and writer on herbal medicine for animals and humans. Settled on the island of Kythera, Greece.

DOLPHIN, MAY I.E.
Poetry of the First World War published during the 1920s.

DOUGLAS, MARY
No biographical information.

DOYLE, CAMILLA (1888–1944)
Born in The Close, Norwich. Daughter of a surgeon. Educated at the Girls' High School, Norwich. Studied at the Slade School and in Paris. Paintings shown at many exhibitions. Lived in Rickmansworth from late 1920s, where she continued to paint and became an established poet; returned to Norwich at the beginning of the war and lived in The Close until her death.

FITZROY, OLIVIA (1921–69)
Born in Christchurch, Dorset. Daughter of Captain the Hon R.O. FitzRoy, who later became Viscount Daventry. Spent her youth at Rockingham Castle. Summer holidays in the highlands of Scotland. Educated at home by a governess. Worked in the library of a London store at the beginning of the war. Served in the WRNS as a fighter direction officer at Yeovilton between 1943 and 1944; Ceylon from the summer of 1944 until late 1945. Travelled with Chipperfield's Circus between 1947 and 1950 to research for her book *Wagons and Horses*, which was published in 1955. Lived in a rented croft in the highlands of Scotland between 1951 and 1956. Married Sir Geoffrey Bates, Bt.

in 1957 and lived in North Wales. Her seven books about the same Scottish family were published between 1942 and 1956; the *Official History of the VIIIth King's Royal Irish Hussars, 1927–1958* was published in 1961.

FRIEDLAENDER, V.H.
Novelist and poet. Wrote poetry during the First World War; reviewed poetry for *Country Life* and other periodicals.

FURSE, JILL (1915–44)
Daughter of Sir Ralph Furse. Granddaughter of the poet Sir Henry Newbolt. Educated in England and Switzerland. Trained as an actress at the Central School. Acting career on the West End stage between 1935 and 1942 showed great promise but was interrupted by intermittent illness, now thought to have been lupus erythematosus. Married Laurence Whistler, the writer and glass-engraver, in 1939. Lived in north Devon and in London during the Blitz. She died a few days after giving birth to their baby daughter.

GALE, ADRIENNE
Lived in Seascale, Cumberland.

GIBBS, BEATRICE RUTH (b. 1894)
Born in Stoodley, Devon. Educated at St Margaret's School, Exeter, and Sherborne School for Girls. Became co-principal of Somerville School, St Leonards, Sussex. Journalist, poet, writer of short stories and books for children.

GRAHAM, VIRGINIA (1910–92)
Born in London. Daughter of Harry Graham, a playwright and lyricist. Educated at Notting Hill High School and privately. During the Second World War she worked with the Women's Voluntary Service as a driver. Contributed to various newspapers and magazines, including *Punch*, and from 1946 was film critic for the *Spectator* for ten years. From childhood she was a close friend of Joyce Grenfell (q.v.) and composed songs for her shows. She married Anthony Thesiger in 1939.

GRANTHAM, ALEXANDRA ETHELDREDA
Poet of the First World War. Writer on Chinese history and art. Married Captain Frederick William Grantham. One of their sons was killed in Gallipoli in June 1915 and another son, an artist, was killed serving in the RAF in June 1942.

GRENFELL, JOYCE (1910–79)

Née Phipps. Born in London. Father an architect. Mother was the sister of Nancy Astor. Educated at Francis Holland School, London, and the Christian Science School in South Norwood and in Paris. Married Reginald Grenfell when she was nineteen. Discovered by Herbert Farjeon, she appeared in three of his revues, the first being *The Little Revue* in 1939. From then on she had many successes on the stage, radio and television. Her range of monologue characters and enormous sense of fun provided rare entertainment. During the war she was a welfare officer at the Canadian Red Cross Hospital at Cliveden; in 1943 she went on the first of two long tours abroad; she performed in hospitals and isolated service units for the Entertainments National Service Association (ENSA) in Malta, Algiers, Sicily, Italy, India and Egypt. During the 1950s she toured the world with her two-hour solo programme. She was a close friend of Virginia Graham (q.v.) for over sixty years; they wrote daily letters to each other whenever they were apart. She retired from the stage in 1973. She was a lifelong Christian Scientist. Appointed OBE in 1946.

GRIFFITHS, GRACE (b. 1921)

Born in Bow, Devon. Educated at Crediton High School. Became a librarian in Exeter Library in 1939. Joined ATS in 1942. Stationed at Shenley, Hertfordshire, and Harrogate. After the war became Librarian at the Teignmouth Branch of the Devon County Library and was later appointed Area Children's Schools' Librarian in South Devon. Wrote *History of Teignmouth* and a number of children's books. Retired in 1981.

HALLETT, OLIVE

No biographical information.

HARRISON, MARY E. (b. 1921)

Born in Derbyshire. Served in the WAAF at Watnall, Nottinghamshire; RAF Nuneham Courteney, Oxfordshire; RAF Medmenham, Buckinghamshire.

HASKINS, MINNIE (1875–1957)

Educated at Clarendon College, Clifton, and the London School of Economics. Poet of the First World War. Taught in London and in India. Tutor at the London School of Economics until she retired in 1944.

HAWKINS, AILEEN (b. 1916)

Born in Dorchester, Dorset. Father William Clough was killed on 1 July 1916, the first day of the Battle of the Somme, when she was three months old. Educated Dorchester County School. As a child met Thomas Hardy at Max Gate. She was an air-raid warden in Weymouth between 1940 and 1942; served as an ATS sergeant in a Heavy Anti-Aircraft Battery of the Royal Artillery on the east coast between 1942 and 1945. Married Edgar William Spencer Hawkins in 1943. Some of her poems written in the Dorset dialect.

HAYCOCK, MYFANWY (1913–63)
Born at Pontnewynydd, near Pontypool, Monmouthshire. Trained at Cardiff School of Art. Freelance journalist, often contributing illustrated poems. During the war became a wages clerk in a munitions factory; a welfare officer in a barrage-balloon factory in Cardiff; an art teacher; a publicity officer in an agricultural college. The last years of the war were spent working for the BBC in London when two of her plays and readings of her poems were broadcast. After the war she returned to freelance writing and illustrating; contributed poems, articles and drawings to national newspapers and magazines; she won several Bardic chairs and on several occasions read her poems on television. Married Dr A.M. Williams, a consultant anaesthetist.

HEBGIN, DAME SCHOLASTICA SYBIL OSB (1894–1973)
Born at Ringland, Norfolk, of East Anglian yeoman stock. Between 1912 and 1915 studied in the Honours English school of Bedford College, London. Became a Catholic during her final year. Worked in a War office in the City between 1915 and 1917. Became a nun at Stanbrook Abbey, Worcestershire, in 1917. Anglo-Saxon and High German scholar. Translated and edited Aelfric's Latin Grammar, one of the treasures of the Worcester Cathedral Library.

HERBERTSON, AGNES GROZIER
Born in Oslo, Norway. Educated privately. Novelist, poet, playwright, writer of short stories and books for children.

HESKETH, PHOEBE (b. 1909)
Born in Preston, Lancashire. Daughter of pioneer radiologist, A.E. Rayner. Educated at Southport and Cheltenham Ladies' College. Married in 1931; three children. During the war she was the women's page editor of the *Bolton Evening News*; looked after evacuees and was a member of the WVS. Taught general studies at the Women's College, Bolton, in the late 1960s and creative writing at Bolton School in the late 1970s. Journalist, BBC scriptwriter, contributor to periodicals; published nine volumes of poetry and two volumes of prose. Elected Fellow of the Royal Society of Literature in 1956.

HEWLETT, AUDREY
Served in the East Sussex branch of the Women's Land Army during the war.

HILLS, JANET (1919–56)
Born at Epsom. Daughter of a doctor. Educated at Stroud High School for Girls, Sidcot and Westonbirt. Went up to Somerville College, Oxford, as a German scholar in 1937 and graduated in 1940. Joined the WRNS and served as an officer in intelligence and then education. At the end of the war spent a year with the British Military Government in Berlin. Became a freelance journalist; in 1949 joined the staff of *The Times Educational Supplement* as a general reporter and feature writer, specialising in school drama and films. She returned to freelance writing in 1951, continued to write regular film articles for the TES and contributed articles to the arts page of *The Times*. A month before she died she had been appointed viewer research officer to the Children's Advisory Committee of the Independent Television Authority.

HOLDEN, MOLLY (1927–81)
Née Gilbert. Granddaughter of the novelist Henry Gilbert. Educated King's College, London. Married Alan Holden, a schoolmaster, in 1949. One son and one daughter. Developed multiple sclerosis and became an invalid in 1964. Wrote poetry and children's novels.

HOLMES, PAMELA
Educated at Benenden School. Lived in Ashford, Kent, during the war. Her first husband Lieutenant F.C. Hall, Rifle Brigade was killed in December 1942; she later married Major Dennis Holmes, Rifle Brigade and their son is Richard Holmes, the biographer. Some of her poems first appeared in *The Sunday Times*, the *Poetry Review*, *Country Life*, the *Spectator*, the *Countryman*, *South East Arts*, the *Literary Review*, the *Field*, *Shepway Writers* and various other magazines and anthologies.

HOOLEY, TERESA (1888–1973)
Born at Risley Lodge, Derbyshire. Father squire of the village and a Justice of the Peace. Educated privately and at Howard College, Bedford. Became a well-known public speaker. Commonwealth Party candidate for Taunton before 1945 general election but stood down in favour of Labour Party candidate. Poems published in national newspapers, magazines and in book form. Lived in Somerset and Derbyshire.

HUNKA, PAMELA (b. 1920)
Born in Lancashire. Became an actress and spent four years in various repertory companies before the war.

JACKSON, ADA
Born in Warwickshire. Contributed poems and articles to various newspapers and periodicals. BBC broadcast two of her poems in 1933 and she read her work on an NBC coast-to-coast broadcast in the United States. In 1943 her poem 'Behold the Jew' won the Greenwood Prize. Americans called her 'the Elizabeth Barrett Browning of our time' and in Britain E.V. Lucas named her 'the English Emily Dickinson'. Poetry published in book form.

JAMES, DIANA (b. 1926)
Born in London. Privately educated. Verse published in the *Spectator* when she was in her teens. Married Peter Gunn in 1953 and has written novels and biographies under the name Elizabeth Gunn.

JARMAN, WRENNE (d. 1953)
Great-granddaughter of the poet Robert Millhouse. Although delicate, she worked on a lathe at the Hawker Aircraft Works, Kingston, during the war. Edited the *Kensington News*. Interested in Left-wing politics and the International Youth Movement. During 1930s visited Russia, Italy and Spain and just before the war made an official tour of Germany as a guest of the Hitler Youth. She said she 'returned from all this reconnaissance sadder and wiser'. Received into the Roman Catholic Church in 1942.

JERROLD, HEBE
Served in the Timber Corps of the Women's Land Army.

JESSE, FRYNIWYD TENNYSON (1888–1958)
Daughter of a clergyman. Great-niece of Alfred, Lord Tennyson. Art student at the Newlyn School in Cornwall. Became a journalist in 1911 and was a reporter on *The Times* and the *Daily Mail*. Book reviewer for *The Times Literary Supplement* and *English Review*. Reported from the front during the First World War. Worked for the Ministry of Information, National Relief Commission and the French Red Cross. Married the playwright, H.M. Harwood in 1918. A novelist, poet and playwright.

KENMARE, DALLAS (d. 1973)
Born at Temple Balsall in Warwickshire. First stories published when she was

twelve. Worked in maternity and child welfare for many years. Novelist, poet and musician. Lived in Tangier after the war and died there.

KING, PAMELA
Born in India. Sister of the novelist Francis King. Married Conan Nicholas in 1943. One daughter. Spent working life teaching. Poetry and short stories published in periodicals.

KNOWLES, SUSANNE (b. 1911)
Born in York. Educated in Italy. Worked as a secretary in the House of Commons. Served in London Auxiliary Ambulance Service during war. Contributed to many periodicals.

LAUGHTON, FREDA (b. 1907)
Born and educated in Bristol. Twice married; first to L.E.G. Laughton and then to John Midgley.

LAWRENCE, MARGERY (c. 1885–1969)
Born in Shropshire. Father a barrister. Educated privately at home and abroad and at art schools in Birmingham, London and Paris. Married Arthur Towle, CBE. Novelist, poet and short-story writer. Shane Leslie called her 'a Bohemian who loved much'.

LEA, BARBARA (1903–45)
Née Pell. Born at Wilburton Manor, Isle of Ely. Married in 1924 and had five children. Served on numerous committees during the war including the Executive Committee of the National Federation of Women's Institutes and Chairman of the Women's Land Army in Worcestershire. She was a Justice of the Peace; awarded the OBE in 1943. She died of cancer.

LEA, MARGERY (b. 1905)
Educated at Elizabeth Gaskell College, Manchester. Taught in schools in Buckinghamshire and Manchester. Inspector of Schools in Manchester. During the war she worked with evacuee children billetted in Shropshire. Later lived in Shrewsbury, Shropshire.

LEDWARD, PATRICIA (b. 1920)
Born in London. Daughter of sculptor Gilbert Ledward, RA, OBE. Educated at St Paul's Girls' School, London, Lausanne University and Morley College, London. Worked near Fleet Street during the Blitz and for a year as an

auxiliary nurse in a sanatorium. Joined ATS in 1942. Trained as a driver near Gresford, North Wales. Poetry published in many periodicals and anthologies and co-editor of *Poems of this War by Younger Poets*, CUP, 1942. After the war worked on staff of Europa, international reference book publishers. Reviewed plays, films and exhibitions. Married Walter Simon, a publisher, in 1948 and had three children. Wrote novels, stories, articles on travel and gardens. From 1975 studied painting and exhibited with local groups.

LENDON, PAULINE (b. 1924)
Born in Hampstead. Educated at Camden School for Girls. Joined WAAF in 1941.

LEVERTOV, DENISE (1923–98)
Born in Essex. Father, a scholar, was a Russian Jew who converted to Christianity and became an Anglican priest. Privately educated at home on a small farm. Became a nurse in London during the war and met her husband Mitchell Goodman, a writer and GI. After the war they lived in France and the USA. During the Vietnam war they spoke out against the US administration; although well aware of the clash with her creative writing as a poet, as a political activist she became increasingly concerned with social issues such as third-world poverty and the anti-nuclear movement. She was divorced in 1975. From 1981 until 1994 she taught creative writing at Stanford University and lived the last few years of her life near her son in Seattle, Washington. Some thirty of her poetry titles are in print.

LEWIS, EILUNED (1900–79)
Born in Newtown, Montgomeryshire. Educated Levana School, Wimbledon and University of London. Became a Fleet Street journalist; on editorial staff of *The Sunday Times*, 1931 to 1936. Her first book *Dew on the Grass* was published in 1934. Married Graeme Hendrey, an engineer, in 1937. During the war her husband continued to work in London but they moved the family home from London to Blechingley on the Kent and Sussex borders; many Doodlebugs fell in the village and when her friend was killed by one she rescued the two small daughters from the house. She worked for the Red Cross libraries and in the local baby clinic, wrote articles and poems and her novel *A Captain's Wife* was set in Pembrokeshire. After the war she continued to write and created the monthly column 'A Countrywoman's Notes' in *Country Life*, the first of which appeared on 27 July 1945 and continued for over thirty years.

LYND, SYLVIA (1888–1952)
Born in Hampstead. Educated at King Alfred School, the Slade School and Academy of Dramatic Art. In 1909 married Robert Lynd, the Irish journalist and essayist. Poet and novelist.

MACKWORTH, CECILY
Born in Llantilo, Monmouthshire. Lived in Paris until the Germans arrived in June 1940. Her journey back to England, via Spain and Portugal, took two months. Worked for the Free French in London. Returned to France after the war. Married the Marquis de Chabannes la Palice, but is now widowed. President of the Association of Paris Welsh. Novelist, poet and journalist.

MANNING, OLIVIA (1908–80)
Born in Portsmouth. Father a retired naval officer. Maternal grandfather a slave-owner on the banks of the Missouri river. Educated at Portsmouth Grammar School. Worked in Portsmouth and then London as a typist. Under the pseudonym Jacob Morrow sold the copyright of three novels for £20 each. Married Reginald Donald Smith, a lecturer with the British Council, and lived in Romania from August 1939; escaped to Greece and then Cairo in 1941 where she was a press officer at the US Embassy; between 1943 and 1945 she was press assistant at the Public Information Office and the British Council in Jerusalem. Her only brother was killed in action during this time. Her best known works were the six novels which comprise *The Balkan Trilogy* and *The Levant Trilogy*. She was appointed CBE in 1976. Died suddenly from a stroke while on holiday on the Isle of Wight in July 1980.

MAYO, FRANCES
No biographical information.

MAYOR, BEATRICE
Born in London. In 1919 published a book of poetry on the First World War.

MITCHISON, NAOMI (1897–1999)
Née Haldane. Born in Edinburgh. Father a physiologist and philosopher. Educated at the Oxford Preparatory School (later the Dragon School) and St Anne's College, Oxford. Worked as a VAD in a London Hospital in the First World War. In 1916, aged eighteen, married Richard (Dick) Mitchison, a lawyer; he was later severely wounded in action. A feminist, member of the Fabian Society and Labour Party and stood as Labour candidate for the Scottish Universities in 1935. In 1931 her husband unsuccessfully contested the

parliamentary seat of King's Norton for the Labour Party. It was won by Barbara Cartland's brother Ronald (q.v.) for the Conservatives; Dick Mitchison was Labour MP for Kettering between 1945 and 1954 when he became a life peer. She spent the war years at their home, Carradale House on the Mull of Kintyre, farming, looking after her family and evacuees and writing. In the 1960s she became 'tribal mother' to the Bakgatla tribe in Botswana. She was active in Scottish local and regional government for many years; she supported the Scottish Nationalists, the Campaign for Nuclear Disarmament in the 1960s and the Greenham Common women in the 1980s. A prolific writer for over seventy years of articles, poetry, drama, children's books, science fiction, biographies, diaries and letters, she was best known for her historical novels. She was appointed CBE in 1985. She had seven children, two of whom died in childhood; her surviving three sons became distinguished scientists and her two daughters became writers.

NAPIER, PRISCILLA (1908–98)
Née Hayter. Father legal advisor to the Egyptian government. She spent early childhood in Cairo. Educated Downe House and Lady Margaret Hall, Oxford. Married Trevylyan Napier, a naval officer, in 1931 and lived in Malta and Dorset. Her husband died of septic endocarditis in 1940, while in command of HMS *Jackal*, a week before their third child was born. She wrote of her grief in *Sheet Anchor* and of bereaved families in *Plymouth in War: A Verse Documentary*, which was broadcast by the BBC in 1994. She wrote other volumes of poetry, biographies on her husband's remarkable forebears and an autobiograhy of her childhood.

NIXON, DAPHNE
Served in the ATS.

OGIER, RUTH
Interned on Guernsey, Channel Islands, during the war years.

PICKTHALL, EDITH (b. 1893)
Educated in Oxton, Birkenhead, Cheshire. Trained as a maternity nurse. During the war she was an emergency midwife and a member of the Red Cross Detachment at Mylor, near Falmouth, which was a reception area for refugees. Village was bombed in 1941 and one of the casualties was a child evacuee.

PITTER, RUTH (1897–1992)
Born Ilford. Father a schoolmaster. Educated at Elementary School, Coburn

School for Girls, Bow. Her poetry first appeared in A.R. Orage's socialist weekly *New Age* in 1911. Junior clerk in the War Office during the First World War. Business in painted furniture and 'gift goods', particularly trays, before and after the Second World War, when she worked in the office of a factory. Her first volume of verse was published in 1920 which was followed by a succession of books of poetry. Created a Companion of Literature in 1974 and CBE in 1979.

POMFRET, JOAN (1913–93)
Born at Darwen, Lancashire. Daughter of a librarian. Educated at Darwen Grammar School and The Park School, Preston. Married Douglas Townsend. Novelist and short-story writer, some in Lancashire dialect. Broadcaster and lecturer. Member of the Lancashire Authors' Association for over sixty years.

POWIS, SYBIL
No biographical information.

PRAEGER, ROSAMOND (1867–1954)
Born and educated in Holywood, County Down, and returned to Ireland after studying art at the Slade School. Artist and sculptor. Published fifteen children's picture books. Appointed MBE in 1939.

PROCTER, IDA
Born in London. Studied book illustration at Kingston School of Art. Draughtswoman in a firm of precision engineers during the war. Married David Fraser Harris after the war. Lived in Cornwall since 1954. Published books on British art; poetry and articles on Cornwall published in periodicals; her book *Visitors to Cornwall* was published in 1982.

RATHBONE, IRENE (1892–1980)
Born in Liverpool. Privately educated. Brief period as an actress. During First World War worked in YMCA canteens in northern France and then trained as a VAD in military hospitals in London. Her fiancé was killed in 1920 while serving in Iraq. She wrote eight books. Her prose poem 'Was there a Summer?' was based on her relationship with Richard Aldington during the 1930s. Her literary friends included Nancy Cunard (q.v.).

READ, SYLVIA
Trained at the Royal Academy of Dramatic Art. During the war she worked with the distinguished concert pianist Doris Hibbert for Army Education in a

series of recitals of music and poetry to troops throughout Britain. Poems published in numerous periodicals, newspapers, anthologies and on BBC Television. Published plays and novels. For over thirty years she and her second husband William Fry have been nationally and internationally known as a two-actor team with their 'Theatre Roundabout' productions. Their adaptations of classics include *Jane Eyre*, *Under Milk Wood*, *Barchester Towers* and *Shadowlands*.

REID, PHYLLIS
Trained at the Central School of Dramatic Art and Speech-Training.

RENSHAW, CONSTANCE (1891–1964)
Poet of the First World War. Contributed to many periodicals.

RHODES, MARGARET ELIZABETH (b. 1915)
Born at Colwyn Bay, North Wales. Educated at Somerville College, Oxford. Married Mark Plummer in 1939. Freelance writer.

RICE, PAULINE
No biographical information.

RIDLER, ANNE (b. 1912)
Née Bradby. Born in Rugby, Warwickshire. Father a housemaster at Rugby School. Educated Downe House School, King's College London and Florence and Rome. Her eldest brother killed at the Battle of Arras in 1917. Worked as an editorial assistant and as secretary to T.S. Eliot at the publishers Faber and Faber. In 1938 married Vivian Ridler, Printer to University of Oxford. Two sons and two daughters. Edited and translated many books; published poetry, librettos and plays and is represented in numerous anthologies.

ROBERTS, LYNETTE (1909–95)
Born in Buenos Aires. Father, of Welsh extraction, general manager of Argentina's Western Railways. Educated at a convent in Buenos Aires and after she returned to England at the Central School of Arts and Crafts and at Constance Spry's Flower School. In 1939 married the writer and editor Keidrych Rhys. They rented a tiny, two-roomed cottage in the village of Llanybri in Carmarthenshire. Here she wrote poetry, researched village dialect and Welsh mythology. From 1943 she had a lively correspondence with Robert Graves which highlights the development of his *The White Goddess: a historical grammar of poetic myth* for which he said she was 'largely responsible';

he had earlier described her as 'one of the few true poets now writing'; he became godfather to her daughter Angharad. Her marriage was dissolved in 1949 and she moved to England with her daughter and son. In 1969 she returned to Carmarthenshire suffering from schizophrenia; she became a Jehovah's Witness and towards the end of her life was elected a member of Yr Academi Gymreig (the Welsh Academy).

ROSCOE, THEODORA (d. 1962)
Privately educated at home. Her husband was in the Army and she travelled with him to various countries. Painter and poet. Contributed to newspapers and magazines. Became Hon Secretary of the Society of Women Journalists. Co-editor with Mary Winter Were (q.v.) of *Poems by Contemporary Women*, published in 1944. Lived in Chalfont St Peter, Buckinghamshire.

ROSS, CHLORIS HEATON
Ran riding stables until the outbreak of war. Joined WAAF in September 1939. Married Sergeant Pilot David Ross who was reported missing three months later over Ceylon. Later married Leslie Morgan. Worked as a fashion journalist. Lived in Chesham, Buckinghamshire.

ROWE, JOYCE
Direct descendant of Nicholas Rowe, Poet Laureate in the early eighteenth century. During the war worked for the BBC Overseas Service. Poet, playwright and writer of scripts for the wireless.

SACKVILLE-WEST, VICTORIA (VITA) (1892–1962)
Born at Knole, the Tudor palace in Kent, that influenced much of her writing. Father became third Baron Sackville; her mother was half Spanish. Educated at home and privately in London. In 1913 she married Harold Nicolson, a diplomat, and they had two sons. In 1930 they bought Sissinghurst, a ruined Elizabethan mansion in the weald of Kent and over the years created 'the most beautiful garden in England' from the wilderness. During the war she joined the Kent committee of the Women's Land Army. She wrote poetry, biographies, novels and books on gardening. In 1948 she was appointed CH for her services to literature.

SAGITTARIUS (PSEUDONYM OF OLGA KATZIN) (1896–1987)
Born of Russian-Jewish parents. An established writer by the time she married Hugh Miller, the actor, in 1921. Two sons and a daughter. In the 1930s she developed her gift for satirical socio-political verse. Lived in London during

the war. She wrote under the pseudonym 'Fiddlestick' for *Time and Tide*, as 'Mercutio' for the *Manchester Guardian*, as 'Scorpio' for the *Daily Herald*; and for more than twenty years as 'Sagittarius' she contributed weekly verses to the *New Statesman*. Her verse was published in book form.

SCOTT, CONSTANCE
Lived in Chatham, Kent.

SCOVELL, E.J. (b. 1907)
Father a canon. Born in Sheffield. Educated at Casterton School, Westmorland and Somerville College, Oxford. Married the ecologist Charles Elton and worked with him in the South and Central American rain forests. Lived in Oxford during the war. Published several volumes of poetry.

SHANNON, SHEILA (b. 1913)
Born in Highgate, London. Educated Henrietta Barnet School and Somerville College, Oxford. Assistant Editor to W.J. Turner producing the *Britain in Pictures Series*, co-editor with Turner and later Patric Dickinson of *New Excursions into English Poetry*. Lived in London during war years. Married Patric Dickinson in 1945. Two children. Reviewed poetry for the *Spectator* and contributed poems to many periodicals.

SITWELL, EDITH (1887–1964)
Born at Scarborough. Father Sir George Reresby Sitwell, fourth baronet. Privately educated. Her brothers Osbert and Sacheverell also became well-known writers. Verse published in the *Daily Mirror* in 1913 and first small volume of poetry in 1915. She collaborated with William Walton to produce *Façade* in 1923. Lived in Paris for some years in the 1930s. Poet, critic, anthologist and writer of a number of prose works. Appointed a Dame of the British Empire in 1954 and a Companion of Literature in 1963. She became a Roman Catholic in 1955.

SMITH, MARGERY (b. 1916)
Born in Nottingham. Educated at Charlotte Mason College, Ambleside. Became a teacher, poet and editor. Served in the ATS during the war. Co-founder of the Nottingham Poetry Society in 1941.

SMITH, STEVIE (FLORENCE MARGARET) (1902–71)
Born in Hull. Daughter of a shipping agent. When the family business failed her father joined the merchant navy and she was brought up by her mother

and aunt. Spent three years in a sanatorium with tuberculosis. Educated at Palmer's Green High School and North London Collegiate School for Girls. For thirty years worked for the publishers Newnes as personal secretary to Sir Neville Pearson, Bt. Poet and novelist, she illustrated much of her work with line drawings. Broadcast on BBC and sometimes sang her poems to her own composition based on Gregorian chants and hymn tunes. Received Queen's Gold Medal for Poetry in 1969.

SPENDER, MARY DOREEN
A schoolmistress and one-time President of London Head Teachers' Association. First woman to be appointed head of a senior mixed school under the London County Council. Educational journalist and reviewer. Awarded MBE for her work in education. Poetry published in periodicals. Looked after evacuees in South Wales during the war. Aunt of Richard Spender, the young poet killed in North Africa.

STAFFORD, SARAH
Lived in London. Taught Belgian children.

STEEN, SHEILA
Born in India. Educated at Cambridge House, Ballymena, Northern Ireland, and at London and Bordeaux Universities. Lived in south-west France. Worked in Fleet Street.

STOPES, MARIE CARMICHAEL (1880–1958)
Father an anthropologist. Educated at St George's, Edinburgh, North London Collegiate School and University College, London. First woman to be appointed to the science staff of the University of Manchester in 1904. In 1907 went to Japan on a Scientific Mission for eighteen months. Married twice; second husband Humphrey Verdon Roe in 1918 and they founded the Mothers' Clinic for Birth Control in London in 1921. Her book *Married Love*, published in 1918, sold millions of copies all over the world; published other books on family planning, botany, plays and poetry.

TOMALIN, RUTH
Born in County Kilkenny, Southern Ireland. Educated at Chichester High School and King's College, London. Served in Women's Land Army 1941 to 1942. Staff reporter on various newspapers, 1942 to 1965, then a freelance press reporter in London courts of law. Early poems appeared in the *Adelphi*, the *Observer*, and other periodicals. Poet, novelist, biographer, writer of

children's stories. Her collected poems *Dormice Again*, celebrating the campaign to return the dormouse to woods in the south and west, is in preparation.

TRINDLES, JOY W. (b. 1922)
Born in London. Educated Fulham High School for Girls. Trained as a nurse at Hammersmith Hospital. Joined Queen Alexandra's Nursing Service Reserve as a sister in December 1943. Soon after D-Day went to France with 29th British General Hospital and landed on Mulberry harbour. Set up a front-line hospital on the Saint Lô Road under dangerous conditions and nursed Germans, Poles, Canadians, British and Free French troops until November; only had two hours off duty each day and operated all day and night when ambulance convoys arrived. Nursed at Eecloo, Belgium, in a convent converted into a hospital. Sent to Belsen and helped set up the first hospital at the camp. Married 1945; at a hospital in Hanover until demobbed in 1946. Qualified as a teacher in 1961 and taught until retirement. A great-grandmother.

VARCOE, JOAN MARY AND J. MITFORD VARCOE
No biographical information.

WADDELL, HELEN (1889–1965)
Born in Tokyo. Daughter of a Presbyterian missionary. Educated at Victoria College for Girls and Queen's University, Belfast. In 1912 her MA dissertation on Milton was examined by Professor George Saintsbury; they only met twice but remained close through correspondence until his death in 1933. She won an Oxford Travelling Scholarship and spent two years in Paris between 1923 and 1925. She researched and wrote works on Catholic medieval Europe which were widely acclaimed by the academic and literary world. Her greatest success was her novel *Peter Abelard*, published in 1933, which was translated into nine languages. She was a distinguished lecturer and received honorary degrees from four universities among many other honours. She also wrote plays, poetry and numerous articles and translated from Latin and Chinese. Became a member of the Royal Irish Academy in 1932.

WARNER, SYLVIA TOWNSEND (1893–1978)
Born in Harrow, Middlesex. Father a master at Harrow School. Privately educated. Worked in a munitions factory in First World War. From 1918 to 1928 member of the editorial board of Tudor Church Music. First book of verse published in 1925; following year her first novel *Lolly Willowes* came out. In 1927 became guest critic of the *New York Herald-Tribune*. Met Valentine

Ackland (q.v.) in 1930 and they became lifelong companions. Became a member of the Communist Party of Great Britain in 1935. In Spain during the Civil War in 1936. Secretary to the Dorchester branch of the WVS during the war. Wrote short stories for the *New Yorker*, and was a biographer and translator, but she is best known for her fiction. Fellow of the Royal Society of Literature.

WELLESLEY, DOROTHY (1889–1956)
Née Ashton. Born at White Waltham, Berkshire. Privately educated. Married Lord Gerald Wellesley in 1914 and became Duchess of Wellington in 1943. One son and one daughter. Wrote poetry, which was much admired by W.B. Yeats, a biography, and an autobiography.

WELLS, ELEANOR
No biographical information.

WERE, MARY WINTER
Kinswoman of Robert Southey. Privately educated. Married Arthur Hughes. Several books of poems and prose published; she was also an essayist, journalist and contributor to many periodicals. Co-editor with Theodora Roscoe (q.v.) of the anthology *Poems by Contemporary Women*, 1944. Daughter served in the ATS during the war.

WESTREN, JO (b. 1914)
Born in Essex. RAMC nurse attached anti-aircraft command, Colchester Military Hospital. Married name Wreford. Published poetry after the war.

WHITE, ELIZABETH
No biographical information.

WHITEHOUSE, PEGGY (PSEUDONYM OF FRANCES MUNDY-CASTLE) (b. 1898)
Born in Belfast. Worked in Ministry of Munitions and Air Ministry and published poetry during First World War. Novelist, playwright and poet.

WILLIAMS, HILDA KATHERINE
Travelled widely. Husband a Deputy Commissioner and they lived in Burma before the war. Probably settled in Jersey in 1935 and lived on the island during the German occupation.

WILLY, MARGARET (b. 1919)
Educated at Beckenham County School for Girls and Goldsmiths' College, London. Served in the Women's Land Army, 1942–46. After the war she became a freelance writer and lecturer.

WINGFIELD, SHEILA (1906–92)
Née Beddington. Born in Hampshire. Educated at Roedean School, Brighton. Self-taught in Greek, French, Russian and English classics. Travelled widely in Europe, the Middle East, West Africa and the USA. In 1932 married Hon M. Wingfield, who later became Viscount Powerscourt. Two sons and one daughter. Five books of poetry published; contributed to many periodicals. Her autobiography was published in 1952.

Select Bibliography

The individual books of poetry and anthologies from which poems were taken will be found under Acknowledgements and the Preface and are not listed again in this Select Bibliography. Place of publication is London unless otherwise stated.

Ackland, Valentine. *The Nature of the Moment*, Chatto & Windus, 1973

Bergonzi, Bernard. *Wartime and Aftermath: English Literature and its Background 1939–1960*, Oxford University Press, 1993

Berry, Paul and Bostridge, Mark. *Vera Brittain, A Life*, Chatto & Windus, 1995

Calder, Angus. *The People's War: Britain 1939–1945*, Pimlico, 1997

Calder, Jenni. *The Nine Lives of Naomi Mitchison*, Virago Press, 1997

Cartland, Barbara. *The Years of Opportunity 1939–1945: Autobiography*, Hutchinson, 1948

Davies, Jennifer. *The Wartime Kitchen and Garden: The Home Front 1939–1945*, BBC Books, 1993

Faulks, Sebastian. *The Fatal Englishman: Three Short Lives*, Vintage, 1997

Gilbert, Martin. *The Holocaust: The Jewish Tragedy*, Fontana paperback, 1987

——. *The Day the War Ended: VE-Day 1945 in Europe and Around the World*, HarperCollins, 1995

——. *Holocaust Journey*, Weidenfeld & Nicolson, 1997

——. *Second World War*, Phoenix paperback edition, 1997

Glendinning, Victoria. *Vita, The Life of V. Sackville-West*, Weidenfeld & Nicolson, 1983

Grenfell, Joyce. *The Time of my Life: Entertaining the Troops, Her Wartime Journals*, edited and introduced by James Roose-Evans, Hodder & Stoughton, 1989

——. *Joyce & Ginnie: The Letters of Joyce Grenfell & Virginia Graham*, edited by Janie Hampton, Hodder & Stoughton, 1997

Grieg, Ian, Leslie, Kim and Readman, Alan (eds). *D-Day West Sussex: Springboard for the Normandy Landings 1944*, West Sussex County Council, 1994

Harman, Claire. *Sylvia Townsend Warner, A Biography*, Chatto & Windus, 1989 and Minerva paperback, 1991

—— (ed.). *The Diaries of Sylvia Townsend Warner*, Chatto & Windus, 1994

Harrisson, Tom. *Living through the Blitz*, Collins, 1976

Hartley, Jenny. *Hearts Undefeated: Women's Writing of the Second World War*, Virago Press, 1994

——. *Millions Like Us: British Women's Fiction of the Second World War*, Virago Press, 1997

Holman, Kate. *Brenda Chamberlain*, University of Wales Press, Cardiff, 1997

Jesse, F. Tennyson and Harwood, H.M. *Letters written to America (July 1940–June 1941)*, Constable & Co. Ltd., 1942

Keegan, John. *The Second World War*, Pimlico edition, 1997

Liddle Hart, B.H. *History of the Second World War*, Cassell, 1970

Lohf, Kenneth A. *Poets in a War: British Writers on the Battlefronts and the Home Front of the Second World War*, The Grolier Club, New York, 1995

Maclaren-Ross, J. *Memoirs of the Forties*, Alan Ross Ltd., 1965

Matanle, Ivor. *History of World War II: 1939–1945*, Tiger Books International, 1994

The Oxford Companion to the Second World War, General Editor I.C.B. Dear, Consultant Editor M.R.D. Foot, Oxford University Press, 1995

Paravisini-Gebert, Lizabeth. *Phyllis Shand Allfrey, A Caribbean Life*, Rutgers University Press, New Brunswick, New Jersey, 1996

Patten, Marguerite. *We'll Eat Again: A Collection of Recipes from the War Years*, Hamlyn, in association with The Imperial War Museum, 1993

Pikoulis, John. *Alun Lewis, A Life*, Poetry Wales Press, 1984

Pinney, Susanna (ed.). *I'll Stand by You, Selected Letters of Sylvia Townsend Warner and Valentine Ackland*, Pimlico, 1998

Raven, Hélène Jeanty. *Without Frontiers*, Hutchinson, 1960

Reilly, Catherine W. *English Poetry of the Second World War: A Biobibliography*, Mansell Publishing Limited, 1986

Reynoldson, Fiona. *Rationing: The Home Front 1939–1945*, Wayland Publishers Ltd, 1990

Sackville-West, Vita. *The Women's Land Army*, Michael Joseph, 1944

Scannell, Vernon. *Not Without Glory: Poets of the Second World War*, The Woburn Press, 1976

Shires, Linda M. *British Poetry of the Second World War*, Macmillan, 1985

Sinclair, Andrew. *War Like A Wasp: The Lost Decade of the Forties*, Hamish Hamilton, 1989

Stansky, Peter and Abrahams, William. *London's Burning: Life, Death & Art in the Second World War*, Constable, 1994

The World at Arms: The Reader's Digest Illustrated History of World War II, 1989

Tyrer, Nicola. *They Fought in the Fields: The Women's Land Army: The Story of a Forgotten Victory*, Arrow Books, 1999

Verrill-Rhys, Leigh and Beddoe, Deidre (eds). *Parachutes and Petticoats: Welsh Women Writing on the Second World War*, Honno, 1992

Wellesley, Dorothy. *Far Have I Travelled: Memoirs*, James Barrie, 1952

Whistler, Laurence. *The Initials in the Heart*, Rupert Hart-Davis, 1964.

ANTHOLOGIES

Hands to Action Stations!: Naval Poetry and Verse from World War II, chosen by John Winton, Bluejacket Books, 1980

I Burn for England: An Anthology of the Poetry of World War II, selected and introduced by Charles Hamblett, Leslie Frewin, 1966

In Time of War: War Poetry selected by Anne Harvey, Blackie and Son Ltd., 1987, and Penguin Books, 1989

Poetry of the Second World War, selected by Edward Hudson, Wayland, 1990

Poetry of the Second World War: An International Anthology, edited by Desmond Graham, Chatto & Windus, 1995

Private Words: Letters and Diaries from the Second World War, edited by Ronald Blythe, Penguin Books, 1993

The Home Front: An Anthology of Personal Experience 1938–1945, edited by Norman Longmate, Chatto & Windus, 1981

The Terrible Rain: The War Poets 1939–1945, an anthology selected and arranged by Brian Gardner, Methuen & Co., Ltd., 1966

The Virago Book of Women's War Poetry and Verse, an omnibus edition of 'Scars Upon My Heart' and 'Chaos of the Night', edited and with a new introduction by Catherine Reilly, Virago Press, 1997

The War Decade: An Anthology of the 1940s, compiled by Andrew Sinclair, Hamish Hamilton, 1989

Wartime Women: An Anthology of Women's Wartime Writing for Mass-Observation 1937–45, edited by Dorothy Sheridan, Heinemann, 1990

Acknowledgements

The editor and publisher gratefully acknowledge the following for permission to reproduce copyright material:

Ackland, Valentine, '7 October 1940' and 'April 1943' from the original typescript of 'War in Progress'. © William Maxwell and Susanna Pinney.

Allan, Mabel Esther, 'I Saw a Broken Town' from *Poetry Quarterly*, Summer 1941.

Allfrey, Phyllis Shand, 'Beethoven in the Highlands' and 'Cunard Liner 1940' from *In Circles: Poems*, The Raven Press, 1940; and 'Colonial Soldiers', first published in *Tribune*, November 1942. Reprinted by permission of Lennox Honychurch.

Anderson, Mary Désirée, 'Dunkirk', 'National Gallery Concert' and '"Blitz"' from *Bow Bells are Silent*, Williams & Norgate Ltd., 1943. Reprinted by permission of Kenneth Anderson.

Arlett, Vera, 'Because they belonged to You' and 'War in Sussex (1944)' from *England 1940 and other poems*, Linden Press, 1958.

Arundel, Honor, 'Paris 1942' from *Poems for France: Written by British Poets on France Since the War*, collected by Nancy Cunard, La France Libre, 1944.

Barry, Alice Frances, 'A Prisoner Returns – 1945' from *Last Poems*, Combridges, Hove 1952.

Barton, Joan, 'First News Reel: September 1939' and 'Newgale Sands 1940' from *A House under Old Sarum: New and Selected Poems*, Harry Chambers/Peterloo Poets, 1981.

Bax, Vera, 'To Richard' and 'Christmas, 1943' from *The Distaff Muse: An Anthology of Poetry written by Women*, compiled by Clifford Bax and Meum Stewart, Hollis & Carter, 1949; 'To Billy, my son' and 'The Fallen' from *Chaos of the Night: Women's Poetry and Verse of the Second World War*, edited by Catherine Reilly, Virago, 1984. Reprinted by permission of Paul North.

Beecham, Audrey, 'Norway' from *Poetry in Wartime: an Anthololgy*, edited by M.J. Tambimuttu, Faber & Faber Ltd, 1942.

Bellerby, Frances, 'The Airman Asleep on the Rocks' from *Plash Mill*, Peter Davies Ltd., 1946. Reprinted by permission of David Higham Associates.

Berington, Olguita Queeny, 'Where is Everybody?' and 'Someone I Know' from *Different Like a Zoo*, Palladium Press, 1949. © the Trustees of the T.M. Berington Will Trust.

Berridge, Elizabeth, 'Conversation', 'Speculation on a Beauty', 'Letter from an Italian Prisoner' from *Triad One*, edited by Jack Aistrop. Dennis Dobson Ltd, 1946. Reprinted by permission of the author.

Bolton, Angela, 'Bengal Summer' and 'The Generals' from *More Poems of the Second World War: the Oasis Selection*, J.M. Dent & Sons Ltd., 1989. Reprinted by permission of the author and The Salamander Oasis Trust; 'The Unknown Soldier' and prose extracts from *The Maturing Sun: An Army Nurse in India, 1942–1945* by Angela Bolton, Imperial War Museum, 1986. Reprinted by permission of the author; and the unpublished poem 'Return from India by Way of the Suez Canal' by permission of the author.

Bowes Lyon, Lilian, 'A Son' from *Tomorrow is a Revealing*, Jonathan Cape, 1941; and 'Headland, 1940' from *A Rough Walk Home and other Poems*, Jonathan Cape, 1946. Reprinted by permission of David Bowes-Lyon.

Briggs, Greta, 'London Under Bombardment' from *Other Men's Flowers: An Anthology of Poetry*, compiled by A.P. Wavell Field-Marshal Earl Wavell, Jonathan Cape, 1944.

Brittain, Vera, 'September, 1939' from *Poems by Contemporary Women*, compiled by Theodora Roscoe and Mary Winter Were, Hutchinson, 1944; extracts from *Testament of a Peace Lover: Letters from Vera Brittain*, edited by Winifred and Alan Eden-Green, Virago Press, 1988; and extracts from *Wartime Chronicle: Vera Brittain's Diary 1939–1945*, edited by Alan Bishop and Y. Aleksandra Bennett, Victor Gollancz, 1989 are included with the permission of Mark Bostridge, her literary executor.

Bryan, Sarah, 'I Admired Him Digging' from *This Living Stone: the Grey Walls Anthology of New Poems*, edited by Wrey Gardiner, Grey Walls Press, 1941.

Bryher (pseudonym of Winifred Ellerman), extract from 'Tourist' from *Life and Letters Today*, Spring Number, April 1941; 'Untitled', and a prose extract from *The Days of Mars: A Memoir 1940–1946*, Calder & Boyars, 1972. Reprinted by permission of Perdita Schaffner and Marion Boyars Publishers, London and New York.

Bulley, Anne, 'Leave Poem' and 'Poem' from *Fleet Poetry Broadsheet*, April 1945. Reprinted by permission of the author.

Burton, Doris, 'Children of War' from *The Incarnation, and other Poems*, Arthur Stockwell Ltd., 1946.

Cartland, Barbara, 'To Ronald' from *Lines on Life & Love*, Hutchinson, 1972; and prose extracts from *Ronald Cartland*, a biography by his sister Barbara Cartland, Collins 1942. Reprinted by permission of the author.

Cawdor, Wilma, 'A Curse' from *Poems for France: Written by British Poets on France since the War*, collected by Nancy Cunard, La France Libre, 1944. Reprinted by permission of The Hon James Campbell and the Cawdor Estate.

Chamberlain, Brenda, 'Dead Ponies' from *Poetry in Wartime: an Anthology*, edited by M.J. Tambimuttu, Faber & Faber 1942; 'For Alun' from *Wales*,

Summer 1944; and extracts from *The Green Heart*, OUP, 1958. Reprinted by permission of Dorothy Chamberlain.

Cherrill, Maud, 'Easter 1942' and 'Christmas 1942' from *Padstow Lights: Poems*, Scrivener Press, Oxford, 1949. Reprinted by permission of Roger Venables.

Churchill, Sarah, '1943' from *The Empty Spaces: Poems*, Leslie Frewin, 1966; and 'Christmas 1943' from *The Unwanted Statue, and Other Poems*, Leslie Frewin, 1969. Reproduced by permission of Lady Soames, DBE, c/o Curtis Brown Ltd, London. Copyright Sarah Churchill 1966, 1969.

Coats, Alice, 'October, 1940' and 'The "Monstrous Regiment"' from *Poems of the Land Army: An Anthology of Verse by Members of the Women's Land Army*, selected by V. Sackville-West, The Land Girl, 1945.

Coleman, Marion, 'Monte Cassino 1945' from *Myself is All I Have*, Outposts Publications, 1969.

Corfield, Joy, 'I Didn't Believe It. . .' and 'Morse Lesson' from *Poems of the Second World War: the Oasis Selection*, J.M. Dent & Sons Ltd., 1985; 'Soldiers' Pets' from *More Poems of the Second World War: the Oasis Selection*, J.M. Dent & Sons Ltd., 1989. Reprinted by permission of The Salamander Oasis Trust.

Cornford, Frances, 'From a Letter to America on a Visit to Sussex: Spring 1942' and 'For M.S. Singing Frühlingsglaube in 1945' from *Travelling Home and Other Poems*, Cresset Press, 1948. Reprinted by permission of the Estate of Frances Cornford and Stephen Stuart-Smith of the Enitharmon Press.

Crosland, Margaret, 'December 1942', 'Reverie at a Main Line Station' and 'Reported Missing (For G.H.)' from *Strange Tempe*, The Fortune Press, 1946. Reprinted by permission of the author.

Cruickshank, Norah K., 'Farewell to X Platoon' from *In the Tower's Shadow*, Oxford University Press, 1948.

Cunard, Nancy, *Relève into Maquis*, The Grasshopper Press, 1944. Reprinted by permission of Anthony R.A. Hobson.

Dane, Clemence (pseudonym of Winifred Ashton), 'Plymouth' from *Poems by Contemporary Women*, compiled by Theodora Roscoe and Mary Winter Were, Hutchinson, 1944. Reprinted by permission of Laurence Pollinger Limited and the Estate of Clemence Dane.

David, Lisbeth, 'Air Sea Rescue' from *Poems of the Second World War: the Oasis Selection*, J.M. Dent & Sons Ltd., 1985; 'Sonnet before D-Day' and 'Forty-Eight Hours', from *More Poems of the Second World War: the Oasis Selection*, J.M. Dent & Sons Ltd., 1989. Reprinted by permission of the author and The Salamander Oasis Trust.

Dawes, Winifred, 'German Boy, 1938' from *The Poetry Review*, No. 1, Vol. XXXVII, 1946.

de Bairacli-Levy, Juliette, 'Killed in Action' from *The Willow Wreath*, Smyrna, Turkey, 1943.

Dolphin, May, 'Norway, 1940' and 'Uncensored' from *Swords and Ploughshares*, Bailes & Sons, Durham, 1947.

Douglas, Mary, 'Blitz on Coventry' from *Verse by the Way*, Walter Barker, Nottingham, 1944.

Doyle, Camilla, 'A Game of Bowls', 'War Time Garden' and 'Damage by Enemy Action' from *Damage by Enemy Action: Poems on the Air Raids of the Second World War*, by Camilla Doyle, collected with an introduction by Richard Lowndes, A Ballivor Book, 1997.

FitzRoy, Olivia, 'Fleet Fighter', 'Piayagala' and 'Sonnet Experiment' from *Selected Poems* by Olivia FitzRoy, privately printed. Reprinted by permission of The Hon Mrs Peter Ormrod.

Friedlaender, V. Helen, 'Trivial Detail' from *Poems by Contemporary Women*, compiled by Theodora Roscoe and Mary Winter Were, Hutchinson, 1944.

Furse, Jill, 'Carol', 'The Days that Forced our Lives Apart' and 'The Rain Falls Silent in the Garden' from *Jill Furse: her Nature and her Poems, 1915–1944*, Chiswick Press, 1945. Reprinted by permission of Laurence Whistler.

Gale, Adrienne, 'Nostalgia' from *The Year*, privately printed, 1942.

Gibbs, Beatrice Ruth, 'The Bomber' and 'To a Country Boy' from *War Poems from the Sunday Times*, printed for private circulation, 1945.

Graham, Virginia, 'Sound the Trumpet', 'Air Raid over Bristol', 'Nanny', and 'Losing Face' from *Consider the Years: 1938–1946*, Jonathan Cape, 1946. Reprinted by permission of the Trustees of Virginia Thesiger Deceased (Virginia Graham).

Grantham, Alexandra Etheldreda, 'War' from *River Roundels*, Joseph Vincent, Oxford, 1943; and 'Crashed' from *Godfrey Grantham*, Joseph Vincent, Oxford, 1942.

Grenfell, Joyce, 'March Day, 1941' from *Poems by Contemporary Women*, compiled by Theodora Roscoe and Mary Winter Were, Hutchinson, 1944. Reprinted by permission of Sheil Land Associates Ltd.

Griffiths, Grace, 'Doodlebugs' from *Poems of the Second World War: the Oasis Selection*, J.M. Dent & Sons Ltd., 1985. Reprinted by permission of The Salamander Oasis Trust.

Hallett, Olive, 'A Good Laugh' and 'Easter Break' from *Topical Tales, and Other Verses*, Cornish Brothers Ltd., Birmingham, 1944.

Harrison, Mary E., 'My Hands' from *More Poems of the Second World War: the Oasis Selection*, J.M. Dent & Sons Ltd., 1989. Reprinted by permission of The Salamander Oasis Trust.

Haskins, Minnie, 'God Knows' from *The Gate of the Year*, Hodder & Stoughton, 1940. Reprinted by permission of Sheil Land Associates Ltd.

Hawkins, Aileen, 'End of D-Day Leave', from *Regency Press Anthology*, 1973. Reprinted by permission of the author.

Haycock, Myfanwy, 'Embarkation Leave', 'Going back to London', '"Killed in Action"', 'Canary in an Air-Raid' from *Poems*, Western Mail & Echo Ltd., Cardiff, 1944. Reprinted by permission of David Williams and Gwladys E. Haycock.

Hebgin, Dame Scholastica Sybil, OSB, 'From the Home Front'. Unpublished poem by permission of Dame Felicitas Corrigan, Stanbrook Abbey.

Herbertson, Agnes Grozier, 'The Return to the Cottage' from *This is the Hour: Poems*, Fortune Press, 1942. Reprinted by permission of Fortune Press/Skilton/ Christchurch Publishers.

Hesketh, Phoebe, 'Spring in Wartime' and 'Post-War Christmas' from *Lean Forward, Spring!*, Sidgwick & Jackson Limited, 1948. Reprinted by permission of the author.

Hewlett, Audrey, 'October, 1940' from *Poems of the Land Army: An Anthology of Verse by Members of the Women's Land Army*, selected by V. Sackville-West, The Land Girl, 1945.

Hills, Janet, 'Autumn by the Sea' and 'To a Friend' from *Fragments*, privately printed, 1956.

Holden, Molly, 'Seaman, 1941' from *Air and Chill Earth*, Chatto & Windus, 1971. © Alan Holden.

Holmes, Pamela, 'Parting in April' and 'War Baby' from *Chaos of the Night: Women's Poetry & Verse of the Second World War*, selected by Catherine Reilly, Virago Press, 1984; 'Missing, Presumed Killed' from *War Poems from the Sunday Times*, printed for private circulation, 1945. Reprinted by permission of the author; and the unpublished poem 'Once' by kind permission of the author.

Hooley, Teresa, 'Christ at Berchtesgaden', 'Regatta' and 'The Singing Heart' from *The Singing Heart: Poems*, Frederick Muller Ltd., 1944. Reprinted by permission of the Estate of Teresa Hooley.

Hunka, Pamela, 'The Time of Dunkirk' from *Modern Reading*, No. 11 & 12, edited by Reginald Moore.

Jackson, Ada, extract from 'Behold the Jew', *The Poetry Review*, July-August 1943.

James, Diana, 'Presage: 1944' and 'The Munition Workers' from *The Tune of Flutes*, Routledge, 1945. Reprinted by permission of Routledge Ltd.

Jarman, Wrenne, 'In Memoriam: Richard Hillary, R.A.F.V.R.' from The *Greenwood Anthology of New Verse*, edited by Herbert Palmer, Frederick

Muller Ltd., 1948; 'Plastic Airman' and 'Target Amiens' from *The Breathless Kingdom: Poems*, Fortune Press, 1948. Reprinted by permission of Fortune Press/Skilton/Christchurch Publishers; and 'Threnody for Berlin – 1945' from *Nymph in Thy Orisons: Poems*, St Albert's Press, Llandeilo, 1960.

Jerrold, Hebe, 'War, which has brought to others fear' from *Poems of the Land Army: An Anthology of Verse by Members of the Women's Land Army*, selected by V. Sackville-West, The Land Girl, 1945.

Jesse, Fryniwyd Tennyson, 'A Tale of St. Peter's Gate' from *The Compass and Other Poems*, William Hodge & Co., 1951. Reprinted by permission of David Evans.

Kenmare, Dallas, 'September, 1939' from *Collected Poems*, Burrow's Press Ltd., Cheltenham, 1953; 'Chestnut-buds and Hazel-catkins' from *Four Words, and Other Poems*, Edward J. Burrow & Co., Ltd, 1940; and 'Home Service June 6th 1944' from *Elegy for Two Voices, and Other Poems*, Burrow's Press Ltd., 1947.

King, Pamela, 'Winter, 1942' from *Oasis*, Summer 1944, edited by John Bate and Conan Nicholas. Reprinted by permission of the author.

Knowles, Susanne, 'The Blitz' from *Poets now in the Services*, Number One, edited by A.E. Lowy, Favil Press, 1943; and 'The ABC of Civil Defence' from *Arpies and Sirens: Verse*, Harrap & Co., Ltd., 1942. Reprinted by permission of Chambers Harrap Publishers Ltd.

Laughton, Freda, 'The Evacuees' from *A Transitory House: Poems*, Jonathan Cape, 1945. Reprinted by permission of Random House, U.K.

Lawrence, Margery, 'Wild Flowers in London' from *Fourteen to Forty-Eight: a Diary in Verse*, Robert Hale Ltd., 1950. Reprinted by permission of David Higham Associates.

Lea, Barbara, 'Barrage Balloon' from *The Urgent Voice and Other Poems*, Fortune Press, 1948. Reprinted by permission of Fortune Press/Skilton/Christchurch Publishers.

Lea, Margery, 'Bomb Story (Manchester, 1942)' from *These Days: Poetry and Verse*, Wilding & Sons Ltd., Shrewsbury, 1969.

Ledward, Patricia, 'In Memoriam' and 'Air-Raid Casualties: Ashridge Hospital' from *Poems of this War by Younger Poets*, edited by Patricia Ledward and Colin Strang, Cambridge University Press, 1942; 'Evening in Camp' from *More Poems from the Forces*, edited by Keidrych Rhys, Routledge 1943; and 'The Dead' from *Khaki and Blue*, No. 4, edited by Peter Ratazzi, Resurgam Books, 1945. Reprinted by permission of the author.

Lendon, Pauline, 'Returned Airman' from *More Poems of the Second World War: the Oasis Selection*, J.M. Dent & Sons Ltd., 1989. Reprinted by permission of The Salamander Oasis Trust.

Levertov, Denise, 'Listening to Distant Guns' from *Collected Earlier Poems, 1940–1960*, Copyright © 1940, 1979 by Denise Levertov. Reprinted by permission of New Directions Publishing Corporation and Laurence Pollinger Limited.

Lewis, Eiluned, 'France, 1940' and 'London Spring, 1941' from *Morning Songs, and Other Poems*, Macmillan & Co., Ltd., 1944. Reprinted by permission of Katrina Burnett, Literary Executor of the Eiluned Lewis Estate.

Lynd, Sylvia, 'RAF, May, 1940' from *Poems by Contemporary Women*, compiled by Theodora Roscoe and Mary Winter Were, Hutchinson, 1944. Reprinted by permission of the Literary Executors of the Sylvia Lynd Estate.

Mackworth, Cecily, 'En Route' from *Poems for France: Written by British Poets on France Since the War*, collected by Nancy Cunard, La France Libre, 1944; and extract from *I came out of France*, Routledge, 1941. Reprinted by permission of the author.

Manning, Olivia, Extract from 'Written in the Third Year of the War' from *Personal Landscape: An Anthology of Exile*, Editions Poetry London, 1945. Reprinted by permission of David Higham Associates.

Mayo, Frances, 'Lament' from *New Lyrical Ballads*, an anthology edited by Maurice Carpenter, Jack Lindsay and Honor Arundel, Editions Poetry London, 1945.

Mayor, Beatrice, 'The Young Actress and Munitions' from *Voices from the Crowd*, Fortune Press, 1943. Reprinted by permission of Fortune Press/Skilton/ Christchurch Publishers.

Mitchison, Naomi, 'Clemency Ealasaid' from *The Bull Calves*, Jonathan Cape, 1947; 'Jim McKinven: March 1941' from *Chapman*, July 1987; 'The Farm Woman: 1942' from *The Cleansing of the Knife, and Other Poems*, Canongate, Edinburgh, 1978; extracts from *Among You Taking Notes . . . : The Wartime Diary of Naomi Mitchison 1939–1945*, edited by Dorothy Sheridan, Victor Gollancz 1985. Reprinted by permission of the late Naomi Mitchison.

Napier, Priscilla, from 'To Michael, Dying' from *Sheet-Anchor* (written under pseudonym 'Eve Stuart'), Sidgwick & Jackson Ltd., 1944; extract from *Plymouth in War: a Verse Documentary*, Denny Bros., Bury St Edmunds, 1978. Reprinted by permission of the late Priscilla Napier and her Literary Estate.

Nixon, Daphne, 'Blandford Camp 1943' and 'In these five years' from *In These Five Years: Poems*, Fortune Press 1946. Reprinted by permission of Fortune Press/Skilton/Christchurch Publishers.

Ogier, Ruth, 'Tomatoes, July 20th 1944', 'Clothes, 1944!', and 'Substitutes' from *Poems on the German Occupation of the Channel Isles*, Arthur Stockwell Ltd., 1946.

Pickthall, Edith, 'Evacuee' from *The Quest for Peace*, Outposts Publications, 1963.

Pitter, Ruth, 'Seagulls in London, January, 1940' and 'The Sparrow's Skull' from *Poems by Contemporary Women*, compiled by Theodora Roscoe and Mary Winter Were, Hutchinson, 1944; 'The Compost-Heap' from *The Rude Potato*, Cresset Press, 1941; and 'Wherefore Lament' from *The Bridge: Poems 1939–1944*, Cresset Press, 1945. Reprinted by permission of the Estate of Ruth Pitter and Stephen Stuart-Smith, Enitharmon Press.

Pomfret, Joan, 'War Weddings' from *Rhymes of the War*, Withy Grove Press Ltd., Manchester, 1940; and 'Knitting' from *The Admiralty Regrets . . . and Other Poems*, Guardian Press, Preston, 1941. Reprinted by permission of The Lancashire Author's Association.

Powis, Sybil, 'Peace Ironical' from *Upland and Valley*, Wilding & Son, Ltd., Shrewsbury, 1941.

Praeger, Rosamond, 'War' from *Old Fashioned Verses and Sketches*, Dundalgan Press, Dundalk, 1947. Reprinted by permission of the Dundalgan Press.

Procter, Ida, 'The One' from *War Poems from The Sunday Times*, printed for private circulation, 1945; and 'Propaganda'. Reprinted by permission of the author.

Rathbone, Irene, 'If you sank . . .' from *Poems for France: Written by British Poets on France Since the War*, collected by Nancy Cunard, La France Libre, 1944. Reprinted by permission of Patricia Utechin.

Read, Sylvia, 'For Women', a previously unpublished poem; 'For the War-Children' from *For those who are Alive: an Anthology of New Verse*, edited by Howard Sergeant, Fortune Press, 1946; 'Second Meeting' from *Khaki & Blue*, No, 4, edited by Peter Ratazzi, Resurgam Books, 1945; and prose extracts from unpublished 'Orkney Diary'. Reprinted by permission of the author.

Reid, Phyllis, 'Fireworks', from *The Distaff Muse: An Anthology of Poetry Written by Women'*, compiled by Clifford Bax and Meum Stewart, Hollis & Carter, 1949.

Renshaw, Constance, 'Ark Royal the Third', from an unidentified newspaper cutting.

Rhodes, Margaret Elizabeth, 'Guernsey', from *Pole-star, and Other Poems*, Hutchinson & Co., Ltd., 1946. Reprinted by permission of Random House, U.K.

Rice, Pauline, 'April Blitz', from *Poetry London X*, 1944.

Ridler, Anne, 'Now as Then', 'At Parting', 'For this Time' and 'Remember Him' from *The Nine Bright Shiners*, Faber & Faber, 1943. Reprinted by permission of the author and Carcanet Press Ltd.

Roberts, Lynette, extracts from *Gods with Stainless Ears*, Faber & Faber, 1951; 'The New Perception of Colour', from *Poetry Wales*, edited by Cary Archard,

Volume 19, No. 2, 1983; 'Crossed and Uncrossed' and 'Poem from Llanybri' from *Poems*, Faber & Faber 1944. Reprinted by permission of Angharad Rhys.

Roscoe, Theodora, 'Written after Visiting Germany in March, 1939' from *The Martinet: Poems*, Ruislip Press, 1940; 'At the National Gallery Concerts' from *Poems by Contemporary Women*, compiled by Theodora Roscoe and Mary Winter Were, Hutchinson. 1944; and 'Old Dorset Women and Tanks' from *From the Chilterns: Poems Old and New*, Ruislip Press, 1946. Reprinted by permission of Nicola Boorman.

Ross, Chloris Heaton, 'Sunday Tea – 1939' and 'Spring in Russell Square' from *A Flat in Bloomsbury*, Favil Press, 1945.

Rowe, Joyce, 'Dieppe' from *Poems for France: Written by British Poets on France Since the War*, collected by Nancy Cunard, La France Libre, 1944; and 'Point of View' from *She Died Alive*, Favil Press, 1945.

Sackville-West, Vita, 'September 1939' from *Selected Poems*, The Hogarth Press, 1941; an extract 'Black-out' from *The Garden*, Michael Joseph Limited, 1946; 'The Wines of France' from *Poems for France: Written by British Poets on France Since the War*, collected by Nancy Cunard, La France Libre, 1944; and prose extracts from *Country Notes in Wartime*, The Hogarth Press, 1940. Reprinted by permission of Nigel Nicolson.

Sagittarius (pseudonym of Olga Katzin), 'Nerves', 'The Descent of Man' and 'All Quiet' from *Sagittarius Rhyming*, Jonathan Cape, 1940; and 'The Passionate Profiteer to his Love' from *Quiver's Choice*, Jonathan Cape, 1945. Reprinted by permission of Jonathan Miller.

Scott, Constance, 'HMS Hood' from *June and a Posy from Kent*, Parrett & Neves, Ltd., Chatham 1941.

Scovell, E.J., 'An Elegy' from *Shadows of Chrysanthemums, and Other Poems*, Routledge, 1944; 'A War-time Story' and 'A Refugee' from *The Midsummer Meadow and Other Poems*, Routledge, 1946. Reprinted by permission of Carcanet Press Limited.

Shannon, Sheila, 'The Artist's Vision', 'Soldier and Girl Sleeping', 'On Pentire Head' and 'On a Child Asleep in a Tube Shelter' from *The Lightning-Struck Tower*, Frederick Muller, 1947. Reprinted by permission of the author.

Sitwell, Edith, extract from 'Still Falls the Rain' from *Street Songs*, Macmillan 1942; and extract from 'Dirge for the New Sunrise' from *Collected Poems*, Macmillan & Co., Ltd., 1957. Reprinted by permission of David Higham Associates.

Smith, Margery, 'Poets in Uniform' from *The Poetry Review*, November/December, 1945. Reprinted by permission of the author.

Smith, Stevie, 'I Remember' from *The Collected Poems of Stevie Smith*, Penguin 20th Century Classics. Reprinted by permission of James MacGibbon.

Spender, Mary Doreen, 'For Richard Spender' from *Poems by Contemporary Women*, compiled by Theodora Roscoe and Mary Winter Were, Hutchinson, 1944.

Stafford, Sarah, 'The Unborn' from *For Those Who are Alive: an Anthology of New Verse*, edited by Howard Sergeant, Fortune Press, 1946. Reprinted by permission of Fortune Press/Skilton/ Christchurch Publishers.

Steen, Sheila, 'True France' from *Poems for France: Written by British Poets on France Since the War*, collected by Nancy Cunard, La France Libre, 1944.

Stopes, Marie Carmichael, extract from *Instead of Tears*, Count Potocki of Montalk at Half Moon Cottage, Little Bookham, 1942; and 'The Doll' from *Wartime Harvest: Poems*, Alexander Moring Ltd., 1945. Reprinted by permission of the Galton Institute, Literary Executors of the Marie Stopes Estate.

Tomalin, Ruth, 'Embroidery, 1940', 'Ladybird, Ladybird', 'Hunting Song' and 'Invasion Spring' from *Threnody for Dormice*, The Fortune Press, 1947. Reprinted by permission of the author.

Trindles, Joy W., 'Until Belsen' from *More Poems of the Second World War: the Oasis Selection*, J.M. Dent & Sons Ltd., 1989. Reprinted by permission of the author and The Salamander Oasis Trust.

Varcoe, Joan Mary and Varcoe, J. Mitford, 'Neighbours' from *London 1940, and Other War Verse*, Houghton & Sons Ltd, 1945.

Waddell, Helen, 'April 20th, 1939' and a short extract from *Helen Waddell: A Biography* by Dame Felicitas Corrigan, Victor Gollancz, 1986; and extract from *Lament for Damon*, privately printed, 1943. Reprinted by permission of Mollie Martin and Dame Felicitas Corrigan, Stanbrook Abbey.

Warner, Sylvia Townsend, extract from her Diary dated 13 June 1940; 'Road 1940' from *Poems for France: Written by British Poets on France Since the War*, collected by Nancy Cunard, La France Libre, 1944; and extract from a letter to Alyse Gregory from *Sylvia Townsend Warner Letters*, edited by William Maxwell, Chatto & Windus 1982. © William Maxwell and Susanna Pinney.

Wellesley, Dorothy, 'Milk Boy' from *Selected Poems*, Williams & Norgate Ltd., 1949; and 'In Memory of Rex Whistler' from *Desert Wells: New Poems*, Michael Joseph Ltd., 1946; extract from *Far Have I Travelled: Memoirs*, James Barrie, 1952. Reprinted by permission of the Trustees of the late Dorothy Wellesley, Duchess of Wellington Will Trust.

Wells, Eleanor, 'For the Undefeated' from *The Best Poems of 1941*, selected by Thomas Moult, Jonathan Cape, 1942. Reprinted by permission of Random House, U.K.

Were, Mary Winter, 'To Saint Francis of Assisi', from *Poems by Contemporary Women*, compiled by Theodora Roscoe and Mary Winter Were, Hutchinson, 1944.

Westren, Jo, 'Brief Sanctuary' and 'Behind the Screens' from *More Poems of the Second World War: the Oasis Selection*, J.M. Dent & Sons Ltd., 1989. Reprinted by permission of The Salamander Oasis Trust.

White, Elizabeth, 'The Parting' from *The Corridors of Dawn, and Other Poems*, Hutchinson & Co. Ltd., 1944.

Whitehouse, Peggy (pseudonym of Frances Mundy-Castle), extracts from *A Democrat's Chapbook* by 'A Quiet Woman', John Lane, The Bodley Head, 1942.

Williams, Hilda Katherine, 'The Sun and the – Luftwaffe' and 'The Cage' from *The Primrose Way: Songs from a Cage*, Bigwoods Ltd., Jersey, 1946.

Willy, Margaret, 'The Reprieved' from *The Invisible Sun*, Chaterson Ltd., 1946.

Wingfield, Sheila, extract from 'Men in War' from *Beat Drum, Beat Heart*, Cresset Press, 1946. With thanks to Viscount Powerscourt and reprinted by permission of David Pryce-Jones, Literary Executor of Sheila Wingfield.

Every effort has been made to trace all copyright holders and we apologise to anyone who inadvertently has not been acknowledged.

I would like to thank my publishers for all their help, in particular Peter Clifford, Jaqueline Mitchell, Alison Flowers, Mary Critchley, Nicola Wood, Martin Latham and Kate Platt.

I am very grateful to the following for their help and kindness:
John Bayliss; Angus Benton; Authors' Licensing and Collecting Society (Gaynor Coules and Susan Williams); Alexandra Berington; staff of the Bodleian Library (particularly Richard Bell, Colin Harris, Christine Mason and Nicky Pound); Richard Bohane, History Department, Hatchards; Book Trust (Suzy Joinson and Sarah Harrington); Charles Causley; Annabel Charlesworth; Aoife Coleman, Rye Old Books; R.L. Cook, The Lomond Press; Johnny Coppin; Christopher Date, British Museum; David and Shirley Edrich; Sister Philippa Edwards, Stanbrook Abbey; Lois Godfrey; Melissa Hardie, Hypatia Trust, Cornwall; Halcyon and Ann-Marie Hine, Ystwyth Books; Eric Holt; Joanne Hook, Victoria and Albert Museum; Celia Kemp; Ann Kennedy; Morine Krissdóttir; Christine Lingard, Language and Literature Library, Manchester Central Library; Richard Lowndes; Don McClen; Alan Martin; Michael Napier; Lizabeth Paravisini-Gebert; Roger Pickard, Curator Royal Signals Museum, Blandford Camp; Cyril Plum; Sara and François Pons; Phillip Powell, Department of Printed Books, Imperial War Museum; The Publishers Association; Robin Ravilious; Rosanne Reeves; Lavinia Robinson; Paul Rodger, Permissions Officer, Random House UK;

Harry Stopes-Roe; Michael Russell; Peter Scupham; Victor Selwyn; Grenville, Amanda and Barnaby Simons; The Society of Authors; Georgina Stonor; Ralph Sunley; David Sutton, Writers and Their Copyright Holders (WATCH), University of Reading; Jeff Tall, Royal Navy Submarine Museum; the late Martin Taylor; Marian Tomlinson; Philip Toogood; Pam Williams, Birmingham Central Library; Joanne Winning; John Winton; Amanda Wood; Caroline Zilboorg.

I am especially indebted to the following friends:

Alan Jeffreys, Department of Exhibits and Firearms, Imperial War Museum, for all the help and research he has undertaken on my behalf; Tony Laurence for his invaluable assistance in checking military details; my warmest thanks to Anne Harvey for her never-ending kindness, advice and support; and to Catherine Reilly for her personal interest and encouragement – *Shadows of War* would not have been possible without her magnificent biobibliography *English Poetry of the Second World War*, and her anthology *Chaos of the Night: Women's Poetry & Verse of the Second World War*.

My final thanks are to my beloved family. To my children and children-in-law, Jonathan and Sarah; Rupert and Clare; and Lucinda and Andrew for all their understanding, support and love. To Jonathan and Rupert for the time they have given in research and general help in so many ways; to Lucinda, my 'problem-solver', for her practical advice, the enormous amount of computer work and hours of research she has undertaken over the last five years. I can never thank my husband Jeremy enough for the huge load he has taken on with infinite patience, tireless efficiency and good humour; his encouragement, care and love have sustained me throughout the many stages of preparation for *Shadows of War*.

Index of First Lines

Index of Authors